Anscombe's *Intention*

OXFORD GUIDES TO PHILOSOPHY

Series Editors
Rebecca Copenhaver, Lewis and Clark College
Christopher Shields, University of Notre Dame
Mark Timmons, University of Arizona

*

Advisory Board
Michael Beaney, Ursula Coope, Karen Detlefsen, Lisa Downing, Tom Hurka, Pauline
Kleingeld, Robert Pasnau, Dominik Perler, Houston Smit, Allen Wood

*

Oxford Guides to Philosophy presents concise introductions to the most important
primary texts in the history of philosophy. Written by top scholars, the volumes in
the series are designed to present up-to-date scholarship in an accessible manner, in
order to guide readers through these challenging texts.

Anscombe's Intention

A Guide

JOHN SCHWENKLER

OXFORD

UNIVERSITY PRESS

OXFORD
UNIVERSITY PRESS

Oxford University Press is a department of the University of Oxford. It furthers
the University's objective of excellence in research, scholarship, and education
by publishing worldwide. Oxford is a registered trade mark of Oxford University
Press in the UK and certain other countries.

Published in the United States of America by Oxford University Press
198 Madison Avenue, New York, NY 10016, United States of America.

Library of Congress Cataloging-in-Publication Data
Names: Schwenkler, John, author.
Title: Anscombe's Intention : a guide / John Schwenkler, Florida State University.
Description: New York : Oxford University Press, 2019.
Identifiers: LCCN 2019010160 | ISBN 9780190052034 (pbk.) |
ISBN 9780190052027 (hardback) | ISBN 9780190052041 (epdf) |
ISBN 9780190052058 (epub) | ISBN 9780190052065 (online)
Subjects: LCSH: Anscombe, G. E. M. (Gertrude Elizabeth Margaret).
Intention. | Intention (Logic)
Classification: LCC B1618.A573 I587 2019 | DDC 192—dc23
LC record available at https://lccn.loc.gov/2019010160

1 3 5 7 9 8 6 4 2

Paperback printed by Marquis, Canada
Hardback printed by Bridgeport National Bindery, Inc., United States of America

Contents

The Commentary

Preface

The aim of this book is to provide a careful, critical, and appropriately contextualized presentation of the main lines of argument in G.E.M. Anscombe's seminal book, *Intention*, at a level appropriate to the advanced undergraduate but also capable of benefiting specialists in action theory, moral philosophy, and the history of analytic philosophy.

Despite the recent renaissance of scholarly interest in Anscombe's work, and even as *Intention* is widely acknowledged as a defining text in the analytic philosophy of action, many philosophers still fail to give her book the close attention it requires, and even when philosophers do engage directly with the arguments of *Intention* they rarely do so on Anscombe's own terms. There are some good reasons for this situation, and also some bad ones. Anscombe's writing does require *very* close attention before her questions, arguments, and conclusions can become clear; she is working in a philosophical context that she rarely references directly and that is anyway quite distant from our own; and her main sources of philosophical inspiration—most notably Aristotle and Thomas Aquinas, as I will document at some length—are mostly left implicit, as Anscombe borrows their ideas without much acknowledgment.[1] Yet when we encounter Anscombe's unapologetically Wittgensteinian style and move quickly to the judgment that her thought is unsystematic, or demand that her text provide arguments against a "causal theory of action" that was nowhere on the philosophical scene when *Intention* was being written, we thereby fail to give her an honest hearing, and all but guarantee that we will come away unpersuaded by what she says.

---

[1] Anscombe's daughter, Mary Geach, gave an explanation for this in her Introduction to a collection of Anscombe's essays: "Anscombe drew on [Aquinas'] thought to an unknowable extent: she said to me that it aroused prejudice in people to tell them that a thought came to him: to my sister she said that to ascribe a thought to him made people boringly ignore the philosophical interest of it, whether they were for Aquinas or against him" (Geach, "Introduction," p. xix).

In order to improve the reader's hermeneutic situation, this *Guide* begins with an Introduction that situates the project of *Intention* in relation to its historical context—in particular, the controversy that Anscombe herself initiated over the University of Oxford's decision to offer an honorary degree to Harry Truman, and the connection she saw between the situation of Oxford moral philosophy and her colleagues' willingness to justify Truman's bombing of Hiroshima and Nagasaki. Throughout the Commentary I also document, extensively but not *nearly* to the extent that was possible, the ways in which Anscombe drew on the thought of Aristotle, Aquinas, and her teacher, Ludwig Wittgenstein, as well as the points at which her argument engages with the work of then-contemporary authors—most frequently, on the reading offered here, the Oxford philosophers R.M. Hare and Gilbert Ryle.

Against this background, the focus of my Commentary is on presenting Anscombe's arguments and assessing the plausibility and philosophical power of the position she develops. Sometimes this involves a detour through other philosophical texts that I think might be in the background of her argument, or through others of Anscombe's own writings where she expands on the ideas in question. In other cases my approach is more speculative, taking the text as a starting point and trying to develop the materials she gives us into a form that I hope will be faithful to her philosophical vision. There is room to challenge my interpretation at any number of points, and I know that there are many instances where my presentation and assessment of Anscombe's views, as well as my choice of what to emphasize in them, reflect my own positions and preoccupations. While I have tried to write in a way that skirts many of the philosophical and interpretive controversies in the existing secondary literature on *Intention*, I do discuss some of these in the body of my Commentary, and others are referenced in the Suggested Readings at the end of each chapter.

Since *Intention* proceeds in the order of discovery, and offers no explicit statement of its main conclusions, the summary interpretation offered in the Précis is likely to be most useful to those who have made their way through Anscombe's book at least once (and then two, three, four, five, six, ... times) before. While Anscombe tends to avoid philosophical jargon, the Glossary of Terms tries to elucidate a number of concepts, identified in boldface in my summary Outline, that play especially important roles in her argument.

Just as a philosopher cannot be engaged with fairly except on her own terms, there is also no serious alternative to reading for oneself the things that a philosopher actually wrote. And while Anscombe's writing is dense and difficult, and its context somewhat foreign to ours, *Intention* does not present nearly the same interpretive challenge as many other great works of philosophy. Next to its going unread, my greatest fear for this *Guide* is that it will preempt some readers from making up their own minds about the substance of Anscombe's position. To anyone who feels tempted to skip that part of the journey, please trust my advice: it's even more worthwhile than the destination.

Acknowledgments

Jimmy Doyle, Kim Frost, Eric Marcus, and Beri Marušić each read this book in draft and provided patient, generous, and insightful feedback that led to enormous improvements. I don't have the words to express my gratitude to them. I apologize to the reader for the handful of places where I failed to follow their excellent advice.

Among the many friends and colleagues whose feedback, advice, and insight I benefited from, Matt Boyle, Stephen Brock, Randy Clarke, Jonathan Dancy, Jeremy Fix, Anton Ford, Jennifer Frey, Matthias Haase, Nathan Helms, Jennifer Hornsby, Paul Hurley, Michael Kremer, Mark LeBar, David McNaughton, Al Mele, Dick Moran, Anselm Müller, Ram Neta, Alva Noë, John O'Callaghan, Sarah Paul, Juan Piñeros, Piers Rawling, Jeremy Redmond, Sebastian Rödl, Angela Schwenkler, Kieran Setiya, Will Small, Nat Stein, Sergio Tenenbaum, Marshall Thompson, Candace Vogler, Brandon Warmke, Eric Wiland, and Rachael Wiseman stand out in my memory as especially deserving of thanks. I am grateful as well to Bob Bishop, Michael Bratman, Michael Brent, Sarah Buss, Nick Byrd, John Campbell, Jeremiah Carey, E.J. Coffman, Jennifer Daigle, Patricio Fernandez, Luca Ferrero, Christopher Frey, Olav Gjelsvik, Nathan Hauthaler, Pamela Hieronymi, David Hunter, Paul Kastafanas, Martin Kavka, John Kelsay, Clayton Littlejohn, Justin Matchulat, Mark Murphy, Antonia Peacocke, Joshua Shepherd, Susanna Siegel, Joshua Stuchlik, Matt Teichman, Michael Thompson, José Torralba, Peter Wicks, and Wayne Wu. Finally, to everyone on Philosophy Facebook, thanks for all the good ideas that you gave me while I was doing my best not to write.

This book would never have come into being without what I learned from all the graduate and undergraduate students who sat patiently through seminars where I assigned *Intention* as the primary text, helping me to work through Anscombe's arguments and sometimes reading drafts of my commentary on it. In addition to Nathan Helms, Jeremy Redmond, and Marshall Thompson, Samantha Berthelette, Richard Creek, Michelle

Gershon, Adam Hamilton, Matthew Jernberg, Andrew Moffatt, Marigny Nevitt, Mirja Pérez de Calleja, Jacqueline Porter, Sam Sims, Nicholas Sparks, George Stamets, and Catherine Vianale all made especially helpful contributions in that context. I also benefited from several discussions with students of Beri Marušić at Brandeis University, and their extensive feedback on a draft of my Précis helped me to improve it significantly.

My colleagues at Florida State University, and earlier at Mount St. Mary's, have encouraged my efforts, indulged my questions, and endured my idiosyncrasies more patiently than I have deserved. In addition to those just mentioned already I owe special thanks to Mike Bishop, Richard Buck, Karen Foulke, Joshua Hochschild, Aline Kalbian, Jessy Jordan, Simon May, Greg Murry, and Drew Watson.

Richard Moran's *Authority and Estrangement*, Sebastian Rödl's *Self-Consciousness*, Michael Thompson's *Life and Action*, and Candace Vogler's *Reasonably Vicious* are four extraordinary books whose influence on this work extends far beyond what I could reasonably document.

I presented material related to this book in a number of forums, including the American Catholic Philosophical Association, Auburn University, Boston University, the Centre for the Study of Mind and Nature at the University of Oslo, the European Society for Philosophy and Psychology, the Florida State University Departments of Philosophy and Religion, a workshop hosted by the Lumen Christi Institute at the Pontifical Gregorian University, the Society for Catholicism and Analytic Philosophy, the Society for the Philosophy of Agency, the Southeastern Epistemology Conference, the St. Louis Annual Conference on Reasons and Rationality, the Thomistic Institute at Yale University, the University of Chicago, Universität Leipzig, and the Values and Agency Conference at the University of Tennessee. I'm thankful for what I learned from audiences on those occasions.

At various times my work on this project was supported by time spent as a *Communitas* fellow at Calvin College, by a First-Year Assistant Professor Fellowship and a grant from the Committee on Faculty Research Support at Florida State University, and by a research grant from the Classical Theism Project, with the support of the John Templeton Foundation. Marshall Thompson prepared the Concordance and Index, and was paid for this work by a grant from the FSU Center for Research and Creativity.

Peter Ohlin has encouraged this project from its inception, responding helpfully to my many questions and dealing appropriately with my too-frequent failure to meet promised deadlines. Becko Copenhaver's invitation to consider being part of the Oxford Guides series provided just the opportunity that I needed to get this thing finally done. Thanks also to Christopher Shields and Mark Timmons for their feedback on the proposal, and for the helpful advice of the four anonymous referees solicited by Oxford University Press.

Finally, and above all—my wife, Angela, and our children, Jack, Daniel, Annie, Dorothy, and Isaac, have supported my work and filled my life with a love that I have too often failed to reciprocate.

I dedicate this book to the memory of those who have been murdered with the blessing of the state.

Abbreviations

BB	Ludwig Wittgenstein, *The Blue and Brown Books.*
CM	Gilbert Ryle, *The Concept of Mind.*
"FP"	G.E.M. Anscombe, "The First Person."
"GW"	G.E.M. Anscombe, "Glanville Williams' *The Sanctity of Life and the Criminal Law*: A Review."
I	G.E.M. Anscombe, *Intention*, 2nd ed. Cited by section, page, and (full or partial) paragraph: e.g., *I*, §1, 1:1.
LM	R.M. Hare, *The Language of Morals.*
"MMP"	G.E.M. Anscombe, "Modern Moral Philosophy."
NE	Aristotle, *Nicomachean Ethics.*
PI	Ludwig Wittgenstein, *Philosophical Investigations.*
ST	St. Thomas Aquinas, *Summa Theologiae.* Cited by part, question, and article: e.g., *ST* I, q. 1, a. 1.
"TD"	G.E.M. Anscombe, "Mr Truman's Degree."
"UD"	G.E.M. Anscombe, "Under a Description."
"WM"	G.E.M. Anscombe, "War and Murder."

Introduction: The Project of *Intention*

Intention is based on a course of lectures that Elizabeth Anscombe delivered at the University of Oxford during Hilary Term of 1957. Her philosophical interest in the topic of intention had crystallized in 1956 during her controversial opposition to the university's decision to award an honorary degree to former US President Harry Truman—a man she regarded as a *murderer* in light of his decision to bomb the cities of Hiroshima and Nagasaki, and thus did not think worthy of the university's honors. "For men to choose to kill the innocent as a means to their ends is always murder," she wrote in a pamphlet explaining her position, "and murder is one of the worst of human actions" ("TD," p. 70). On this ground she objected "vehemently ... to *our* action in offering Mr Truman honours, because one can share in the guilt of a bad action by praise and flattery, as also by defending it" (p. 70).

Anscombe saw a great deal of self-serving flattery among those who stood in defense of honoring Truman. But she thought as well that some distinctly philosophical errors lay behind their willingness to praise or excuse him, and her project in *Intention* is ultimately in the service of combating these false doctrines. However, in Anscombe's view the fundamental errors in need of correction were not in moral theorizing, but rather in the philosophical *psychology* that contemporary moral philosophy tends to assume. Her 1958 paper "Modern Moral Philosophy" singles out for special criticism the definition of intention in Henry Sidgwick's *Methods of Ethics*:

> [Sidgwick] defines intention in such a way that one must be said to intend any foreseen consequences of one's voluntary action. ... He uses [this definition] to put forward an ethical thesis which would now be accepted by many people: the thesis that it does not make any difference to a man's responsibility for something that he foresaw, that he felt no desire for it, either as an end or as a means to an end. ("MMP," pp. 34–35)

There are two quite straight paths from Sidgwick's definition of intention to the praise of Truman as one who acted courageously in the face of frightful necessity. The first is that, by erasing the difference in responsibility between the foreseen and intended effects of an action, Sidgwick's position renders incoherent the very idea of exceptionless prohibitions against certain *types* of things that a person may never do, no matter the circumstances she is in. This is because any such prohibition will necessarily concern what a person *intentionally* does, in contrast to what is brought about as a side-effect of her action: thus, e.g., the prohibition against killing innocent persons is taken not to be violated by a person who pushes someone off a cliff when he is menacing her life, or by a doctor who administers a palliative drug that hastens the death of a patient.[2] According to a view of human action in which this distinction is erased, the only thing that can recommend against an action is the overall badness of what will happen if one does it—which means that the general badness involved in doing a certain sort of thing can always be overwhelmed, in the right circumstances, by the badness of the consequences that would result from doing anything else. Anscombe's pamphlet unfolds the logic here:

> The action was necessary, or at any rate it was thought by competent, expert military opinion to be necessary; it probably saved more lives than it sacrificed; it had a good result, it ended the war. Come now: if you had to choose between boiling one baby and letting some frightful disaster befall a thousand people—or a million people, if a thousand is not enough—what would you do? Are you going to strike an attitude and say "You may not do evil that good may come?" ("TD," pp. 64–65)

It is not, however, the project of *Intention* to defend the ancient prohibition against doing evil in pursuit of a good end. Rather, the point at issue is that if we assume a view of intention like Sidgwick's then the question cannot even *arise* whether a given act might fail to be justified by the balance of evil it avoids and good it brings about—cannot arise, that is, because it cannot even be *formulated* within the conception of act and intention that Sidgwick provides. Here he is in *The Methods of Ethics*:

> Moralists of all schools, I conceive, would agree that the moral judgments which we pass on actions relate primarily to intentional actions regarded as intentional. In other words, what we judge to be "wrong"—in the strictest ethical sense—is not any part of the actual effects, as such, of the muscular movements immediately caused by the agent's volition, but the effects which he foresaw in willing the act; or, more strictly, his volition or choice

---

[2] For these examples, see "WM," pp. 54–55.

of realising the effects as foreseen. When I speak therefore of acts, I must be understood to mean—unless the contrary is stated—acts presumed to be intentional and judged as such.[3]

Anscombe agrees with Sidgwick on this much: that among the things a person does or brings about, the only things for which the person can be credited or blamed are those which she knew or believed[4] that her action would involve or bring about. Her criticism is that Sidgwick does not make a further distinction, within this category of things that a person knows or believes that she will do or bring about, between those that are and are not intended. If we do not make this distinction, then the *only* thing that we can do in evaluating the actions of a Truman is to compare the numbers of lives and other goods foreseeably "saved" to those foreseeably "sacrificed" among the courses of action available to him. If Sidgwick is right, then *all* the consequences that are foreseen in a choice are equally part of the agent's intention. Had Truman chosen to continue the war by "conventional" means, understanding that in this choice some civilian deaths would result, he would have intended those deaths no less than he intended the deaths of the civilians in Hiroshima and Nagasaki. At least as far as life and death are concerned, the only thing for him to do was choose the option that appeared to have the most favorable body count.

Among Anscombe's contemporaries, her Oxford colleague R.M. Hare was especially straightforward in endorsing the upshot of this Sidgwickean conception of choice. Here is Hare in his 1952 book *The Language of Morals*:

suppose I am an employer, and am wondering whether or not to sack a clerk who habitually turns up at the office after the hour at which he has undertaken to turn up. If I sack him I shall be depriving his family of the money on which they live, perhaps giving my firm a reputation which will lead clerks to avoid it when other jobs are available, and so on; if I keep him, I shall be causing the other clerks to do work which otherwise would be done by this clerk; and the affairs of the office will not be transacted so quickly as they would if all the clerks were punctual. These would be the sorts of consideration I should take into account in making my decision. They would be the effects on the total situation of the alternative actions,

---

[3] Henry Sidgwick, *The Methods of Ethics*, Bk. III, ch. 1, pp. 201–202.

[4] Or, perhaps, *ought* to have known or believed. Anscombe argues that this addition matters quite a lot: here see her paper "On Being in Good Faith." But it would not be enough to save Sidgwick's view from the present criticism.

sacking him or not sacking him. It is the effects which determine what I should be doing; it is between the two sets of effects that I am deciding. The whole point about a decision is that it makes a difference to what happens; and this difference is the difference between the effects of deciding one way, and the effects of deciding the other. (*LM*, pp. 56–57)

For Hare as for Sidgwick, a decision is simply a choice between effects; and it is the balance of the effects that determine what should be chosen. Given this view, he *must* treat as equivalent the choice to kill one person as a means of preserving the lives of some others, and the choice to knowingly allow or bring about the death of one person as the consequence of a life-saving act. Except insofar as we wish to follow the advice of our received moral traditions, the only thing there is to decide between these choices is the foreseeable effects of each one.

The other way that Sidgwick's definition of intention leads straight to the justification of wartime atrocity is in the way that it requires us to frame the distinction between "legitimate and illegitimate objects of attack" in a military context (see "TD," p. 63). On the classical view that Anscombe is out to defend, no person may be targeted in an attack who is *innocent* from the perspective of those waging war—which is why an army may sometimes bomb a military base but never do the same to a village, and why soldiers can justifiably be taken prisoner while civilians cannot. However, the concept of "innocence" at work in these distinctions does not have to do with a person's moral character: the point of the restrictions is not that armies should attack bad people rather than good ones, but rather that they may attack only those people who are actively involved in the military conflict. Thus Anscombe:

What is required, for the people attacked to be non-innocent in the relevant sense, is that they should themselves be engaged in an objectively unjust proceeding which the attacker has the right to make his concern; or—the commonest case—should be unjustly attacking him. Then he can attack them with a view to stopping them; and also their supply lines and armament factories. But people whose mere existence and activity supporting existence by growing crops, making clothes, etc., constitute an impediment to him—such people are innocent and it is murderous to attack them, or make them a target for an attack which he judges will help him towards victory. For murder is the deliberate killing of the innocent, whether for its own sake or as a means to some further end. ("WM," p. 53; and cf. "TD," p. 67 for a similar account)

The problem once again is that it is simply impossible to draw this line in the right place without an appropriate understanding of act and intention. For suppose it were to be accepted, within a consequentialist framework like Hare's, that the deaths of innocents are more to be avoided than other deaths, since they are in some way a worse thing to have happen. But *who* are the innocents? If the answer comes: They are those who are not fighting and not engaged in supplying those who are with the means of fighting, then we need a way to delineate these categories. And by treating all the foreseen consequences of a person's action as part of the content of her intention, a philosopher who accepts the Sidgwickean view of intention will draw this line in entirely the wrong place. If a farmer grows crops, *foreseeing* that these will be sold to a conglomerate and then eaten by the troops who fight, then on a view like Sidgwick's the effects that her farming contributes toward the war effort count as *intentional* actions or consequences no less than those of the soldiers and the generals. And the same will hold in turn for any civilian who understands that *something* she is doing is likely to contribute in *some* way to her nation's military efforts. It is only those who are very young, or otherwise blissfully unaware of the wartime situation, who will fail to satisfy this condition—but then many such innocent lives will likely be "lost" no matter how a war proceeds, and so the choice to kill some of them will often be justified by appeal to the total situation that this brings about.

The project of *Intention* is, once again, not to establish any exceptionless moral principles or defend a robust concept of legal innocence, but rather to make it possible at least to *ask* coherently whether, for example, it is a worse thing to target civilians directly than to act in a way that one foresees will result in civilian deaths—a question that we naturally take to be an important part of moral evaluation, but which cannot even be raised intelligently within a framework like Sidgwick's. Indeed, questions like this one remain important for philosophers who hold that all moral principles admit of possible exception, as long as they accept that the intrinsic nature of an act has *some* special bearing on the permissibility of performing it. For example, in his paper "What Makes Right Acts Right?," the Oxford philosopher W.D. Ross rejects the "ideal utilitarianism" of G.E. Moore, according to which the *only* moral duty is that of producing good effects, and argues instead that there are a number of other "*prima facie* duties" that are significant in moral deliberation. Ross gives as examples the duties to keep one's promises, make reparation for wrongful acts, express gratitude for services done, and not injure or do harm to others.[5] On Ross's view, none of these duties are binding in every possible circumstance: that is, they are all such that it *can* be right to violate them in order to prevent a great enough evil or bring about a great enough good. Even so, Ross needs a robust distinction between intention and foresight in order to get his non-absolutist position of the ground, as we cannot understand what these supposed duties even *concern* without distinguishing a person's intentional action from its foreseen consequences. The requirements that, for example, we not "kill one person in order to keep another alive, or ... steal from one in order to give alms to another" (p. 22), even if they bind only prima facie, cannot be made so much as *intelligible* if we do not distinguish an intentional killing from a death that foreseeably results from a choice not to kill, or intentional theft from a person's foreseen poverty.[6]

At the same time as she opposes the collapse of the categories of intention and foresight, Anscombe also opposes any account that identifies a person's intention with the *mental state* that is she is in before or during the time when she acts. In a couple of places in *Intention*, as well as a pair of other essays that she wrote around the same time,[7] she singles out for special criticism the idea that intention consists in an "interior movement" (*I*, §25, 42:1) of saying to oneself "I *mean* to be doing such-and-such." This conception of intention is "false and absurd" ("GW," p. 247), she says, since according to it simply *thinking* in the right manner about one's actions turns out to be "a marvellous way ... of making any action lawful" ("WM," p. 59). But this is not the only way that a conception of intention as something interior to an agent can lead a philosopher into absurdity.[8] Consider the following from Judith Jarvis Thomson:

> Suppose a pilot comes to us with a request for advice: "See, we're at war with a villainous country called Bad, and my superiors have ordered me to drop some bombs at Placetown in Bad. Now there's a munitions factory at Placetown, but there's a children's hospital there too. Is it permissible for

[5] See W.D. Ross, "What Makes Right Acts Right?," pp. 19–22. Anscombe references Ross's account, though not Ross by name, in discussing recent "productions of Oxford moral philosophy" in the penultimate paragraph of "Mr Truman's Degree."

[6] For a more contemporary example of a position with this form, see Warren Quinn's defense of a non-absolutist Doctrine of Double Effect in "Actions, Intentions, and Consequences."

[7] See *I*, §§25 and 27, together with "War and Murder" (1961) and her unpublished review of Glanville Williams's 1958 book *The Sanctity of Life and the Criminal Law*.

[8] Thanks to Juan Piñeros for prompting what follows, and to numerous philosophers on Facebook for helping me work through the details.

me to drop the bombs?" And suppose we make the following reply: "Well, it all depends on what your intentions would be in dropping the bombs. If you would be intending to destroy the munitions factory and thereby win the war, merely foreseeing, though not intending, the deaths of the children, then yes, you may drop the bombs. On the other hand, if you would be intending to destroy the children and thereby terrorize the Bads and thereby win the war, ... then no, you may not drop the bombs." What a queer performance this would be! Can anyone really think that the pilot should decide whether he may drop the bombs by looking inward for the intention with which he would be dropping them if he dropped them?[9]

Anscombe will of course disagree with Thomson over whether this case shows the moral irrelevance of the distinction between intention and foresight. She does agree, however, that it is *entirely* wrong to look "inward" rather than "outward" in evaluating the permissibility of an act—whether one's own or that of another person. One reason for this is the one I just gave earlier: advice of the sort that Thomson imagines giving to the pilot practically invites him to focus on getting his *attitudes* aligned in a way that will allow him then to act as he wishes.[10] What makes this introspective concern so perverse is that the badness of murder has to do with what is *done*—that is, with the kind of *event* or *happening* that it consists in—and not with the inner state of the person who carries it out. And Thomson's advice represents the situation as if there were two distinct things to consider here: as if what the pilot *does* will be the same whether he intends the civilian deaths or merely foresees them, and the difference between the cases lies in the attitude that he has toward this effect. Yet surely it is not *himself* that the pilot should be concerned with in deciding whether or not to destroy a hospital full of children!

As we will see, Anscombe allows that there are circumstances in which the intention with which a person acts, conceived as something somehow

[9] Judith Jarvis Thomson, "Self-Defense," p. 293. Thomson does confuse one very important point here: it is no part of the traditional position she is challenging that civilian casualties are permissible *whenever* they are not intended. Indeed, as I discuss in what follows, Anscombe follows tradition in holding that one may be a *murderer* even in bringing about a death that one did not intend, as long as one acts with indifference to human life. (For this point see *I*, §25, 45:3, as discussed in section 3.4 of the Commentary.) This is just what we should say of someone who would destroy an entire city in order to get rid of the military targets that were present in it.

[10] Thus it is that many Catholics, myself included, who were raised on the teaching that mortal sin requires "full knowledge and consent" have discovered the strategy of keeping oneself selectively ignorant in order that one's sins be "merely" venial. Anscombe criticizes this teaching in her essay "On Being in Good Faith."

distinct from what they actually do, can be relevant in moral evaluation. Section 25 of *Intention* quotes a passage from Wittgenstein's *Philosophical Investigations* that points us to this phenomenon:

> Why do I want to tell him about an intention too, as well as telling him what I did?—Not because the intention was also something which was going on at the time. But because I want to tell him something about *myself*, which goes beyond what happened at the time. (*PI* §659; quoted in *I*, §25, 45:4)

It is, however, a central thesis of Anscombe's book that the *primary* role of our concept of intention is quite different from the one that Wittgenstein describes here. On her view, the main use of the concept of intention is not to characterize the state of mind of an agent, but rather to describe *what happens* in a way that reveals the means–end order that an agent's (real or proposed) action embodies. As we will see, Anscombe holds that the ethically relevant difference in a case like Thomson's is simply between (1) destroying a building because it is full of civilians and (2) destroying a building because it is near to a munitions factory. And neither of these descriptions has reference to the agent's state of mind: the difference between them is a difference in *what is done*. For Anscombe, it is insofar as he *acted* in ways that fall under descriptions like the first one that Truman violated the prohibition against the intentional killing of innocents. To bring someone's action under such a description is *thereby* to describe that person as acting with the intent to kill. And the importance of this description is not what it says about the inner state of the agent. In contexts like these, the use to which we put the concept of intention is simply in describing what people actually do.[11]

There is some danger in framing the project of *Intention* against the background of these ethical debates. For as we have seen, the mistakes that Anscombe means to correct in her book have to do with the way that concepts like "action" and "intention" are conceived in philosophical *psychology*,[12] and it is no part of her project to develop an *ethical* theory that justifies exceptionless prohibitions or gives weight to the difference between intended and foreseen consequences. Here is how Anscombe describes her situation in a memorable passage from "Modern Moral Philosophy":

---

[11] For further discussion of the difference between Anscombe and Thomson over the interpretation of the intention/foresight distinction, see T.A. Cavanaugh, "Anscombe, Thomson, and Double Effect." For a different way of replying to Thomson's argument, see Matthew Hanser, "Permissibility and Practical Inference."

[12] That is, what today we would call "philosophy of action" and "philosophy of mind."

In present-day philosophy an explanation is required how an unjust man is a bad man; to give such an explanation belongs to ethics; but it cannot even be begun until we are equipped with a sound philosophy of psychology. For the proof that an unjust man is a bad man would require a positive account of justice as a "virtue." This part of the subject-matter of ethics is, however, completely closed to us until we have an account of what *type of characteristic* a virtue is—a problem, not of ethics, but of conceptual analysis—and how it relates to the actions in which it is instanced: a matter which I think Aristotle did not succeed in really making clear. For this we certainly need an account of what a human action is at all, and how its description as "doing such-and-such" is affected by its motive and by the intention or intentions in it; and for this an account of such concepts is required. ("MMP," p. 29)

Her idea, then, is that in order (a) to understand what makes a person bad we should first (b) give positive accounts of certain virtues. This, however, requires accounts of both (c) what virtue is and (d) how virtues relate to virtuous actions, which in turn require understanding (e) what human action is and (f) how the correct description of an action is affected by the agent's motives and intentions. This, finally, requires (g) accounts of what motives and intentions themselves are. And Anscombe insists that we approach this task by considering these questions "simply as part of the philosophy of psychology," and so "*banishing ethics totally* from our minds" ("MMP," p. 38), in order that our account of these concepts not be colored by our prior ethical commitments when in fact the proper dependence is the other way around.

If I am correct in the account I have outlined thus far of Anscombe's position on these matters, then the project of *Intention* is radical indeed, and much more so than is usually recognized. For, thanks in large part to her influence, philosophers today are quite different from Anscombe's contemporaries in taking the concept of intention very seriously within moral theory and the philosophy of mind. But it is common ground in these discussions that whatever intention is, it is a mental state, and that the distinguishing characteristics of intentional action must lie in some connection between the mental state of the agent and the things that she does because of this.[13] Like the ground beneath our feet, we proceed from these assumptions so steadily and consistently that we tend to be forgetful of the

---

[13] For an exception that proves the rule, see Part II of Michael Thompson's *Life and Action*.

use we put them to. We have not *really* engaged with Anscombe on her own terms until we have given her the chance to shake this ground.

Suggestions for further reading

- For a systematic overview of Anscombe's philosophical thought, see Roger Teichmann, *The Philosophy of Elizabeth Anscombe*.
- For further discussion of the project of *Intention* in relation to the controversy over Truman's degree, see Anthony Kenny, "Elizabeth Anscombe at Oxford"; Rachael Wiseman, *Guidebook to Anscombe's Intention*, chapters 1–2; and Wiseman, "The Intended and Unintended Consequences of *Intention*."

Interpretive Précis

Intention is a philosophical inquiry into the concept named in its title. This is a concept that we put to work in a number of different ways, including treating certain statements as expressions of the intention to do something, categorizing certain actions as intentional and others as not, and describing the intentions with which people act as they do. What constitutes the unity among these forms of thought?

A natural answer is that the word "intention" refers to a *mental state* that is operative in all these things: it is the state *expressed* in expressing an intention, the state that *causes* or otherwise qualifies the execution of an intentional action, the state that a person is *in* when she acts with the intention to do such-and-such. But Anscombe turns this common picture on its head. On her view, the primary use of the concept of intention consists in a distinctive manner of describing *what happens* in the world.

The distinctive *form of description* which we engage in when we employ the concept of intention can be elucidated by reflecting on the special sense of *"Why?"* expressed in queries like the following:

(Q1)   Why are you going to marry her?
(Q2)   Why are you sawing that plank of Smith's?
(Q3)   Why did you step on my toe just then?

A positive answer to one of these questions will give one's *reason for acting* in the manner described, e.g.:

(A1)   To get at her parents' money.
(A2)   Because I am building him a birdhouse.
(A3)   In order to get your attention.

As statements given in answer to the previous questions, each of (A1), (A2), and (A3) represents two events as standing in some connection:

(B1)   I am *going to marry her* to *get at her parents' money*.

(B2)   I am *sawing Smith's plank* because I am *building him a birdhouse*.

(B3)   I *stepped on your toe* in order to *get your attention*.

The connections represented in (B1), (B2), and (B3) are all relations of dependence: each one says that I *would not* do, be doing, or have done, one thing if I *were not* thereby doing another, and likewise that my doing the latter thing is or was to be a *consequence* of my doing the former. And all these relations are in some sense causal—thus it is no accident that the same word "because" appears both in (B2) and in

(B4)   The tree is falling because it was damaged in the storm.

But the *sort* of causal relation represented in a statement like (B4) is different from the sort represented in (B2): while (B4) presupposes a general (though not exceptionless) law to the effect that storm-damaged trees have a tendency to fall, (B2) could be true even if when I saw planks it is almost always because I am making bookshelves, and birdhouses I generally make out of plastic instead. What is the sort of causal dependence that is represented in these statements, and in virtue of what does it obtain?

Anscombe's answer to the first question is that the dependence represented in statements like (B1), (B2), and (B3) is *teleological*: it is the dependence of a means on an end that it serves. And her answer to the second is that this dependence obtains in virtue of *the agent's own understanding* of what she is doing and why—that is, that it is only because the speaker of (B1), (B2), and (B3) endorses these statements in their first-personal guise that the corresponding third-person statements are true:

(B1*)   He is going to marry her to get at her parents' money.

(B2*)   She is sawing Smith's plank because she is building him a birdhouse.

(B3*)   Tommy stepped on your toe in order to get your attention.

There seems to be room for exception here: couldn't (B1*), for example, be true of someone who doesn't understand what he is really after? But in cases like this we do not take a person to be *wholly* ignorant of his or her motivations: e.g., if the true reason I am marrying someone is that I want to get at her parents' money, then I must know "at some level" that I am moved by this desire, even if I won't *admit* it to myself or to others. It is thus quite unlike a case where, e.g., I sign away my inheritance because someone has tricked me into doing this—in which case I am *simply* unaware that this is the true account of what I do.

Similar questions arise in connection with one of the best-known theses of *Intention*, which we may abbreviate here as the *Knowledge Thesis*:

(KT)   A person does something intentionally only if she knows, without observation, *that* she is doing it and *why*.

The truth of (KT) would account for the possibility of delineating the class of intentional actions according to the applicability of "Why?"-questions with the special sense expressed in (Q1), (Q2), and (Q3). For if questions of that sort are answered positively with descriptions that have the distinctive form of (B1), (B2), and (B3), and the truth of these depends on the agent's own knowledge of the causality that they represent, then the domain of an agent's self-knowledge will overlap with that of the "Why?"-question's application.

Anscombe treats (KT) as an exceptionless principle, and rejects any attempt to prop it up by restricting the scope of an agent's self-knowledge to an inner mental state, or the domain of agency to a proximate trigger of outward events. Her thesis attributes to an agent first-personal knowledge of *what happens*, brought under the form of description we employ in representing an action's means–end structure. As such, it can be hard to square (KT) with cases where an agent's self-knowledge of her act seems to fall short of the worldly happenings that constitute the execution of her intention. Is it really true, for example, that (B2*) could be true of someone only if she *knows without observation* that she is sawing Smith's plank? How could this be, given the fallibility of our active powers and the ineliminable role of perception in the knowledgeable performance of such an act?

The answer to this challenge is supposed to lie in the characterization of an agent's self-knowledge as *practical* knowledge, knowledge that is (in the phrase that Anscombe borrows from Aquinas) the cause of what it understands. This knowledge is the *measure* of its object, setting the standard by which action is judged as a success or failure: thus a person who judges (B2) when the plank she is sawing is not really Smith's will be making a mistake in what she *does*. It is the principle of its object's *form*, constituting what would otherwise be a mere "chaos" of events into the means–end unity represented in the agent's practical reasoning: thus an agent's self-knowledge of her act is what makes it possible to bring it under the special form of description we have explored. And it is also the *efficient* cause of the agent's movements and their effects—as fire is the cause of heat, and God's knowledge the cause of the things he creates.

It is not easy to say whether this defense of (KT) is sufficient. One of the main contentions of my Commentary is that (KT) cannot, after all, hold up as Anscombe meant it, and that we should treat it instead as a principle describing what holds "for the most part," and admitting of possible exceptions. Only so, I argue, can we hold on to the idea that the proper domain of an agent's self-understanding is the material reality of her act.

Outline of the Text

Terms that appear in boldface are discussed in the Glossary of Terms.

§1: Three ways to employ a concept of "intention": (i) treating a statement as the **expression of intention**, (ii) categorizing **action as intentional**, (iii) describing the **further intention** with which a person acts. What constitutes the unity among these?

§2: Consideration of heading (i). A statement of the form "I am going to do X" may express either the intention to do X or the mere **estimate** that one is going to do this. In both uses the statement offers a **prediction**—it describes *what one will do*, and not the state of mind one is presently in. Only in the first use, however, does the possibility arise of a **mistake in performance**—that is, a case in which *what one does* can be criticized or "impugned" for not being in accordance with what one says.

§§3–4: The difficulty of characterizing what is *expressed* in expressing an intention by appeal to the mental state of the speaker. Intention is something more than mere desire—but in what does the difference consist? We do not recognize our own intentions by introspecting our psychology. And one of the best ways to tell another person's intentions is simply by looking at her actions and describing what she does—in the usual cases, you will *thereby* report some of what she intends.

§5: Intentional actions can be defined as those about which it is possible to ask **"Why?,"** in a sense that would be answered positively by giving a **reason for acting**. The difficulty in explicating the latter phrase without appeal to action- and intention-concepts.

§§6–8: Beginning to elucidate the relevant sense of "Why?" by identifying ways of **refusing its application**. (1) Claiming that one did not know that she was doing the thing in question—as when I saw Smith's plank, not knowing that it belongs to him. (2) Claiming that one knew she was doing this only by **observation**—as when I operate the traffic lights in crossing the road. (3) Claiming that it was only by observation that one knew the cause of her doing it—as when a tap from the doctor's hammer causes my leg to kick. Action as intentional only **under descriptions**: namely, those under which it is nonobservationally known.

§§9–16: A further way to refuse application of the question "Why?": (4) Stating that one's action was merely the result of a **mental cause**. Consideration of this last concept, and of the difference between acting from a mental cause and acting from a **motive**. The possibility of arguing against motives in a way that mental causes cannot be argued against. A tentative proposal: action from motive is distinguished by the way that thoughts of what is good and bad are involved in it.

§§17–18: Consideration of **"for no reason"** and **"I don't know why I did it,"** as possible responses to the question "Why?". Answers like these are not ways of refusing the question's application.

§19: An argument that action is not intentional in virtue of an *extra feature* that exists when it is performed.

§§20–21: An argument that our original headings (i), (ii), and (iii) are connected. There could not be a concept of intentional action, as something to which a special sense of "Why?" is given application, if it were not possible to answer this question by expressing intention for the future and describing the further intention with which one acts.

§§22–24, 26: Further discussion of these two ways of answering the question "Why?": with a wider description of what one *is doing*, and with a description of something else that one is *going to do*. The **"break"** separating descriptions of these two sorts. The unity of an action as revealed in the **A–D order** in a series of descriptions of the action that stand to one another as means to end. The special sense of "How?" that seeks to discover the means by which something is done.

§§25, 27: Consideration of "I didn't care about that" as a way of refusing application of the question "Why?" The distinction between one's intention and the foreseen consequences of one's act does not depend on a conception of intention as an interior movement.

§§44–45: The practical knowledge of action as "**cause of what it understands.**" Two senses in which this formula may apply: knowledge of an act as productive or *efficient* cause of an agent's movements and their effects, and knowledge of an act as the *formal* principle of its unity, in virtue of which it falls under descriptions that are subject to the question "Why?"

§§46–48: The term "intentional" relates to a *form of description* of events. We employ this form of description in representing things as intentionally done, including with special concepts of human action and with the use of words like "by," "because," and "in order to," where these give *reasons for acting* in the sense sought after by our question "Why?"

§49: The relation between the intentional and the voluntary. Merely voluntary action as movement that falls outside the scope of an agent's practical knowledge.

§§50–52: Further consideration of the expression of intention for the future, now understood as a statement of what one will do to which our question "Why?" has application, and that is justified by reasons for acting. How to think about the possibility of failing to do what one intends. What could be meant in saying, e.g., "I am going to do this ... unless I do not." St. Peter's conflicted view of his future, when the conclusion of his own practical reasoning is opposed by the prophecy of Christ.

The Commentary

1

Preliminaries

Anscombe begins her book by introducing three different ways we "employ a concept of 'intention'" (*I*, §1, 1:1): we treat certain statements describing what a person will do as the *expression* of the speaker's intention to do that thing; we describe *actions* as intentional and distinguish them from things that people do without intending to do them; and we characterize people's intentions *in* acting, or the *further* intentions *with which* they act as they do. Having introduced her topic in this way, in Sections 2–3 she briefly considers the nature of expressions of intention, emphasizing how intention is expressed through a description of *what one will do* and not of one's present state of mind. Following this, she proposes in Section 4 that the concept of intentional action—that is, of "what physically takes place, i.e. what a man actually does" in acting intentionally (§4, 9:2)—is the most promising starting-point for a philosophical inquiry into the concept of intention.

This methodological priority is not that of a philosophical behaviorist.[1] For Anscombe explicitly allows that there is such a thing as "purely interior" intention that a person never even attempts to execute (see §4, 9:2), and later on she will argue that there could not be a robust concept of intentional action without a way of describing a person's further aims and future ends.[2] But she recommends her *action-first* approach as a way to avoid what she calls "dead ends" (§3, 5:4, 6:2) that we can be led into by construing intention as "something whose existence is purely in the sphere of the mind" (§4, 9:2). On this latter approach, the task of the philosopher is first to characterize this interior state and only then to consider "what physically takes place, i.e. what a man actually does" (§4, 9:2) in doing something intentionally. Anscombe's recommended starting-point is precisely the opposite of this.

---

[1] This accusation comes up in conversation more often than it appears in print—but for an example of the latter, see Michael Bratman, *Intention, Plans, and Practical Reason*, pp. 5–7. Also, in "Davidson's Theory of Intention," Bratman describes Anscombe's discussion of reasons and causes as "rooted in strong behaviouristic assumptions" (p. 210).

[2] This is the thesis of Sections 20–21, as discussed in section 3.2.

1.1 The three headings (§1)

Consider three different ways that we use a concept of "intention" in everyday life (see *I*, §1, 1:1):

1. We treat intention as something that can be *expressed*, paradigmatically by saying what one is going to do;
2. We characterize *actions* as intentional, distinguishing intentional activity from things that people do non-intentionally; and
3. We describe people as acting *with* intentions, e.g., boiling water for tea or studying for the bar exam because one plans to become a lawyer.

The first thing to notice is the sheer variety of the list: heading (1) describes an instance of *linguistic* behavior as an expression of the speaker's intention; (2) describes an instance of *overt* behavior as itself intentional or not; and (3) describes—well, how should we put it?—the *aim* of an action or of an agent, i.e., something that a person acts in pursuit of, such that her action can be understood in relation to this further thing. On the other hand, there seems to be a *unity* within this variety, insofar as talk of "intention" isn't just equivocal between (1), (2), and (3)—as it is with talk of "bank" in statements like "My money is in the bank," "She hit a bank shot," and "The flow of water is eroding the bank." An adequate philosophical account of intention needs to reveal the connections among these three forms of understanding.

An essential thing to observe here, which Anscombe's initial presentation tends to obscure, is that very often we "employ a concept of 'intention'" (§1, 1:1) in some of the ways she describes without using the *language* of "intention" in doing so. This is easiest to see in connection with heading (1), as outside of philosophical contexts a person will not usually (or ever!) use the *phrase* "expression of intention" to characterize the meaning of a statement. Consider Anscombe's example from the start of Section 2:

> if I say "I am going to fail in this exam." and someone says "Surely you aren't as bad at the subject as that", I may make my meaning clear by explaining that I was expressing an intention, not giving an estimate of my chances. (§2, 1:3–2:1)

Faced with a confusion like this, what a person would most likely *say* to explain her meaning is not "Oh, I was expressing an intention," but rather something like "Oh no, it's not that—I am just so tired of all the pressure that my parents have been putting on me, and I need to show them ...." This clarification *is* a way of saying that one was expressing an intention, and anyone who can offer or appreciate such a clarification will have to draw on her grasp of that concept, but all this can be done even if the phrase "expression of intention" never occurs in the exchange. In a similar way, as we will see later, Anscombe's route to discovering our ordinary concept of intentional action is not to explore the circumstances in which we *call* actions "intentional," but rather to investigate the conditions under which we regard an action as suited to a request for reason-giving explanation. In each case our pre-theoretical grasp of these intention-concepts is put to use in ordinary practices where words like "intention," "intentional," etc., will occur only rarely.

So now we are to ask: *What do we mean* when we speak, implicitly or explicitly, of the expression of intention, of doing things intentionally, of the intentions with which people act? How are these ways of speaking, and the other human practices that are bound up with them, interrelated? And which of the three should be the starting-point of our philosophical investigation?

1.2 Predictions and expressions of intention (§§2–3)

Sections 2 and 3 take up the first of Anscombe's three headings—expressions of intention—and consider how these relate to *predictions* of what will happen in the future. It is worth reading this discussion alongside §§629–632 of Wittgenstein's *Philosophical Investigations*, where there are several distinctions, examples, and argumentative turns that are mirrored by Anscombe's arguments in Section 2 especially. In particular, we should notice that according to both Anscombe and Wittgenstein the expression of an intention to do something *is* a kind of prediction (*Voraussage*) of what will happen, albeit of a kind that is somehow different from the kind of prediction given in what Anscombe calls "estimates" of the future. Why are we supposed to think this?

To begin, consider again the example from the start of Section 2. I say I am going to fail an exam, and then when told that I'm not so bad at the subject, I "make my meaning clear by explaining that I was expressing an intention, not giving an estimate of my chances" (*I*, §2, 2:1). Such an explanation usually *will* clarify my meaning, which shows that we have an "intuitively clear" (§2, 1:3) understanding of the difference between expressing an intention and estimating what is going to happen. In everyday life we rarely have trouble employing this distinction to understand what people say. But *what* do we understand, when we understand this? What sort of distinction are we drawing?

A natural answer, which Anscombe wants us to resist, is that expressions of intention are distinguished from estimates of the future by the different ways that they relate to the *mental state* of the speaker. She suggests two ways to develop this idea:

> Suppose it is said "A prediction is a statement about the future". This suggests that an expression of intention is not. It is perhaps the description—or expression—of a present state of mind, a state which has the properties that characterise it as an intention. (§2, 2:2)

The first suggestion here is that expressions of intention differ from predictions in what they *describe*: whereas a prediction describes what will happen in the future, the expression of intention describes the "present state of mind" of the one who speaks. And the second is that these things differ in what they *express*—that is, in the state of mind *from which* one speaks, and which is manifested or given voice in one's verbal behavior.[3] Implicit in both suggestions is the assumption that we already have a working concept of intention as a *mental state*, and can appeal to this concept in explaining the distinction in question. The aim of Sections 2 and 3 is to undermine our confidence in taking such a concept for granted.

So let us ask: under what conditions is a statement like

(1)   I am going to fail this test

the *expression of an intention* to fail, rather than an estimate of one's chances? According to the first *mentalistic* analysis suggested at the start of Section 2, this will be the case whenever such a statement *describes the speaker's state of mind*:

---

[3] A further possibility, which Anscombe does not mention here, but which would also be called into question by her arguments in these sections, would be to say that an expression of intention is a *prescriptive* claim about how the world *should* be. The discussion of commands in Section 2 (see 2:4–3:1) reveals the inadequacy of this analysis, by arguing that descriptions of the future can also function as orders (e.g., "Nurse will take you to the operating theatre," said by a doctor in the presence of the nurse: §2, 3:1), and thus that "the indicative (descriptive, informatory) character is not the distinctive mark of 'predictions' *as opposed to* 'expressions of intention,' as we might at first sight have been tempted to think" (§2, 3:1).

(M) An estimate is a description of what will happen in the future, while an expression of intention is rather a description of the speaker's state of mind.

The first and most obvious reason to resist this proposal is simply that it seems wrong on its face. For a statement like (1), where this expresses the intention to fail, at least *appears* to have the same sort of descriptive content as any other indicative statement about the future state of the world, such as

(2)   It is going to rain tomorrow.

A statement like (2) might be justified by, or true in virtue of, an aspect of how the world presently is: for example, it might be because of a front that is presently over the Gulf of Mexico that, tomorrow, Florida is going to get some rain. Nevertheless this statement does not *describe* the present at all—it is, rather, simply a description of what is going to happen in the future. And the same seems to be true of (1): even if this statement is justified by, or true in virtue of, the speaker's present mental state, it does not *describe* such a state, but only describes what the speaker will do. At least on the face of things, *what one describes* in expressing an intention with a statement like (1) is the very same thing one describes in predicting or "estimating" a future happening that one does not intend: in each case, one's statement is simply a description of what is going to happen.

Anscombe notes, however, that there is a further and "deeper rooted" (§2, 4:2) objection to saying that intention is expressed in a prediction. Here is how she puts it:

> If I do not do what I said I would, I am not supposed to have lied; so it seems that the truth of a statement of intention is not a matter of doing what I said. (§2, 4:3)

If this conclusion of this little argument were correct, then the expression of intention would have to be something other than a description of a future happening—for any statement *describing* what will happen can be *true* only if things happen as it says they will. But Anscombe goes on to argue that the line of reasoning here is fallacious (for this rebuttal see §2, 4:4–5:1). It is true that someone who says she will do something that she then does not do has not necessarily *lied* in what she said—for her statement may have been *sincere* as long as she really had the intention to act in this way. But this does not show that her statement was really a *description* of her intention, any more than the possibility of offering a sincere but mistaken forecast of the weather shows that an estimate of the future is really a description of one's belief. (If I utter (2) and tomorrow it is dry, this does not mean that I have lied—for I may really have believed that it would rain. Nevertheless my statement was a *description* of tomorrow's weather, and not of my belief about it.) In both cases, while the speaker's state of mind determines the *sincerity of what* she says, the *truth* of her statement turns on what happens in the world—and this would not be true if these statements merely described the speaker's intention or belief.

Through these arguments, Section 2 thus opposes the mentalistic analysis (M) and supports instead what I will call a *factualist* analysis of the expression of intention:

(F)   Like a prediction or estimate of the future, an expression of intention is a description of what is going to happen.

The factualist analysis holds that in expressing the intention to do something, *what* a person says is simply that something *will happen*—namely, that she will do what she says she will. This, I suggest, is what Anscombe has in mind when she follows Wittgenstein in saying that the expression of intention is a species of prediction. And it helps her to mark an important difference between intention and mere appetite or desire: when a person expresses the intention to do something by saying that she is going to do it, she says something quite different than if she just said that she wanted or desired to do it—for she has described what she is going to *do* and not merely the internal state that she is in. It is thus that the analysis of the content of expressions of intention is supposed to keep us out of the "dead ends" that we can get into by thinking of intention first as a psychological state (see §3, 5:4–6:2): we find a clue that intentions are different from emotions or "drives" in the fact that the expression of intention parallels the expression of *belief*. The expression of intention is not merely a manifestation of how things are within oneself, but a sign that points beyond one's own psychology and represents how things are or will be in the world.[4]

---

[4] This is also what Anscombe has in mind when, at the end of Section 2, she corrects Wittgenstein's remark in the *Investigations* about the "natural expression of intention," saying instead that the expression of intention "is purely conventional," and that as a consequence non-linguistic animals, though they do have intentions and engage in intentional action, cannot have "any distinct expression of intention" (see §2, 5:3; and cf. §47, 86:2–87:1 for more on the intentions of non-linguistic animals). That is, Anscombe's position is that while intention can be *manifested* in non-verbal behavior (as when a cat is "crouching and slinking along with its

One might wonder, however, whether the factualist analysis (F) also applies to cases where a person expresses her intention by saying that she *intends* (or means, plans, etc.) to do something, and not simply that she will do it. An example (compare §2, 5:2) might be saying

(3)   I intend to go for a walk.

Doesn't a person who says something like (3) express an intention by describing her state of mind? Recalling the parallel with the expression of belief can help dislodge this intuition. If, for example, a person says

(4)   I believe that it is going to rain tomorrow,

her statement functions quite differently from a superficially similar statement that attributes a belief to someone else. To see this, notice that the conjunction in

(5)   She believes that it will rain tomorrow, but it will not

is in no way strange, but the first-personal counterpart

(6)   I believe that it will rain tomorrow, but it will not

has the ring of paradox.[5] A plausible explanation of this is that a statement like (4) is usually not a *mere* description of one's belief in the same way as one like

(7)   She believes that it will rain tomorrow

is *merely* a description of the belief of someone else. And as Anscombe points out toward the end of Section 2, something similar holds for talk of what one *intends* to do: thus a statement like

(8)   I intend to go for a walk but shall not go for a walk

"does sound in some way contradictory" (§2, 5:2), whereas there is no such appearance of contradiction in a corresponding statement about someone

eye fixed on [a] bird and its whiskers twitching" (§47, 86:2)), the expressive resources available to a non-linguistic creature do not allow for a way to *express* intention that is distinct from the expression of mere desire. A non-linguistic creature whose expressive resources are limited to behaviors like laughing and whimpering can express emotions like joy and sadness, and these can of course be clues to its intentions. But something further is available to us: we can use language to say what we are going to do.

[5] Here we might compare Wittgenstein's remarks on Moore's paradox in *Philosophical Investigations* II.x. I discuss this parallel at length in chapter 7.

else. Exactly how a statement like (8) is contradictory (if it really is at all) is a question Anscombe will return to later on.[6] For now it is enough to note the difficulty of accounting for this appearance of contradictoriness on the supposition that a statement of the form "I intend to *F*" does not offer any description of what one will in fact do.

A final objection one might raise to the factualist analysis (F) is that there seems to be a difference between the *kind* of thing which, in expressing an intention, one says is going to happen, and the kind of thing which one says is going to happen when one describes future happenings other than one's intentional actions. More specifically, one might suggest that the future state of the world one describes in expressing an intention will be one "in which the speaker is *some sort of agent*" (§3, 6:3; emphasis added), whereas this is not the case in an estimate of the future. While this suggestion seems right as far as it goes, there are some difficulties with it. For one thing, if a person says something like (1) and means it as an estimate of the future, clearly she is *some* sort of agent in the future she describes. More importantly, making good on this suggestion would require an explanation of what it is to *be* an agent in the relevant sense, which would take us to the second heading in Anscombe's initial division, i.e., the concept of intentional action. This will be the focus of our inquiry beginning in the next section.

First, however, we need to look more closely at two dense but important paragraphs where Anscombe gestures at a pair of ideas that will turn out to be crucial later on, namely that expressions of intention might differ from estimates of the future in respect of *(1)* how they are *grounded or justified* (see §2, 3:5–4:1) and *(2)* the way they establish a *standard of correctness* for the events they describe (see §2, 4:5–5:1). In what follows, I will consider each point in turn.

(1) Anscombe introduces the first distinction as follows:

> there is a difference between the types of ground on which we call an order, and an estimate of the future, sound. The reasons justifying an order are not ones suggesting what is probable, or likely to happen, but e.g. ones suggesting what it would be good to make happen with a view to an objective, or with a view to a sound objective. (*I*, §2, 3:5–4:1)

As Anscombe's wording makes clear, *soundness* here is a different concept from *truth*. A statement is *sound* in the sense at issue here to the extent that it is *justified* by the considerations that are supposed to support it—and thus, e.g., a well-informed weather forecast may be sound even if it turns out to be incorrect. And so Anscombe's point is that when a person expresses the intention to do something, the considerations that are supposed to support her statement are similar to those that would support an *order*: "not [considerations] suggesting what is probable, or likely to happen, but e.g. ones suggesting what it would be good to make happen with a view to an objective" (§2, 4:1). That is, the "description of something future" offered in an expression of intention will be grounded in "reasons for acting, sc. reasons why it would be useful or attractive if the description came true, not by evidence that it is [or will be] true" (§3, 6:3). Anscombe says briefly that "What is meant by 'reason' here is obviously a fruitful line of inquiry" (§3, 7:2), but she sets it aside for now.

(2) The second difference between expressions of intention and estimates of the future is that when a person fails to do what she says she will, the *fault* or *mistake* may lie not in what she said, but rather in her failure to *act* as she said she would. This is not just a reiteration of the earlier point that a person can be truthful in expressing the intention to do something she doesn't eventually do. What Anscombe observes now is when this happens, the speaker can be faulted or criticized *for failing to act* in the way that she says she will—a possibility that does not arise concerning a mere estimate of the future, where the speaker can be faulted only for what she said. As Anscombe puts it, in the first sort of criticism "the facts are, so to speak, impugned for not being in accordance with the words, rather than *vice versa*" (*I*, §2, 4:5–5:1). And she identifies three ways that there may be such a lack of accordance (I have added the bracketed numbers for ease of reference):

> This is sometimes so when [1] I change my mind; but another case of it occurs when [2] e.g. I write something other than I think I am writing; as Theophrastus says (*Magna Moralia*, 1189b 22[7]), the mistake here is one of performance, not of judgment. There are other cases too: [3] for example, St. Peter did not *change his mind* about denying Christ; and yet it would not be correct to say he made a lying promise of faithfulness. (§2, 5:1)

---

[7] The passage Anscombe cites here is from Book I, ch. xvii of the *Magna Moralia*: "No one debates with himself how the name of Archicles should be written, for that is already defined; so that errors arise, not in the conscious Understanding [*dianoia*], but in activity of writing." The authorship of this text is still disputed.

The differences between these three phenomena—of changing one's mind, failing to execute an action that one attempts to perform, and acting against an intention without changing one's mind—will be explored at length later on,[8] but there are two points that are important to appreciate right now. First, the possibility of "impugning the facts" seems to arise *only* in connection with commands and expressions of intention, and not with estimates of the future. And second, notice that in saying that the *mistake* in these cases "is one of performance, not of judgment," Anscombe does not abandon her factualist analysis of the expression of intention—that is, she does not deny that a person who expresses the intention to do something which, in the end, she does not, will have said something untrue. Indeed she says just the contrary: the possibility of mistaken performance "only shows that *there are other ways of saying what is not true*, besides lying and being mistaken" (§2, 4:3; emphasis added).[9] Her position is that even though, for expressions of intention no less than estimates of the future, it *is* the case that "if I don't do what I said, what I said was not true" (§2, 4:5), expressions of intention make room for a *kind* of fault or mistake that estimates of the future do not. We will consider in more detail later on how Anscombe thinks this distinctive kind of mistake is to be understood.

So far my discussion of these sections has focused on explaining how Anscombe's factualist analysis of the expression of intention challenges the idea that in expressing an intention a person offers "a description ... of a present state of mind" (§2, 2:2). But what about the other possibility that we considered: that while the expression of an intention *describes* what will happen, rather than the speaker's state of mind, what distinguishes these statements from estimates of the future is the state of mind that the speaker is *in* when she makes them—that is, in the state of mind that these statements *express*? The simple answer is that this strategy would require us to go beyond the first of Anscombe's three headings, since it would depend on a prior understanding of the concept of intention as a mental state. But this is not where Anscombe turns next: she proposes to focus first on the concept of intentional *action* rather than the mental state of intention. Why?

---

[8] Once again, see Sections 31–32 and 50–52, discussed in sections 4.3 and 7.2.

[9] Compare as well the last sentence in the entry for Section 2 in the Table of Contents: "The falsity of expressions of intention in the simple future tense *(a)* as lying and *(b)* as falsity because the intention is not carried out" (*I*, p. iii).

1.3 Action first (§§3–4)

If expression of intention is the wrong place to begin our inquiry, which of the other two headings should we consider first instead? At the end of Section 4, Anscombe indicates some of the reasons why we might want to start with the concept of further intention. In particular, she notes that often when we want to understand a person's intentions our interest is "not just in [that person's] intention *of* doing what he does, but in his intention *in* doing it," and moreover that "a man can form an intention which he then does nothing to carry out, either because he is prevented or because he changes his mind: but the intention itself can be complete, although it remains a purely interior thing" (*I*, §4, 9:2). The effect of this is

> to make us think that if we want to know a man's intentions it is into the contents of his mind, and only into these, that we must enquire; and hence, that if we wish to understand what intention is, we must be investigating something whose existence is purely in the sphere of the mind; and that although intention issues in actions, and the way this happens also presents interesting questions, still what physically takes place, i.e. what a man actually does, is the very last thing we need consider in our enquiry. (§4, 9:2)

This approach seems attractive. But Anscombe says that it is backward: what we should really consider first is intentional action itself. What are her reasons for favoring this *action-first* approach?

In these early sections of *Intention* the main reasons given in favor of Anscombe's strategy are epistemological. For example, she argues in Section 4 that it is simply not the case that intention is *in general* something "purely interior," since if it were we would not be able to know a person's intentions in the way we very often do, namely by observing their overt behavior:

> if you want to say at least some true things about a man's intentions, you will have a strong chance of success if you mention what he actually did or is doing. For whatever else he may intend, or whatever may be his intentions in doing what he does, the greater number of the things which you would say straight off a man did or was doing, will be things he intends. (§4, 8:1)

The point Anscombe is making here is not merely that a person's intentions are often revealed in what she does. Rather, her point is that in many everyday situations the most natural ways we have of describing what a person does will already implicate intention-concepts: the ascription of intention to a person is something we engage in *simply* in describing what happens when a person acts. She gives an example: a person who sees Anscombe at work on her book will say that she is sitting in a chair writing, and will not talk about her mere bodily movements or the way that they are "affecting the acoustic properties of the room" (§4, 8:2). Yet to say that Anscombe *is writing* is already to say something about the intention with which she acts. This description of what she is doing is already a description of her intention.

It might be objected, however, that this argument overlooks what is distinctive in the way we know *our own* intentions—for this knowledge seems not to require observing our own behavior, and its scope extends far beyond what we are evidently doing at a moment, encompassing as well our further intentions and intentions for the future. While *we* can see Anscombe writing, and so know that she has the intention of doing this, *she* also knows exactly *what* she is writing, as well as her purpose in writing this and what she intends to do next, and so on. Doesn't this first-person perspective provide a window into something that is real but "purely interior"?

The objection gets this much right: the knowledge of one's own intentional actions is not knowledge by observation, or at least is not usually dependent on observation in the same way as knowledge of the actions of others; and it usually extends well beyond what one is observably doing at any given moment. What Anscombe wants us to resist, however, is the interpretation of these phenomena in terms of privileged first-personal access to the contents of an inner domain. One reason for this is that *what* we know (1) when we know what we are doing or are going to do is not anything interior: for otherwise it would not be knowledge of what we are *doing* or are going to do. Second, while no doubt there is an "intuitively clear" (§2, 1:3) difference (2) between intending to do something and not intending to do it, in attempting to *explain* what we understand in grasping this distinction "we are likely to find ourselves in one or another of several dead ends," e.g.: psychological jargon about 'drives' and 'sets'; reduction of intention to a species of desire, i.e. a kind of emotion, or irreducible intuition of the meaning of 'I intend'" (§3, 5:4–6:1). (What makes the attempted explanations "dead ends" is that they do not aid in our understanding but only shift the location of our ignorance. What *sort* of motivation or "drive" is involved in intention? *Which* species of desire is it?) Finally, serious philosophical difficulties arise for any attempt to (3) explain the self-knowledge of intention as a matter of *recognizing* one's inner mental state:

If this were correct, there would have to be room for the possibility that
[one] misrecognizes. Further, when we remember having meant to do
something, what memory reveals as having gone on in our consciousness
is a few scanty items at most, which by no means add up to such an
intention; or it simply prompts us to use the words "I meant to . . .," without
even a mental picture of which we judge the words to be an appropriate
description. (§3, 6:2)[10]

This is not a behaviorist argument, or even an argument that the mental states
of intention or meaning ever lack a distinctive "cognitive phenomenology".
Rather, the point of the argument is that this is not what we *understand*
when we understand what an intention is, nor is it a means by which we
identify our own mental states as intentions rather than, say, beliefs. Together,
these considerations make clear the difficulty in giving an illuminating
philosophical explanation of the concept of an aim or purpose that does not
presuppose a prior grasp of intentional action as something that happens in
the world.

   Nothing in these considerations is likely to yield to a decisive argument
in favor of an action-first approach. But since the stakes here concern
philosophical strategy rather than matters of substance, it is not clear that
we should demand anything more than this—we may learn a lot from
Anscombe's approach even if a different one could also have yielded good
fruit. It is, however, worth noting two more reasons to favor an action-first
approach over one that prioritizes the concept of intention as a psychological
state. First, since in having an intention a person intends *to do* something, and
not merely that something happen merely by accident or chance, it might be
that the concept of intentional action is required to explicate the content of
the state of intention.[11] Second, it is widely acknowledged that attempts to
explain intentional action in terms of an agent's mental states have trouble
accounting for the possibility of "deviant causal chains," in which a person's
mental states give rise to an action of the sort they rationalize, but not in
a way that renders that action intentional.[12] While this problem might not

---

[10] As Anscombe notes, these arguments are indebted to Wittgenstein. See, e.g., *PI*, §§633–638.

[11] For an argument in this vein, see Matthew Boyle and Douglas Lavin, "Goodness and Desire."

[12] For example: "A climber might want to rid himself of the weight and danger of holding another man on a rope, and he might know that by loosening his hold on the rope he could rid himself of the weight and danger. This belief and want might so unnerve him as to cause him to loosen his hold, and yet it might be the case that he never chose to loosen his hold, nor did he do it intentionally" (Donald Davidson, "Freedom to Act," p. 79).

show that we cannot analyze intentional action in terms of the mental states that cause it, it does give reason to think that any understanding of how intention is the cause of intentional action will likely presuppose a prior understanding of intentional action itself. Together these arguments seem like reason enough to take the action-first approach seriously and follow Anscombe's arguments to see what fruit they bear.

1.4 Summary discussion

The principal aim of these opening sections is to show the necessity for a philosophical inquiry into the concept of intention, by exploring some of the puzzles, confusions, and dead-ends into which our thinking about these matters can lead us. Despite their aporetic character, these sections do plant seeds for some of the most important ideas that Anscombe will go on to develop in the remainder of the book. These include:

- The focus on *what happens* in the world, rather than on the mental state of a speaker or agent, in the analysis of how the concept of intention is usually deployed;
- The idea that statements about what will happen—and, as we will see, statements about what *has* happened in the past or *is* happening now—can be justified by *reasons for acting* rather than evidence about what will come to pass; and
- The distinction between mistakes in *judgment* and mistakes in *performance*, as two different ways to falsify an expression of intention.

The second of these ideas will play a central role in the discussion of intentional action that begins in Section 5.

Suggestions for further reading

- For a close reading of Anscombe's discussion of the expression of intention, see Richard Moran and Martin Stone, "Anscombe on Expression of Intention: An Exegesis."
- For an illuminating account of the Wittgensteinian method that Anscombe employs in her opening sections, see chapter 3 of Rachael Wiseman's *Guidebook to Anscombe's Intention*.

2

Beginnings of an Account

Section 5 begins our inquiry into the concept of intentional action. Rather than opening with a consideration of what it means to *say* that something was done intentionally, Anscombe's point of departure is a consideration of the way we ask and answer questions about *why* we act as we do. As I will suggest in what follows, the rationale behind this strategy is that the primary use to which we put the concept of intentional action is not in the explicit categorization of certain things as done intentionally, and others as not. Rather, we most often deploy this concept in explaining, and seeking explanations of, the *reasons why* people act as they do—as when, e.g., I ask, "Why are you chopping those carrots?," and you answer that it's because you're making chicken soup. Anscombe will argue, however, that this concept of a "reason for acting" (*I*, §5, 9:3) is not one that we can simply take for granted in our inquiry. The reason for this is that we speak of many things other than intentional actions as explicable by "reasons" as well, and so the relevant concept of a reason *for acting* is itself an action-concept, or at least a concept that depends on a prior concept of what it is to act (for this argument, see §5, 9:3–11:2).

In order to find a way out of this circle, Anscombe turns in Section 6 to an analysis of what a person must *know* about what she is doing, in order for a question like "Why are you doing that?", meant in a way that asks for the person's reason for acting, to be given application to what she does. It is in this context that Anscombe advances one of her best-known theses, that in doing something intentionally a person must have *non-observational knowledge* of what she is doing and why. It also leads to important discussions of the difference between reason-giving explanations and explanations that identify the *causes* of what takes place, and of whether it is possible to act intentionally but for no reason, or for reasons of which one is unaware.

2.1 "Why?"-questions (§5)

Anscombe opens Section 5 by posing the question that she has said should be considered first in her inquiry: "What distinguishes actions which are intentional from those which are not?" (*I*, §5, 9:3). This question is asked in a philosophical spirit rather than a scientific one: it presumes that we already have a working mastery of the concept of intentional action, and can draw on this mastery to identify the actions that fall under this concept and explore their distinguishing characteristics. In what, however, does this working mastery consist? An example from Section 19 reveals that our most common way of deploying the concept of intentional action is not in applying *words* like "intentional" and "unintentional" to things that people do:

> E.g. if I saw a man, who was walking along the pavement, turn towards the roadway, look up and down, and then walk across the road when it was safe for him to do so, it would not be usual for me to say that he crossed the road intentionally. But it would be wrong to infer from this that we ought not to give such an action as a typical example of an intentional action. (§19, 29:3)

One of the morals that Anscombe draws from this example is that "[t]he question does not normally arise whether a man's proceedings are intentional; hence it is often 'odd' to call them so" (§19, 29:3). And this is surely right: in general we *call* actions intentional or unintentional only when a person has done something untoward and we are trying to determine how to assign blame.[1] This suggests that we cannot reliably determine the extension of this concept just by considering the use of these particular words. What other approach is there to take?

The answer Anscombe suggests in Section 5 is that in ordinary circumstances people categorize actions as intentional, not by applying the words "intentional" or "intentionally" to them, but rather by treating them as events "to which a certain sense of the question 'Why?' is given application" (§5, 9:3). In the background here is the idea that there is a difference in the meaning of "Why?" between questions like

(1)   Why did that man cross the road?

---

[1] Indeed, in a 2006 study Bertram Malle surveyed the use of the words "intentional" and "intentionally" in news stories, and found that "94% of all instances concerned negative or socially undesirable events, 88% in the case of intentional, 99% in the case of intentionally" ("Intentionality, Morality, and Their Relationship in Human Judgment," p. 95).

and

(2)   Why did that man slip and fall?

In appreciating the difference in the meaning of these questions, we also appreciate that there is a difference in the sort of positive answer that is appropriate to each: thus statements like

(3)   Because he was going to look in that shop window

and

(4)   Because the floor had a wet spot on it

will have different meanings depending on which of these questions they are given in answer to. That is, giving (3) as an answer to (1) would suggest that the man was crossing the road *in order to* look in the shop window, whereas in answer to (2) it would suggest that it was *on the way* to looking in the window that he stepped on something that made him slip. Similarly, (4) in response to (1) would suggest that the man crossed the road to avoid the wet spot, or perhaps to clean it up, whereas in answer to (2) it would suggest that he slipped and fell when he stepped on the spot. Anscombe characterizes this difference by saying that only when a statement like (3) is given in answer to a question like (1) does the answer "give[. . .] a *reason for acting*" (§5, 9:3; emphasis added). The idea, then, is that we regard an action as intentional when we regard it as something that *could* be explained by giving a reason why it was done—that is, as something concerning which a request for such an explanation is appropriate.

Yet Anscombe notes right away that this proposal is insufficient as it stands, since we sometimes talk of *reasons* in querying and explaining non-intentional behaviors too. For "we readily say e.g. 'What was your reason for starting so violently?'" (§5, 10:1)—and a positive answer to this question, such as

(5)   I thought I saw a face at the window and it made me jump,[2]

would not carry any implication that the action in question was intentional. Yet we cannot *explain* why this is by saying, e.g., that "Giving a sudden start [. . .] is not *acting* in the sense suggested by the expression 'reason for acting'" (§5, 10:1), since it is just this sense of "acting" that the appeal to the concept

---

[2] For this example see §5, 9:4.

of a reason for acting was supposed to help us illuminate. Since "the question 'What is the relevant sense of the question "Why?"' and 'What is meant by "reason for acting"?' are one and the same" (§5, 9:3), it is only if we can "find the difference between the two kinds of 'reason' *without* talking about acting" (§5, 10:1; emphasis added) that we can explain one concept in a way that allows us to shed light on the other. This "danger of moving in a circle in our explanations of 'reasons for acting' and 'action'"[3] is illustrated throughout the remainder of Section 5, and sets the stage for the all-important sections that follow.

For ease of terminology, let us define a *"Why?"-question* as a question that asks "Why?" in the special sense that is our interest here. That is, a *"Why?"-question* is a question that would be answered positively by giving a *reason for acting* in the manner in question—but we still have to clarify the meaning of this latter phrase. So the working hypothesis proposed in Section 5 is that *an action is intentional if and only if a "Why?"-question has application to it.* If this hypothesis is correct, then we can identify the conditions under which an action is *not* intentional by identifying the conditions under which a "Why?"-question concerning it would be refused application. For such a refusal "is not indeed a proof (since it may be a lie), but a claim, that the question ... has no application" (§6, 11:4), and thus the conditions that would justify such a claim must be ones that would render the action non-intentional. Corresponding to each such condition will be a *necessary* condition of intentional action—that is, a condition that an action must satisfy in order for a "Why?"-question to have application to it. In what follows we will consider how Anscombe implements this strategy in order to find a way out of the circle described above.

2.2 The three epistemic conditions (§§6–8)

Our task is to explain the sense of "Why?" in which, e.g.,

(1)   Why did that man cross the road?

asks a different *sort* of question than, e.g.,

(2)   Why did that man slip and fall?

---

[3] See the entry for Section 5 in the Table of Contents: *I*, p. iii.

We need, however, to do this without appealing to any terms like "intention," "action," or "reason for action," since all these come from the family of concepts we are trying to elucidate. Beginning in Section 6, Anscombe's ingenious strategy for resolving this difficulty is to identify several ways of refusing application of a "Why?"-question that can be analyzed in *epistemic* terms, and thus without presupposing any action- or intention-concepts. Focusing for now only on cases where the person answering the "Why?"-question is also the person whose action is under consideration,[4] the first three ways she considers are:

- Saying that one *did not know* that she was doing the thing in question;
- Saying that one knew *only through observation* that she was doing this; and
- Saying that one needed observation to know *why* she was doing this.

Anscombe's proposal is that statements like these are all ways of *refusing application of the "Why?"-question*—that is, they are ways of saying that a question like "Why are you (/is she) doing that?" or "Why did you (/she) do that?," asked of the relevant action in the sense where a positive answer to this question would give one's reason for acting, *lacks application*. If such a statement is truthful, then any request for a reason for acting would be akin to asking of a person without a pocket how much money her pocket contains, or asking who was the winner of a non-competitive game:[5] the question *lacks application* because the action under consideration is not the kind of thing that is *suitable* to be understood in this way. According to the working hypothesis introduced previously, such a statement therefore carries the implication that this action is not intentional. Because of this, Anscombe takes these three ways of refusing application of a "Why?"-question to yield the following three necessary conditions on intentional action:

(C1) A person does something intentionally only if she *knows* that she is doing it.

(C2) A person does something intentionally only if she *knows without observation* that she is doing it.

---

[4] We should notice, however, that we could reach the same conclusions by considering third-personal "Why?"-questions and answers instead, as, e.g., the question "Why is *she* sawing Smith's board?" (cf. *I*, §6, 11:5–12:1) can be refused application by saying that *she* doesn't know it is Smith's.

[5] I owe the latter example to Marshall Thompson. For the former, see §17, 25:3.

(C3) A person does something intentionally only if she *does not need observation to know why* she is doing it.

Since much of the remainder of *Intention* is devoted to elaborating these conditions and defending them against various objections, my aim in the rest of this section will be not to argue in their favor, but only to say a bit more about how they should be understood, and what the intuitive motivation is for each.

Condition (C1)

Anscombe motivates her first condition by claiming that a "Why?"-question "is refused application by the answer 'I was not aware I was doing that'" (*I*, §6, 11:4). (Notice that, as in ordinary English, the relevant sense of "being aware" is simply equivalent to knowing—indeed, Anscombe switches to talk of knowledge by the end of the following paragraph.) As she points out right away, the knowledge-condition in (C1) relates to another important feature of intentional action that is also discussed in Section 6, namely that action is intentional only *under a description* (or some set of descriptions) of what a person does. That is, even if (in a non-technical sense) a person's doing *F* and her doing *G* describe "a single action" (§6, 11:5), still she might be doing *F* intentionally and *G* only by mistake. For example, a person may be sawing a plank intentionally, and the plank may be one of Smith's, but still she might not *intentionally* be sawing one of *Smith's* planks—for she may not know that the plank is Smith's (cf. §6, 11:5–12:1), and so a "Why?"-question might not have application to her action under that description, though it would have application under the description "sawing a plank." Since knowledge is also sensitive in this way to the description of what is known—that is, since a person can know (or believe) that *p* without knowing (or believing) that *q* even if *p* and *q* are, in a non-technical sense, one and the same fact—the thesis that intentional action requires knowledge of what one is doing helps to explain this characteristic of it.

While Anscombe presents her condition (C1) as a truism, there are several ways philosophers have objected to it. One of these objections is worth considering right away, since it will lead to an important clarification of Anscombe's view. This objection is that (C1) is violated in the case of some *automatic* or *absent-minded* actions, which may be intentional even though the agent lacks any conscious awareness of what she does. David Armstrong offers an oft-quoted description of this sort of automaticity:

> If you have driven for a very long distance without a break, you may have had experience of a curious state of automatism, which can occur in these conditions. One can suddenly "come to" and realize that one has driven for long distances without being aware of what one was doing, or, indeed, without being aware of anything. One has kept the car on the road, used the brake and clutch perhaps, yet all without any awareness of what one was doing. (Armstrong, "The Nature of Mind," p. 12)

If we accept, as seems plausible, that in Armstrong's case the actions of keeping the car on the road, using the brake, etc., are intentional—that is, that Anscombe's "Why?"-question has application to them—then his claim that the driver *lacks awareness* of these actions makes the case seem like a counterexample to condition (C1). What should we say in reply to this?

There are three points worth making. The first is that as I noted earlier, "awareness" in the sense Anscombe uses it in *Intention* is simply equivalent to "knowledge," and because of this condition (C1) does not have any implications for what a person's *conscious* mental life must be like at the time when she acts. Just as one may "come to" the realization that one knows a certain fact, say that Trenton is the capital of New Jersey, even if she has known this for a long time, so the phenomenon of "coming to" the realization that she has been doing something does not show that she was doing it unknowingly.[6] Since there are many things we take a person to know beyond what she is consciously considering at a given time, the phenomenon described by Armstrong does not provide an easy route to a refutation of condition (C1).

The second point to make about the phenomenon of absent-minded action is that at least some of the cases that philosophers present as instances of self-ignorant action might rather be cases of swift *forgetting*—that is, cases in which a person knows what she is doing while she does it, but doesn't make this an object of attention in a way that leads to its being "stored" in long-term memory. If, for example, I get in my car and simply can't remember whether I locked the door of my house, that does not show that when I *was* locking the door I was entirely unaware—that is, ignorant—of doing so. This is why, as Anscombe notes (cf. *I*, §6, 11:4), the way to refuse application of

---

[6] No doubt this concept is vague at the boundaries. (Do I already know, before I think about it, that 3 x 267 = 801, that zebras can't dance ballet, and that "The door was left open by an elephant in a red bikini" is a grammatical sentence in English? Or is my thinking about these things also a way of figuring them out?) And there is certainly room for a philosophical exploration into the conditions of implicit or "tacit" knowledge. But nothing in Anscombe's position hinges on the possibility of clarifying this concept in a way that would yield an exact account.

a "Why?"-question concerning a past action (that is, a question of the form "Why *did you do* that?") is to say that one *did not* (then) know that one was acting in the way described, rather than that one *does not* (now) know this. And condition (C1) says nothing about our propensity to remember things that we were doing earlier on.

③ My final observation is that there can be something self-undermining in the way that philosophers present the phenomenon of absent-minded action as evidence that intentional actions are not necessarily self-known. The moral of Armstrong's example is supposed to be that in this "state of automatism" one may not be aware of anything at all—or, perhaps, that one is aware only of whatever happens to occupy her thoughts. And if this is granted, then it follows that *one* of the things that an absent-minded agent will not be aware of is her own knowledge or ignorance of what she does! This suggests that a person's post hoc testimony that she did not know that she was doing something is precisely *not* something we should treat as definitive evidence of her cognitive state at the time, and not only because she may have forgotten what she previously knew. For it could be that in acting absent-mindedly we know what we are doing, but *without being aware that we know this*—since our minds are elsewhere at the time, if indeed they are anywhere at all. And (C1) does not bring any requirement of second-order knowledge or awareness.

Condition (C2)

Having argued that knowledge of what one is doing is a necessary condition of intentional action, Anscombe turns in Section 7 to consider the class of things that are done *knowingly but not intentionally*—things like, for example, jumping in fright when one sees a face in the window (cf. *I*, §5, 9:4). While such actions sometimes described as "involuntary" (see §7, 12:2), this usage won't help us here, as the concept of involuntary action is, again, just the sort of action-concept we are trying to elucidate.[7] It is in this context that

---

[7] Another remark in this passage—that we should "reject a fashionable view of the terms 'voluntary' and 'involuntary', which says that they are appropriately used only when a person has done something untoward" (§7, 12:3)—is likely directed against Gilbert Ryle, who argues just this in chapter 3 of *The Concept of Mind*; and cf. J.L. Austin's claim in "A Plea for Excuses" (presented in 1956 as his Presidential Address to the Aristotelian Society) that there is "No modification without aberration"—that is, that terms like "voluntary," "intentional," etc., are appropriately applied to an action "[o]nly if we do the action named in some *special* way or circumstances, different from those in which such an act is normally done" (pp. 15–16). As I noted in fn. 1, Ryle and Austin are probably right that we tend use the *words* "intentional," "voluntary," etc., in

Anscombe introduces one of the most important concepts in *Intention*, namely that of *non-observational knowledge*, as a better way to delineate the category of known-but-unintentional actions. She introduces this concept with the following example:

> a man usually knows the position of his limbs without observation. It is without observation, because nothing *shews* him the position of his limbs; it is not as if he were going by a tingle in his knee, which is the sign that it is bent and not straight. Where we can speak of separately describable sensations, having which is in some sense our criterion for saying something, then we can speak of observing that thing; but that is not generally so when we know the position of our limbs. (§8, 13:4; and cf. §28, 49:2–50:1)[8]

These remarks are opaque, and a great deal of ink has been spilled both exploring what Anscombe meant and debating whether she could have been correct in what she says here about bodily self-knowledge.[9] And that situation presents an enormous difficulty: for if we can't pin down what Anscombe is saying about how we know the position of our limbs, or understand how what she says could be correct, then it is hard to see how we can use the example of bodily self-knowledge to help us understand what it is to know something without observation.[10] Moreover, even if we could resolve these difficulties it seems that this characterization of non-observational knowledge fails to isolate what is really distinctive in the knowledge of one's intentional actions. For example, knowledge by inference, hearsay, and intuition all seem not to involve any "separately describable sensation" through which one comes to know, but none of these are ways in which a person usually comes to know what she is intentionally doing. So a proper construal of criterion (C2) should explain why they are ruled out.

these ways, but this does not show that our *concepts* of intentional or voluntary action have this inherently evaluative structure.

[8] A likely inspiration here is Wittgenstein: see *PI* §§624–626, as well as the discussion in Part II, section viii of the *Investigations* of the idea that "My kinaesthetic sensations advise me of the movement and position of my limbs."

[9] For discussion of these questions, with copious reference to Anscombe's writings as well as the surrounding literature, see Rachael Wiseman, *Guidebook to Anscombe's Intention*, pp. 84–92.

[10] Notice that this difficulty is especially acute for anyone sympathetic to the idea that the character of perception is "diaphanous" or "transparent"—that is, the idea that *in general* it is not possible to describe the character of perceptual sensations except by reference to what they are, at least apparently, perceptions of: for in that case won't it *always* be impossible to give a "separate" description of the sensations in virtue of which, through perception, we come to know things?

As interesting as these questions are, we need not let them detain us here. For Anscombe's purpose in introducing the concept of non-observational knowledge is to characterize the way we know our *actions*, not the way we know the position and movements of our bodies. And the idea that there is something distinctive in the knowledge of one's intentional actions can be worked out, in a way that is both philosophically rigorous and faithful to Anscombe's text, without having to consider what sort of "sensations" this knowledge is grounded in. Consider as a starting-point this famous passage from Wittgenstein's *Blue Book*:

There are two different cases in the use of the word "I" (or "my") which I might call "the use as object" and "the use as subject." Examples of the first kind of use are these: "My arm is broken," "I have grown six inches," "I have a bump on my forehead," "The wind blows my hair about." Examples of the second kind are: "*I* see so-and-so," "*I* fear so-and-so," "*I* try to lift my arm," "*I* think it will rain," "*I* have toothache." One can point to the difference between the two cases by saying: The cases of the first category involve the recognition of a particular person, and there is in these cases the possibility of an error, or as I should rather put it: The possibility of an error has been provided for . . . . It is possible that, say in an accident, I should feel a pain in my arm, see a broken arm at my side, and think it is mine, when really it is my neighbour's. And I could, looking into a mirror, mistake a bump on his forehead for one on mine. On the other hand, there is no question of recognizing a person when I say I have toothache. To ask "are you sure that it's *you* who have pains?" would be nonsensical. (*BB*, pp. 66–67)

One purpose of this passage is to draw a distinction between two different ways we have of knowing things about ourselves. To know oneself "as object" is to know that one is *F*, but in a way that provides for the possibility that it is really someone else's being *F* that one knows about in this way—thus, e.g., if I know that my arm is broken by seeing, among a pile of bodies, a broken arm at my side, it *could* be that I mistook my neighbor's arm for my own. By contrast, a person knows herself "as subject" when she knows herself in a way that does not provide for such a possibility—as when I simply feel a pain in my arm and thereby know that I am hurt.[11] Ways of knowing oneself as object therefore include routes to knowledge like perception, hearsay, and

---

[11] Notice that this form of invulnerability to mistake does not necessarily equate to infallibility—for example, I might *merely* be feeling a pain, and so not be hurt after all. The point is that the pain in my arm does not leave open the question of *who* is hurt, if indeed anyone is.

inference, while ways of knowing oneself as subject include interoceptive bodily awareness as well as whatever the usual ways are of knowing one's sensations and psychological states. Understood in this way, the point of saying that the knowledge of one's actions is *non-observational knowledge* is to place this knowledge in the second of these categories: it means the knowledge of oneself "as agent" is knowledge of oneself *as subject*, and so that we do not come to have this knowledge in the same way as we come to know about the actions of other people. This is just the sort of characterization that Anscombe herself offers in an important passage in Section 28, where she writes that "in so far as one is observing, inferring, etc. that [something] is actually taking place, one's knowledge is not the knowledge that a man has of his intentional actions":

> By the knowledge that a man has of his intentional actions I mean the knowledge that one denies having if when asked e.g. "Why are you ringing that bell?" one replies "Good heavens! I didn't know *I* was ringing it!" (*I*, §28, 50:3–51:1)

The emphasis on "I" is in the original text: Anscombe seems to be indicating that part of what distinguishes the knowledge of one's intentional actions is that it is a kind of knowledge that does not leave open *whose* actions these are, as it is in the nature of this knowledge that the actions known are those of she who knows them. She also advances this position in her 1974 paper "The First Person," where bodily action is frequently used as an example of something that is an object of self-knowledge or self-consciousness:

> I have from time to time such thoughts as "I am sitting," "I am writing," "I am going to stay still," "I twitched." There is the question: in happenings, events, etc. concerning what object are these verified or falsified? The answer is ordinarily easy to give because I can observe, and can point to, my body; I can also feel one part of it with another. "This body is my body" then means "My idea that I am standing up is verified by my body, if it is standing up." And so on. But observation does not show me which body is the one. Nothing shows me that. ("FP," pp. 33–34)

If Anscombe is right in what she says here about the usual way of knowing that one is sitting, writing, staying still, etc., then it might make sense to deny this knowledge the label "observational," since it seems to be part of the concept of observation that it can be directed across a range of different objects. Most importantly for our purposes, the idea that bodily self-knowledge, and the knowledge of one's actions, are distinctive in *this* way doesn't depend on any controversial theses about the nature of the sensations in which these forms of knowledge are or are not grounded.

Another way to see why Anscombe would have been interested in this concept of a distinctively first-personal way of knowing is by putting Gilbert Ryle's work in the background. In chapter 6 of *The Concept of Mind*, Ryle argues at length against a conception of first-person authority according to which a person necessarily has privileged access to the states of her own mind and only a problematic, inference-based knowledge of the minds of others. Against this conception, Ryle holds that though we usually know more about ourselves than we know about other people, the *ways* we know these things are one and the same: thus he famously remarks that "in principle, as distinct from practice, John Doe's ways of finding out about John Doe are the same as John Doe's ways of finding out about Richard Roe" (*CM*, p. 138). And in Ryle's view this is no less true of the knowledge of our voluntary or deliberate actions:

> in almost the same way as a person may be, in this sense, alive to what he is doing, he may be alive to what someone else is doing. In the serial operation of listening to a sentence or a lecture delivered by someone else, the listener, like the speaker, does not altogether forget, yet nor does he have constantly to recall the earlier parts of the talk, and he is in some degree prepared for the parts still to come, though he does not have to tell himself how he expects the sentence or lecture to go on. Certainly his frame of mind is considerably different from that of the speaker, since the speaker is, sometimes, creative or inventive, while the listener is passive and receptive; the listener may be frequently surprised to find the speaker saying something, while the speaker is only seldom surprised; the listener may find it hard to keep track of the course taken by the sentences and arguments, while the speaker can do this quite easily. While the speaker intends to say certain fairly specific things, his hearer can anticipate only roughly what sorts of topics are going to be discussed. (*CM*, p. 160)

The "almost" in Ryle's first sentence here should not be given much weight. Indeed, immediately following this passage he explains that all these self/other asymmetries "are differences of degree, not of kind," and boil down to the fact that the person performing an action "is in a very good position to know what [another person] is often in a very poor position to know" (p. 160).

On Ryle's view, while being "alive" to what one is doing is a mark of intelligent or skillful action, and while we ordinarily know our own actions *better* than those of other people, the knowledge that an agent has of herself is not any distinctive *kind* of knowledge, but only a matter of turning a general-purpose mind-reading capacity toward the observation and interpretation of one's own behavior.

Despite sharing Ryle's antipathy to any "Cartesian" understanding of the scope of self-knowledge and its difference from the knowledge of others, Anscombe does not agree at all that the distinctiveness of self-knowledge is exclusively a matter of degree. Read in light of this disagreement, her thesis that "the class of intentional actions is a sub-class of ... the class of things known without observation" (*I*, §8, 14:2) amounts to the claim that the way a person knows what she herself is intentionally doing is different *in kind* from her ways of knowing about other matters, including the intentional actions of others. It is because this knowledge is a form of *self*-knowledge that it cannot be knowledge by observation, nor by "inference, hearsay, superstition or anything [else] that knowledge or opinion are ever based on" (§28, 50:3)—for none of these are ways of knowing oneself "as subject." Nevertheless the *object* of an agent's self-knowledge is something that can also be known about in any of these other ways, as Anscombe noted earlier: for if, e.g., I am sitting in a chair and writing, then "anyone grown to the age of reason in the same world would know this as soon as he saw me" (§4, 8:2). *His* knowledge would be knowledge by observation, but it would be knowledge of the very same thing that I myself knew "without reflection, certainly without adverting to observation" of my own behavior (§4, 8:2). This difference does not guarantee that an agent's judgment of what she is doing is infallible—a point that will become crucially important later on. Rather, the idea is only that insofar as we are *not* mistaken, the knowledge we have of what we are intentionally doing is arrived at in a quite different way from the way in which someone else may come to know the very same thing.

Notice that this is a purely negative characterization of "the knowledge that a man has of his intentional actions" (§28, 50:3–51:1): condition (C2) says that this knowledge is *not* knowledge by observation, which means it is *not* the sort of knowledge we have of most things in the world, including what other people are doing. We have to wait until later on for a positive characterization of what makes this knowledge distinctive—and also for a fuller explanation of how it is *so much as possible* for a person to know "from within" without adverting to inference, hearsay, or observation, the very same thing that can be known "from without" by a person who observes her behavior.

Condition (C3)

Recall the task at hand. It is to delineate, without appeal to any action- or intention-concepts, the conditions in which a question like "Why did you do that?" or "Why are you doing that?," where this question asks for a person's reasons for acting, is appropriately given application. Conditions (C1) and (C2) help to do this, by showing that the question does *not* have application to something that the agent did not know she was doing, or knew she was doing only through observation. But Anscombe argues at the start of Section 8 that these conditions are not sufficient, since some *involuntary* actions will satisfy them both: for example, "you would know even with your eyes shut that you had kicked when the doctor tapped your knee, but cannot identify a sensation by which you know it" (*I*, §8, 14:3–15:1). In this case an action (of a sort) is known without observation (here, through interoceptive awareness of a bodily movement), but it is not something one intentionally does. In the final paragraphs of Section 8, Anscombe introduces condition (C3) as a way to rule some of these cases out:

(C3)   A person does something intentionally only if she *does not need observation to know why* she is doing it.

The idea here is that while a person usually will not need observation to know, e.g., that she has kicked her leg, that this motion is *due to the doctor's tap* is something she will know only through observation or inference. Anscombe fleshes this idea out further in Section 17, where she explains that an action will fail to satisfy this third condition

> if the only way in which a question as to [its] cause was dealt with was to speculate about it, or to give reasons why such and such should be regarded as the cause. E.g. if one said "What made you jump like that?" when someone had just jerked with the spasm which one sometimes gets as one is dropping off to sleep, he would brush aside the question or say "It was involuntary—you know, the way one does sometimes jump like that"; now a mark of the rejection of that particular question "What made you?" is that one says things like "I don't know if anyone knows the cause" or "Isn't it something to do with electrical discharges?" and that is the only sense that one gives to "cause" here. (§17, 25:2)

This passage makes clear something I have alluded to already, namely that in speaking of non-observational knowledge Anscombe means not only knowledge that isn't grounded immediately in sensory perception, but also knowledge that isn't verified by "inference, hearsay, superstition," and so forth (§28, 50:3). Her position is that *any* "third-personal" or non-self-specific way of knowing cannot be a person's way of knowing either what she is intentionally doing or why she is doing it. And once again there is a helpful contrast to be drawn with Ryle, on whose view there will be no difference in kind between the way an agent can give an explanation of her own actions and the way they might be explained by an outside observer: in each case this explanation is just a matter of subsuming what happened under a general law, and the way one does this in the first-person case is no different from the way one does it in the case of someone else.[12] Anscombe's third condition denies this: it says that if the only way you can explain an action is to speculate as to why you did it, or to give explanations that are based in evidence (i.e., "reasons why such and such should be regarded as the cause" (§17, 25:2)), then this action cannot have been intentional under that description. And the reason for this is that all those ways of working out the explanation of an action are, paradigmatically, ways we have of working out explanations of what *someone else* is doing, or why something is happening in the physical world around us. While we *can* also use these as ways of finding explanations for what we ourselves are doing, condition (C3) tells us that when this is the *only* way a person has to explain a given action, it cannot be something she intentionally does.

In addition to the questions raised already about the knowledge-condition and the concept of knowledge without observation, the introduction of condition (C3) raises a challenging question that refers us back to the original difficulty raised in Section 5 concerning the concept of a "reason for acting." The trouble, as Anscombe put it at the start of Section 9, was that

> there are contexts in which there is some difficulty in describing the distinction between a cause and a reason. As e.g. when we give a ready answer to the question "Why did you knock the cup off the table?"—"I saw such and such and *it made me jump.*" (§9, 15:4–16:1; and cf. §5, 9:4 for the first occurrence of this example)

---

[12] For this thesis see *CM*, pp. 76–77. I discuss this passage further in section 2.3.

Intuitively this answer does not give a *reason* for acting in the sense that we are out to explain—that is, it is not the kind of positive answer that gives application to Anscombe's question "Why?" Nor, however, in a case like this does one need observation (or inference, hearsay, etc.) to say either what one was doing or why—so all of the first three conditions are satisfied. Because of this, in order to explain how this response can be a way of *refusing* the application of the "Why?"-question that it is an answer to, we will need a further condition beyond the three introduced so far. It is in order to provide this that Anscombe now turns to consider more directly the concept of doing something *for a reason*.

So much for our preliminary discussion of conditions (C1), (C2), and (C3). We must bear in mind that it is *only* preliminary, and that much of the remainder of *Intention* is focused on the task of developing these conditions in more detail and defending them against various objections. We will consider all of this in due course.

2.3 Reason, motive, and cause (§§9–16)

At the start of Section 5, Anscombe noted an important difficulty in her task of explicating the sense of "Why?" in which a positive answer to questions like "Why are you doing that?," "Why did you do that?," or "Why are you going to do that?" will "give[. . .] a reason for acting" (*I*, §5, 9:3). The difficulty was that a person's answer to such a question may, in *a* perfectly ordinary sense of "reason", give a reason for her action, even though the action was not intentional, as with, e.g.:

(1)   Why did you knock the cup off the table?

answered by

(2)   I thought I saw a face at the window and it made me jump.

Since a startled jump is not an intentional action, the statement in (2) should be a way of *refusing* application of the "Why?"-question in (1), and *not* a way of giving one's reason for acting. This requires us to explain the sense of "reason for acting" in which the answer in (2) does not give one—and, again, to do this without appealing directly to any of the action- or intention-concepts that we are supposed to avoid taking for granted.

The introduction of conditions (C1), (C2), and (C3) helped to make some headway in this task of explication. Those conditions do not, however, manage to address the original problem case, as it seems to satisfy all three of them: a person who jumps in this way usually knows without observation that she does this, and does not need to rely on observation, inference, testimony, etc., to say why this is.[13] The overarching aim of Sections 9–16 is to introduce and defend one last condition that will explain why such *involuntary* behaviors do not count as intentional actions:

(C4)   An action is intentional only if it is not merely the effect of a mental cause.

Anscombe's endorsement of (C4), and her arguments for it, are often taken to show that she is an "anti-causalist" about intentional action explanation—that is, that on her view "the concept of cause that applies elsewhere cannot apply to the relation between reasons and actions."[14] I will argue later on in this section that such an interpretation of Anscombe's position is simply incorrect. In order to see this, however, we will first have to consider what condition (C4) means and why Anscombe thinks we should accept it.

 (1) To begin: condition (C4) says that an intentional action cannot *merely* have had a *mental cause*. What is the meaning of the italicized phrases? I will consider them in reverse order.

  Concerning the second phrase, one thing we know is that mental causes are supposed to be causes that satisfy (C3), and so the efficacy of mental causes must be known without observation—that is, when M is the mental cause of S's action A (or thought T or feeling F; cf. I, §10, 16:3), S will know without observation that M was the cause of A.[15] Beyond this, Anscombe says that what further distinguishes mental causes is that a mental cause is always a conscious mental occurrence, i.e., "something perceived by the person affected" (§11, 17:2). Thus she writes that giving the mental cause of an action or thought or feeling is a way of answering "the specific question: what produced this action or thought or feeling on your part: what did you see or hear or feel, or what ideas or images cropped up in your mind, and led up to it?" (§11, 17:2–18:1).

---

[13] Thus "the cases where this difficulty arises are just those in which the cause itself *qua* cause (or perhaps one should rather say: the causation itself) is in the class of things known without observation" (§9, 16:2).

[14] See Donald Davidson, "Actions, Reasons, and Causes," p. 9.

[15] As Anscombe puts it, in the cases at issue "the cause itself *qua* cause (or perhaps one might say: the causation itself) is in the class of things known without observation" (§9, 16:2).

Concerning the first emphasized term, the force of "merely" in condition (C4) is simply to allow that mental occurrences of the sort just described can be *part* of the account of why something was intentionally done—so what the condition requires is only that in order for an action to be intentional it must be possible *also* to explain it by giving one's reasons for acting.[16] For example, Anscombe imagines a case where "a feeling of desire to eat apples affects me and I get up and go to a cupboard where I think there are some" (§11, 17:1). In this case the feeling of desire would count as a mental cause in the relevant sense, and so condition (C4) allows that it could be appealed to in answering a question like "Why did you open the cupboard?" The condition requires, however, that in order for such a "Why?"-question to have application to this action it must be possible to answer it positively by describing something else, too—though at this point we are still waiting on Anscombe's positive account of what this other sort of answer is like. So the presupposition of condition (C4) is that *a description of the mental causes of an action is not itself a description of the agent's reasons for acting*. Because of this, a claim that an action can be explained *only* in terms of mental causes, as in a statement like (2) earlier, amounts to a refusal of the application of the "Why?"-question to it.

(2) What should we think of this proposal? One thing that seems clear enough is that an action's being explicable in terms of reasons for acting does not *require* its having had any mental causes in Anscombe's sense of that term. That is, not in *every* case can an explanation of the form "'I did so and so in order to ...' [...] be backed up by [e.g.] 'I *felt* a desire that ...'":

> I may e.g. simply hear a knock on the door and go downstairs to open it without experiencing any such desire. Or suppose I feel an upsurge of spite against someone and destroy a message he received so that he shall miss an appointment. If I describe this by saying "I wanted to make him miss that appointment" this does not necessarily mean that I had the thought "If I do this, he will ..." and that affected me with a desire of bringing it about,

---

[16] Indeed, Anscombe claims later on that the possibility of mental-causal explanation is a necessary condition of a "Why?"-question's application—that is, that an action is *not* intentional if there is "no room for ... mental causality" in the explanation of it (§17, 25:2). Her idea there is that if an action admits of a reason-giving explanation it must also make sense to consider "what went on in [the agent's] mind and issued in the action" (§11, 17:1). By contrast, there will be "no room" for mental causality if, e.g., "the only way in which a question as to cause [is] dealt with [is] to speculate about it, or to give reasons why such and such should be regarded as the cause" (§17, 25:2)—that is, if the explanation of an action, thought, or feeling cannot be known *without observation*.

which led up to my doing so. This may have happened, but need not. (*I*, §11, 17:1)

There is, once again, nothing suspiciously behaviorist here—Anscombe's claim is only that reason-giving explanations do not always rest on an appeal to what is *consciously* thought or felt. But the more difficult thing to understand is why explaining an action by describing its mental causes is not even a *kind* of reason-giving explanation in the sense at issue. Why, that is, should we think that an explanation of an action that gives one's reasons for acting is a different *sort* of explanation than an explanation of an action in terms of its mental causes?

I believe that we can better understand why Anscombe says this if we situate her argument in its immediate historical context, contrasting it especially with Ryle's account of psychological explanation in chapter 4 of *The Concept of Mind*. Ryle distinguishes there between what he calls *causal* explanations, which represent two events as standing in the relation of cause and effect, from explanations that appeal to *dispositions*, which on his analysis represent "law-like propositions" concerning what has a general propensity to happen. Thus he writes:

> We ask why the glass shivered when struck by the stone and we get the answer that it was because the glass was brittle. Now "brittle" is a dispositional adjective; that is to say, to describe the glass as brittle is to assert a general hypothetical proposition about the glass. So when we say that the glass broke when struck because it was brittle, the "because" clause does not report a happening or a cause; it states a law-like proposition. *People commonly say of explanations of this second kind that they give "the reason" for the glass breaking when struck.* (CM, p. 74; emphasis added)

What matters for our purposes is to see how, for Ryle, the sense of "because" in which we say that a glass broke *because it was struck* is different from the sense in which we say that it broke *because it was brittle*.[17] In the first case our explanation "reports an event" (*CM*, p. 74) that is the *cause* of the thing we explain. In the second, our explanation appeals to a general *tendency* of the glass to do a certain sort of thing—namely, break—in the circumstance

---

[17] Thus: "There are at least two quite different senses in which an occurrence is said to be 'explained'; and there are correspondingly at least two quite different senses in which we ask 'why' it occurred and two quite different senses in which we say that it happened 'because' so and so was the case" (CM, p. 74). Surely Anscombe was aware, and expected her readers to be aware, of how her remarks about the different senses of "Why?" echo this passage.

it was in. And, according to Ryle, it is the second sort of explanation that is commonly said to give a "reason" for what happened.[18]

Ryle's distinction between causal and dispositional explanations is likely to appear rather strained. For surely there is *a* perfectly good sense of "causal" in which "The glass broke because it was brittle" gives a causal explanation of what happens! But we should not interpret him as denying this truism. Ryle is pointing out that a standing dispositional characteristic like the fragility of an object is a different *sort* of causal-explanatory factor than a triggering event like its being struck, and thus that we are making a different sort of claim—a claim whose "grammar" is different, we might say—when we explain what happens in terms of dispositions and triggering events, respectively. What Ryle somewhat artificially calls "reasons" are *explanatory factors of the dispositional variety*, and reason-giving explanations in his sense are explanations that appeal to dispositions. And my suggestion is that in distinguishing reason-giving explanations of action from mental-causal ones, Anscombe is doing something similar: her claim is that the description of a person's reasons for acting gives a different sort of explanatory factor than the description of the conscious events that led up to what she did. Understood in this way, the force of condition (C4) is that in order for an action to be intentional it must be suited to be explained in terms of something other than its triggering causes.

Anscombe departs from Ryle, however, on the matter of whether describing someone's reasons for acting is simply a matter of attributing to that person an underlying *disposition* that her action was a manifestation of. Citing Ryle's suggestion that "he boasted from vanity" be analyzed as "he boasted ... and his doing so satisfies the law-like proposition that whenever he finds a chance of securing the admiration and envy of others, he does whatever he thinks will produce this admiration and envy" (*CM*, p. 75), Anscombe remarks that this analysis "is rather curious and roundabout in expression":

---

[18] John Hyman (*Action, Knowledge, and Will*, pp. 117–118), points to a discussion in Wittgenstein's *Blue Book* that is also relevant in this context. There, Wittgenstein says that a causal explanation is always "a hypothesis" based on some inductive evidence, whereas the explanation of an action in terms of a reason or motive is not. He continues: "The double use of the word 'why,' asking for the cause and asking for the motive, together with the idea that we can know, and not only conjecture, our motives, gives rise to the confusion that a motive is a cause of which we are immediately aware, a cause 'seen from the inside,' or a cause experienced" (*BB*, p. 15). And cf. also *PI* II, p. 191: "What is the difference between cause and motive?—How is the motive *discovered*, and how is the cause?"

it seems to say, and I can't understand it unless it implies, that a man could not be said to have boasted from vanity unless he always behaved vainly, or at least very very often did so. But this does not seem to be true. (*I*, §13, 21:1)

As an objection to Ryle this is not very potent: for the claim that vanity is a disposition does not entail that a vain person must always or often behave vainly, any more than the dispositional character of fragility means that a fragile vase must always or often shatter.[19] But Anscombe's more decisive criticism of Ryle's view is in her demonstration of how a dispositional analysis fails to distinguish between several different *kinds* of motives, which explain a person's actions in correspondingly different ways. This point emerges in Sections 12–13, where Anscombe argues that we have to distinguish between:

- *Backward-looking* motives, as, e.g., when a person explains why she killed someone by saying "He killed my brother" (§13, 20:2). Here, "something that *has happened* (or is at present happening) is given as the ground of an action or abstention that is good or bad for the person ... at whom it is aimed" (§13, 20:2).

- *Forward-looking* motives, as, e.g., when a person does something "from the motive of gain" (§12, 18:3), or perhaps "'to release him from this awful suffering,' or 'to get rid of the swine'" (§12, 18:4). Explanations of this sort cite the *future objective* of an action in order to identify the "spirit in which" it was done (§12, 18:4).

- *Interpretative* motives (which Anscombe also calls "motive-in-general"), as when, e.g., a person signs a petition out of "admiration for its promoter" (§13, 20:3). Here the admiration is neither a past or present happening that is being responded to, nor does it refer to a future state of affairs that is to be brought about. The purpose of explaining actions in this way is rather to *interpret* the actions or "put them in a certain

---

[19] Another thing Anscombe might have said here is that on Ryle's view there should be no difference between the way a person knows her own motives or reasons for acting and the way we know such things about anyone else, since in each case our knowledge is of a general tendency that we would need a mix of observation, interpretation, and inference to discover. Ryle says this explicitly about "long-term motives" at *CM*, p. 76; and similarly he writes of the way "I discover my or your motives" (*CM*, pp. 152–153). From Anscombe's perspective, what Ryle gets wrong is not that we are *never* mistaken about our motives, or never have to resort to observation, interpretation, and inference in order to understand why we act as we do—indeed those are all claims that Anscombe herself denies, e.g., at *I*, §12, 19:2. Rather, the problem for his view is that one doesn't *in general* need observation or inference in order to know, say, why one is opening the cupboard or crossing the road.

light" (§13, 21:2). Anscombe notes it is "notoriously difficult" to say when such descriptions are accurate (§13, 21:2).

- And *mixed* cases involving a combination of two or three of these categories (see §13, 21:3). For example, explaining someone as motivated by spite or despair will both appeal to something past and offer an interpretation of the present "spirit" with which she acts, and explaining someone as motivated by curiosity will both characterize her objective and say something about her present orientation to it. The first explanation combines backward-looking and interpretative aspects, the second is both forward-looking and interpretative.

A strictly dispositional analysis of motive-explanation is sorely inadequate to account for the variety that Anscombe displays here. In particular, while the operation of forward- and backward-looking motives is usually not *causal* in the Rylean sense, nor on the other hand do such motives usually stem from any general tendency or *disposition* whose manifestation follows a law-like pattern. We can see this clearly by considering one of Ryle's own examples, which nicely illustrates what Anscombe would call a forward-looking motive:

A person replying to an interrogation might say that he was delving into a ditch in order to find the larvae of a certain species of insect; that he was looking for these larvae in order to find out on what fauna or flora they were parasitic; that he was trying to find out on what they were parasitic in order to test a certain ecological hypothesis; and that he wanted to test this hypothesis in order to test a certain hypothesis about Natural Selection. At each stage he declares his motive or reason for pursuing certain investigations. And each successive reason that he gives is of a higher level of generality than its predecessor. He is subsuming one interest under another, somewhat as more special laws are subsumed under more general laws. (*CM*, pp. 76–77)

It is entirely implausible to analyze this explanation as resting on a series of general hypothetical propositions to the effect that whenever I am in state X, I tend to do Y: for the explanation does not presuppose that I have any *tendency* to delve into ditches when I wish to find the larvae of an insect species, or to look for insect larvae when trying to find out what they are parasitic on, or anything else of the sort.[20] Rather, all these descriptions can give the *reasons*

[20] Nor does it help if the putative dispositions are flexible or "multi-track" (see *CM*, pp. 31–33). It is rather that there need be no dispositions *at all* to underwrite this sort of explanation.

why I act in these ways even if there are no underlying dispositions that my behavior manifests. And the same holds for the explanation of an action in backward-looking fashion as a response to something that happened in the past: for example, if asked why I killed someone I say that it was because he killed my brother, this answer does not imply that I have any general tendency to kill those who kill my siblings. Even if *some* of what motivates us can be understood in terms of underlying tendencies whose manifestation follows an approximately law-like pattern, this clearly is not a presupposition of motive-explanation in general.

(3) Let us now return to the question raised earlier. Especially given her rejection of Ryle's dispositional analysis, what ground does Anscombe have for holding that an explanation of an action that gives the person's reasons for acting is a different *sort* of explanation than the explanation of an action that gives only its mental causes? That is, even if we accept that a person's reasons for acting are not just a matter of underlying dispositions or conscious mental events that triggered her behavior, what should prevent us from analyzing reasons for acting in terms of elements of a person's mind or psychology that may not themselves have a conscious character, but that nevertheless "issue in action" in roughly the same way as mental causes do?

At this point in Anscombe's inquiry, the first part of her answer is simply that we don't *know* whether we should accept this analysis, as we haven't yet said enough about the nature of reason-giving explanation to pronounce confidently on it. Nor, Anscombe adds, do we know enough about the nature of causality, since in her view this topic "is in a state of too great confusion" to make any very sharp distinctions involving it (*I*, §5, 10:2).[21] But in Section 14 she does identify *a* clearly significant difference between explanations of action by reasons and mental causes, namely that the intelligibility of saying that a person did something for a certain reason, or out of such-and-such a motive, usually requires attributing to that person certain *evaluative* attitudes, whereas mental-causal explanation does not depend in the same way on this:

> E.g. if I am grateful to someone, it is because he has done me some good, or at least I think he has, and I cannot show gratitude by something that I intend to harm him. In remorse, I hate some good things for myself; I could not express remorse by getting myself plenty of enjoyments, or for something that I did not find bad. If I do something out of revenge which

[21] This is a fundamental difference between Anscombe's approach and Donald Davidson's. Davidson was so confident that the only variety of causation was a relation between events that he appealed to this metaphysical thesis as a premise in his arguments.

is in fact advantageous rather than harmful to my enemy, my action, in its description of being advantageous to him, is involuntary. (§14, 21:5–22:1)

The three examples Anscombe considers here—of gratitude, remorse, and revenge—are all ones of acting from a backward-looking motive, and her point is that in each case the explanation of the action by the past state of affairs assumes that the agent regards that state of affairs as somehow good or bad, and regards her action "as doing good or harm of some sort" (§14, 22:2) that is an appropriate response to that original goodness or badness.[22] And a similar point seems to hold for the explanation by forward-looking and interpretative motives as well: for example, to do something from the motive of gain I must think that I have something (good) to gain by it; and to act out of admiration for someone I must both have a certain (here, in some sense positive) view of that person, and understand what I do as somehow reflecting or arising from that view. (That is, in the latter case I must regard my action as, say, the sort of thing that this person would do herself, or as something that she would want me to do, or that will help her to get the recognition that she deserves, etc.) Anscombe's argument is that absent such attitudes, while a person may be *in* a psychological state like anger or admiration, she cannot act *from* that attitude in a way that would make it count as her motive. There is a point of contrast here with purely dispositional explanations, such as saying that someone did something because she's a "hothead."[23] Hotheadedness is a *dispositional* characteristic in Ryle's sense: roughly, you are a hothead if you have a general tendency to get angry when provoked. It is not, however, usually a person's *motive* in the sense that Anscombe has given to that term, since when we say that a person did something because she's a hothead we don't attribute to her any evaluative attitudes that serve to "rationalize" her behavior. If you do something because you're a hothead, you do it simply because a certain stimulus "set you off," in the way that people like you are prone to. And—this is the crucial point—the same point of contrast exists with the explanation of action by mental causes, at least in paradigm cases like that of jumping when one is startled: for while one who does such a thing must have perceived a certain stimulus as in some sense bad or fearful, she need not have taken such a view of *her own action* in order for it to count as a consequence of her fear.

---

[22] This is not to say that acting for a reason depends on any specifically *moral* thinking. Rather, the relevant concepts of "good" and "bad" are *formal* concepts in a sense that I will introduce in section 5.4.

[23] I am very grateful to Catherine Vianale for suggesting this excellent example.

So this is our clue: for Anscombe, what distinguishes reason-giving explanations from explanations in terms of mental causes is the role played in reason-giving explanations by considerations of goodness and badness. This explains why we cannot *argue* against a mental-causal explanation in the way we can argue against an explanation by a reason or motive (cf. §15, 24:2). That is, if, e.g., you tell me that your act was one of revenge and I reply that it turned out to benefit your enemy, then your explanation "ceases to offer a reason, except prefaced by 'I thought'" (§14, 22:4). But "[n]o such discovery would affect an assertion of mental causality" (§14, 22:4)—and thus my saying that the face at the window wasn't really scary doesn't undermine the claim that it *made you jump*. Admittedly this is not enough to disprove the psychologistic analysis outlined earlier, since we have not shown that the evaluative attitudes involved in acting for a reason are not elements in a causal process from which action results. It does, however, yield an important constraint on what such an analysis would have to look like.

Despite the importance that she places on this distinction, Anscombe is clear that she does not mean to have demonstrated that acting from a reason involves judgments of good and harm, whereas acting from a mental cause does not. One reason for this is that she does not take herself to have proved that "*in general* good and harm play an essential part in the concept of intention" (§14, 22:4; emphasis added)—rather, she has shown only that they are part of what marks the distinction between motives and mental causes. Another reason is that in Section 15 she identifies a range of cases that cannot be classified neatly as ones of acting from reasons rather than mental causes, or vice versa. These borderline cases (see §15, 23:4) include doing something because someone told you, or because someone else was doing it, or in response to a forceful or striking stimulus. Anscombe says that whether explanations like these should be counted as reason-giving rather than merely causal "appears to depend very much on what the action was or what the circumstances were," and that "we should often refuse to make any distinction at all between something's being a reason, and its being a cause of the kind in question" (§15, 23:4)—that is, that "in many cases the distinction would have no point" (§15, 24:1). The existence of such hard-to-categorize cases means that even if condition (C4) is correct, it will not always allow us to draw a sharp line between intentional and non-intentional actions. This is, however, no objection to the condition as long as the cases where it is unclear or indeterminate whether (C4) is satisfied are also cases where it is similarly unclear or indeterminate whether the action in question is intentional. Meanwhile, the presence of what Anscombe calls "full-blown" cases (§15, 24:2) that fall clearly on either side of the distinction and are sorted correctly by (C4) is sufficient to justify appeal to this condition at this stage in her inquiry.

(4) Now we can consider the question I raised at the start of this section, namely whether Anscombe's arguments for condition (C4), and the distinction she draws between reason-giving explanations and causal ones, show that she is an "anti-causalist" about intentional action-explanation. If anti-causalism is the philosophical thesis that reason-giving explanations are non-causal, i.e., that "*the* concept of cause that applies elsewhere" in non-psychological explanation does not apply to the reason-giving explanation of action,[24] then the arguments of Sections 9–16 clearly do not support such a reading. The conclusion of these sections is only that there is *a* causal concept—namely, the concept of a triggering event—that we use in explaining what happens in the physical world as well as some of our thoughts and behaviors, and which is not the same as the causal concept we use in explaining what people do by appeal to their reasons. Moreover, at this point in the text Anscombe has neither given her own account of acting for a reason nor clarified the concept of causality in a way that would do away with any of our "great confusion" (*I*, §5, 10:2) about it. *All* she has done is argued that paradigmatic or "full-blown" cases of reason-giving explanation can be distinguished in a *rough* way from similarly "full-blown" cases of explanation of action by mental causes, by the role of normative or evaluative attitudes in explanations of the first sort:

> Roughly speaking, it establishes something as a reason if one argues against it; not as when one says "Noises should not make you jump like that: hadn't you better see a doctor?" but in such a way as to link it up with motives and intentions: "You did it because he told you to? But why do what he says?" Answers like "he has done a lot for me," "he is my father," "it would have been the worse for me if I hadn't" give the original answer a place among reasons.... Thus the full-blown cases are the right ones to consider in order to see the distinction between reason and cause. But it is worth noticing that *what is so commonly said, that reason and cause are everywhere sharply distinct notions, is not true.* (§15, 24:2; emphasis mine)[25]

---

[24] This is how Davidson summarizes the view that he is targeting in "Actions, Reasons, and Causes," p. 9, emphasis added.

[25] One philosopher who seems to have held this common view is Ryle—see the lines quoted in fn. 17.

Having argued only this much so far, it remains an open question whether there is some clear and useful sense of "cause" in which descriptions of a person's reasons for acting would fall under the broad umbrella of causal explanation.

2.4 "For no reason" / "I don't know why I did it" (§§17–18)

Sections 17–18 conclude Anscombe's discussion of the ways that a "Why?"-question can be refused application. She begins by considering whether a "Why?"-question is rejected with answers like "I just thought I would," "It was an impulse," "For no particular reason," and "It was an idle action"—that is, answers saying, in one way or another, "that there is *no* reason" for what one did (*I*, §17, 25:3). Following this, she considers the significance of an answer like "I don't know why I did it," where this "does not mean that perhaps there is a causal explanation one does not know" (§17, 25:4)—that is, an explanation in terms of underlying causes that one could know only through inference, testimony, or observation. How should we understand statements like these, and what do they reveal about the nature of intention and intentional action?

Anscombe's treatment of the first class of answers is straightforward. If asked why one did something, the answer that one did it merely idly or impulsively, or for no particular reason or "just because I thought I would," does not give a reason for acting, but nor does such an answer *refuse application* of the "Why?"-question in its special sense. And this seems right: a question like "Why did you do that?" or "Why are you doing that?," asked in a sense where a positive answer would give one's reason for acting, does not *fail to apply* in a circumstance where there isn't such a reason—"any more than the question how much money I have in my pocket is refused application by the answer 'None'" (§17, 25:3), or the question "Who won the game?" is refused application by saying that the participants weren't keeping score. As a pocket is something about which one can sensibly ask what it contains, and a competitive game something about which one can sensibly ask who won, so an intentional action is something about which one can sensibly ask for a reason-giving explanation.[26] This does not mean, however, that there

---

[26] For another illustration of the idea, see Anton Ford's discussion of concepts of quantity in his paper, "The Arithmetic of *Intention*," Ford suggests that the concept of a countable quantity or *multitude* is marked in English by the question "How many?," while the concept of a measurable quantity or *magnitude* is marked by the question "How much?" Thus it makes sense to ask *how*

must *be reasons* for everything we intentionally do—though Anscombe will argue soon that we could not have a meaningful concept of intentional action unless it were possible *sometimes* to answer the question "Why?" by giving the "reason or purpose" with which one acts.[27]

The second way of answering "Why?"-questions that Anscombe considers in Section 17 is with a statement to the effect that one *doesn't know* why she did the thing in question. This is supposed to be different from the sort of answer that motivates condition (C3), since it does not mean that there is perhaps a causal explanation out there, like the explanation of the hypnic reflex by "something to do with electrical discharges" (§17, 25:2), that one simply cannot give. Rather, Anscombe says that this sort of answer "goes with 'I found myself doing it,' 'I heard myself say . . .'"—answers suggesting a "surprise at one's own actions" (§17, 25:4), which is somehow a different *sort* of surprise from the surprise one feels upon learning that she has been standing on a hose-pipe, operating the traffic lights, or sawing Smith's plank. What sort of surprise or puzzlement is this?

There are in fact several relevant things that a person can mean with a phrase like "I don't know why I did it."[28] Some uses of this phrase convey either (i) that an action was impulsive or out of character, or (ii) that whatever reason one may have had for doing something now seems like a *bad* reason for doing it. However, in neither of these cases is a person *literally* saying that she doesn't know why she acted as she did—and thus the fact that they can be given in answer to a "Why?"-question does not show that Anscombe's condition (C3) admits of counterexamples. A third way to use such a phrase is (iii) in connection with what I earlier called automatic or absent-minded action, as "one may say: 'Now why did I do that?'—when one has discovered that, e.g., one has just put something in a rather odd place" (§17, 26:2). And similarly to what I suggested earlier,[29] the ignorance here is only of the reason for a *past* action whose rationale, if it wasn't simply accidental, the agent will have understood at the time she was acting. (I may in fact have put the keys in the cupboard to keep them away from the baby, but no longer remember

---

much, but not how many, water is in a glass, and to ask *how many*, but not how much, children are in someone's family. In neither case is the question *denied application* by the answer "None."

[27] This is the conclusion of Section 20, as discussed in section 3.2.

[28] What follows in this paragraph and the one following is my reading of the very condensed passage at §17, 26:2–3. My (i), (ii), and (iii) are the uses that Anscombe discusses in the first part of 26:2 (up to ". . . in a rather odd place"), and (iv) covers the remainder. Thanks to Jennifer Frey for some useful feedback on an earlier version of this discussion.

[29] See the discussion of Armstrong's case in section 2.1, pp. 22–24.

that this was my purpose in doing it.) As such, this too is not really a way of saying that Anscombe's condition (C3) was not met.

The final possibility, which is more difficult to supply an adequate account of, is one where (iv) a phrase like "I don't know why I did it" is used

> by someone who does not *discover* that he did it; he is quite aware as he does it; but he comes out with this expression as if to say "It is the sort of action in which a reason seems requisite." As if there were a reason, if only he knew it; but of course that is not the case in the relevant sense; even if psychoanalysis persuades him to accept something as his reason, or he finds reason in a divine or diabolical plan or inspiration, or a causal explanation in his having been previously hypnotised. (§17, 26:2)

We can make some sense of this very difficult passage by reading Anscombe as concerned with the phenomena of self-ignorance that are often discussed under the headings of repression, self-deception, the Freudian unconscious, and so on. While we say of cases like these that they involve a failure to understand or appreciate the reasons why we think and do things, we do not think of this as *mere* ignorance, like ignorance of the causes of the hypnic reflex: thus explaining someone's behavior in a Freudian manner is not like giving "a causal explanation that [the agent] does not know" (§17, 25:4). Nor is it like ignorance of the "reasons" of a hypnotist or a divine planner or diabolical manipulator: for the reasons that explain one's behavior here are supposed to be *one's own*. That is precisely why these are not described *straightforwardly* as cases where a person is ignorant of why she acts as she does. As Anscombe says, we only speak of them *as if* this were so.

These phenomena are far too puzzling for us to expect an account of them in a book of ninety-four pages—or even one of a thousand.[30] What makes them so hard to pin down is that the status of a putative reason-giving explanation of an action (or belief, intention, etc.) is generally tied to the agent's capacity to give such an explanation herself. This is why the question "Why?" is paradigmatically addressed *to the one who acts*, and why we take it that the knowledge expressed in answering it is a self-specific knowledge different in kind from knowledge of the actions of others. A consequence of this is that being ignorant or unaware of one's reasons for doing something is not at all like being ignorant of *someone else's* reasons for acting, where it is perfectly intelligible how *she* could have acted for those reasons even though

---

[30] For a good start, which I take to be in line with what I suggest in what follows, see Eric Marcus, "Reconciling Practical Knowledge with Self-Deception."

I happened not to know this. Nor is it like being ignorant of the (non-mental) causes of one's involuntary actions, or of autobiographical facts like one's name or the color of one's underwear—facts which usually a person is in a particularly good position to speak to, but which there is nothing especially puzzling in the idea of someone's having forgotten. Though there may be such a thing as ignorance of what one does and why, such ignorance can only be partial, and a special sort of explanation, often in terms of a species of psychological disfunction, will be required in order for it to be intelligible why the self-knowledge that is usually unproblematically available to an agent is thwarted or repressed in this particular case. (It is here that we might use the language of "repression," "denial," or "not owning up" to something that one knows "on some level.") And to the extent that such ignorance *does* seem to be total, and the agent can become aware of her reason *only* in a third-personal way, we lose our handle on its *really* having been *her* reason—and, perhaps, *her* intentional action—after all. Here, Anscombe says, we have "a curious intermediary case: the question 'Why?' has and yet has not application; it has application in the sense that it is admitted as an appropriate question; it lacks it in the sense that it has *no answer*" (§17, 26:3; emphasis added). No doubt this reply leaves a great deal more to be said. But doing this would be a project for another occasion.

2.5 Summary discussion

Section 5 introduced the concept of a *"Why?"-question* as a way to delineate our ordinary concept of intentional action. We regard an action as intentional, Anscombe proposes, when we treat it as suitable to be explained by giving a reason for acting, and as non-intentional when we refuse the application of a "Why?"-question to it. However, since the concept of a reason for acting is not one that we can take for granted at this stage of our inquiry, we need another way of delimiting the conditions under which a "Why?"-question is given application. And this is what the three epistemic conditions that are introduced in Sections 6–8 are supposed to help us do. Taken together, the three conditions yield the thesis that a person who does something intentionally will necessarily *know, without observation, both what she is doing and why*. The introduction of condition (C4), which also avoids direct appeal to any action- or intention-concepts, adds further that this knowledge of "why" will involve something more than an understanding of the *mental causes* of her action. And with this, we have now "roughly outlined the area of intentional actions" (*I*, §18, 28:2). (*Roughly.*)

We should notice, however, that so far the outline we have drawn has been mainly negative, as the focus in these sections has been on answers to a "Why?"-question that *refuse* its application, which were those that yielded conditions (C1) to (C4). By contrast, our working list of answers by which "Why?"-questions are *given* application looks like quite a motley bunch. In summarizing her conclusions so far, Anscombe says that answers in the latter category may either:

(a) simply mention past history, e.g. "He killed my father";

(b) give an interpretation of the action, e.g., "lovingly" or "out of friendship"; or

(c) mention something future, e.g., "to make him miss that appointment."[31]

Sections 17 and 18 then add one more sort of answer to this list, namely one that

(d) says something like "For no reason," "I just thought I would," etc.

As we have seen, Anscombe holds that an answer like (d) is a way to *grant the applicability* of a "Why?"-question while *denying that one acted for a reason*. Because of this, the answers that give "Why?"-questions application "are ... more extensive in range than the answers which give reasons for acting" (§18, 28:2)—for it is, again, only a *positive* answer to a "Why?"-question that will necessarily give such a reason. This is what answers of the forms (a), (b), and (c) all do: (a) gives a backward-looking motive rather than a mental cause to the extent that "the ideas of good or harm are involved in its meaning as an answer" (§16, 24:3–25:1), while in (b) and (c) "the answer is already characterised as a reason for acting" (§16, 24:3)—that is, the answer gives an interpretative motive in (b) and a forward-looking motive, or intention (see §13, 21:3), in (c).

But what *unifies* the sorts of answer listed in (a), (b), and (c), such that all of them count as doing the same sort of thing, namely *giving a reason for acting*? This is one of the main questions that Anscombe begins to answer in the pages that follow. Having done this, in Section 28 she will revisit her epistemic conditions, attempting to address the discomfort that readers

---

[31] For this list, see §16, 24:3.

will have felt in the thesis that there can be *non-observational knowledge* of action.

Suggestions for further reading

- Anscombe discusses the concept of causation at length in her paper "Causality and Determination," given originally as a lecture in 1971.

- For illuminating discussion of the dialectical role of Anscombe's question "Why?," see Lucy Campbell, "Two Notions of Intentional Action? Solving a Puzzle in Anscombe's *Intention*," and Anton Ford, "The Arithmetic of *Intention*."

- Donald Davidson's seminal paper "Actions, Reasons, and Causes" puts forward an influential argument that reason-giving explanations must be causal, as otherwise there would be no difference between having a reason for an action that one performs, and performing the action for that reason. For critical evaluation of Davidson's position see Eric Marcus, *Rational Causation*, chapter 4, and John Hyman, *Action, Knowledge, and Will*, chapter 5.

3

The Unity of Action

The hypothesis advanced in Section 5 was that intentional actions are those to which a "Why?"-question can be given application, and that a positive answer to such a question will give not a mere cause of action, but one's *reason for* doing the thing in question. So far this concept of a reason for acting has been elucidated through a motley group of examples that include backward-looking reference to something that happened in the past, interpretative characterization of the spirit in which one acted, and forward-looking reference to one's aim or objective. The last of these forms of explanation will occupy a central place beginning in Sections 20–21, where Anscombe argues that in order to have a robust concept of intentional action it must be possible to explain our actions in terms of *further* things that we are intentionally doing, as well as things that we intend to do *in the future*. The subsequent sections then put these concepts to work in exploring what constitutes action as a *unity*—that is, what makes it the case that the flurry of movement involved in our intentional activity amounts to doing *something* in particular.

3.1 An extra feature? (§19)

Section 19 sets the stage for this discussion by offering a difficult argument against the thesis that in categorizing an action as intentional one thereby attributes to it "extra feature attaching to an action at the time it is done" (*I*, Table of Contents, Entry for §19, at p. v). Taking a lead from Jennifer Hornsby,[1] let us call this position the *dualistic* view of action. It holds that any intentional action comprises two parts: on the one hand the aspect of the action that *happens in the world*, where the nature of this happening can

---

[1] Hornsby, "Dualism in Action." As Hornsby explains there, materialist views that identify properties of the mind with those of the brain are no less dualist, in the sense relevant to the present discussion, than Cartesian views that locate the mind in an immaterial soul.

be characterized by a "fundamental description" (§19, 29:2) that is neutral as to whether it is an aspect of someone's intentional activity; and on the other some *mental or psychological characteristic* of the agent in virtue of which she counts as doing a certain thing intentionally. The conclusion of Section 19 is that this dualistic view is incoherent.

Two important questions arise here. First, how should we understand Anscombe's argument in this section? And second, what alternative conception of intentional action does she propose in place of the dualistic one? Here is a plausible representation of her argument:

(1)   Let us suppose, for *reductio*, that the dualistic view is correct—that is, that what makes an action intentional is the presence, alongside some "preintentional" physical events such as the contraction of a person's muscles, of an "extra feature which exists when [the action] is performed" (§19, 28:4). We are to call this extra feature "*I*."

(2)   Our supposition, then, is that the combination of "preintentional movement + *I* guarantees that an intentional action is performed" (§19, 28:4; italics modified).

(3)   And since, as was observed in Section 6, "the same action can be intentional under one description and unintentional under another" (§19, 28:4), this combination must determine the description (or descriptions) under which the action is intentional.

(4)   But that description is not determined by the character of the preintentional movement, since "nothing about the [agent] considered by himself in the moment of contracting his muscles, and nothing in the contraction of his muscles, can possibly determine the content of that description" (§19, 28:4–29:1).

(5)   Therefore it must be determined by the character of the feature *I*—which therefore "must be interpreted as a description, or as having an internal relation to a description, of an action" (§19, 28:4).

(6)   However, from (4) and (5) it follows that the relation between what a person actually does, i.e., what *happens in the world* when she acts, and the description under which what she does is intentional, is entirely inexplicable. That is, "it is a mere happy accident that an *I* relevant to the wider context and further consequences *ever* accompanies the preintentional movements in which a man performs a given intentional action" (§19, 29:1).

(7)   And since the conclusion in (6) is absurd, the original
             supposition in (1) should be rejected.

Clearly the force of this argument turns on premise (6)—that is, our focus
should be on the claim that the alleged *distinctness* of the feature I from
the preintentional bodily movements that it accompanies entails that these
components are entirely unrelated. Anscombe glosses this premise by saying
that according to the dualistic view, "[w]hat makes it true that the man's
movement is one by which he performs such and such an action will have
absolutely no bearing on the I that occurs" (§19, 29:1; italics modified)—but
does the dualistic view really entail this? She imagines trying to resist this
move by saying that there is "a mechanism by which an I appropriate to the
situation is able to occur because of the man's knowledge of the situation—he
guesses e.g. that his muscular contractions will result in his grasping the
hammer and so the right I occurs" (§19, 29:1). And her reply is that this is
unreasonable, since "a man may very likely not be so much as aware of his
preintentional acts" (§19, 29:1), and also because on this account there will
be no way for the feature I to have any "effect on what occurs" (§19, 29:1).
Thus, she concludes, the dualistic view is mistaken.

But the trouble with this defense of premise (6) is that it overlooks
the possibility that the connection between the feature I and the agent's
bodily movements might be established in some other way than the one
just imagined. For example, it is commonly supposed in psychology that
subpersonal motor systems in the human brain work to generate movements
that satisfy an agent's mental representation of her goals. If we identify
these goals with the agent's intention (that is, the hypothesized feature I),
then this process would establish a mechanism by which an appropriate
correspondence between the content of a person's intention and the character
of her bodily movements is something more than a lucky accident, but not
because the agent herself is aware either of her preintentional actions or of
the connection between her having a goal and "its description's coming true"
(§19, 29:1). On such a view, what makes it more than an accident that we do
what we intend is that *intention leads reliably to movements* that bring about
the intended results.

It is hard to identify materials in the argument of Section 19 that
challenge this last position directly. Some interpreters have suggested that
Anscombe is tacitly appealing to the possibility of "deviant causal chains" that
interrupt the proper connection between a person's intention and her action,
or that since her feature I is internal to the agent it must have a "narrow"

content that does not represent things in the world outside her.[2] But even if these ideas could help to flesh out her argument, there is scant textual evidence that they were at work in Anscombe's own thinking.

A less anachronistic way to fill in the gap might be by appeal to Anscombe's doctrine that in acting intentionally a person knows without observation what she is doing and why. The argument would be that if the connection between an agent's mental state and her intentional action is secured through the operation of subpersonal mechanisms, then there will be no reason why the agent herself, who on this view is merely the arena in which these subpersonal operations are taking place, will be in a position to know in any distinctive way what results from these operations. Such an argument would connect the dualistic view of action to what Kevin Falvey has helpfully termed the *two-factor thesis* concerning agential knowledge.[3] According to the two-factor thesis, an agent's self-knowledge does not extend to her action itself but only to what she intends or is trying to do—which is just what we might expect to be the case if, as on the dualistic view of action, *what happens* when a person acts is a causal consequence of her inner mental state. Once again, however, considerations like this don't make any appearance in Anscombe's argument as she herself presents it. Nor, for that matter, can we simply assume that there is no way to account for the possibility of non-observational knowledge of one's intentional actions within the framework of the dualistic view.[4] Absent a lot of further development, the argument of Section 19 is simply inconclusive.

Beyond our evaluation of the argument itself, what should we say about the contrast of positions that lies behind it? Anscombe sums up her conclusion by saying that

> in describing intentional actions as such, it will be a mistake to look for *the* fundamental description of what occurs—such as the movements of muscles or molecules—and then think of intention as something, perhaps very complicated, which qualifies this. The only events to consider are intentional actions themselves, and to call an action intentional is to say

---

[2] For the first interpretation, see Candace Vogler, "Nothing Added." It is true that Anscombe makes reference to deviant causal chains in a later paper challenging causal theories of action, and in *Intention* she notes that "an intended effect just occasionally comes about by accident" (§23, 39:1), implying that in such a case the bringing about of that intended effect would not be intentional. But none of this figures in her argument in Section 19. For the second interpretation, see Rosalind Hursthouse, "Intention."

[3] See Falvey, "Knowledge in Intention."

[4] For a recent attempt at doing just this, see Sarah Paul, "How We Know What We're Doing."

it is intentional under some description that we give (or could give) of it.
(*I*, §19, 29:2)

By contrast, the underlying assumption of the dualistic view is that we *can* describe the non-psychological component of intentional action merely as a flurry of muscular or molecular motions, and that we postulate something "extra" in addition to events like these when we describe someone as performing an intentional action. And it may seem incredible that Anscombe could deny this. For, we might object, *of course* this much is true: molecular movements of the same sort that take place when a person acts *could* also take place in the absence of any intentional action, either as a chance occurrence or through the control of some extra-personal or non-agential mechanism. Isn't this enough to show that intentional action involves a mental component that is *additional to* those purely physical happenings?

Implicit in this objection is a way of thinking that Wittgenstein gives expression in a famous passage in the *Philosophical Investigations*, which Anscombe likely intends her argument in Section 19 to evoke. Wittgenstein writes:

Let us not forget this: when "I raise my arm," my arm goes up. And the problem arises: what is left over if I subtract the fact that my arm goes up from the fact that I raise my arm? (*PI*, §621)

Wittgenstein's "problem" is usually read as an invitation to do a bit of philosophical arithmetic. We are to suppose that since my arm can go up whether or not I raise my arm, therefore this event—that is, the event of my arm going up—is something that can be "subtracted" from the event of an intentional arm-raising. The inevitable conclusion is that what is "left over" in this equation will be mental or psychological aspect of action. And this, of course, is just how the dualistic view would have it.

But is this inference sound? To see how we might resist it, let us compare Wittgenstein's question with the following variant on it:

When a car is red, it is colored. And the problem arises: what is left over if I subtract the fact that the car is red from the fact that it is colored?

The question will seem bizarre on its face. But it begins from an intuition similar to what inspires Wittgenstein's question: there is a natural sense in which a car's being red amounts to something *more* than its having some color or another. It is easy, however, to spot the mistake in supposing that there must therefore be two distinct facts involved here—the car's *being red* and its *being colored*—such that one can be "subtracted" from the other, leaving something extra behind. The reason for this is that when we say that a car is red, we do not predicate a feature that it has *in addition* to its being colored, but rather attribute to it a *specific* or *determinate* form of what is predicated only indeterminately when we say only that it is colored, and not what specific color it has.[5]

The suggestion I wish to make on behalf of Anscombe's conclusion in Section 19 is that a similar analysis might hold concerning the relationship between, e.g., the description of someone as *raising her arm* and the description of her arm as *going up* (or *rising*). This broadly *disjunctivist* picture accepts that *if* someone raises her arm, *then* her arm rises, but denies that this is because raising one's arm involves two components—a "mere" arm-rising plus a further psychological feature that stands in a suitable relation to it. Rather, on the alternative analysis offered here, this entailment holds because someone's raising her arm is one of the *ways* that her arm can go up, just as a car's being red is a *way* that it can be colored. If this is correct, then in saying that someone raised her arm we do not add *something extra* to what we say when we say merely that her arm went up—that is, we do not postulate any extra *feature* beyond what is described in saying only that her arm rose. What we do instead is further *specify the sort* of arm-rising that this was—we describe it as an intentional movement rather than something that merely took place.

It might be objected, however, that this attempted analogy between the cases of color and of movement is problematic.[6] For after all, there *can* be such a thing as a "mere" bodily movement that is not an action, whereas no object can "merely" be colored without being some determinate color or another. But such an objection would beg the very question at issue. The disjunctivist picture does not question whether there can be bodily movements that are not intentional actions, but only whether these consist in a determinate kind of movement that is also present in corresponding intentional actions, rather than standing *alongside* intentional actions as a distinct species of the genus of movement in general. If the latter analysis is correct, then nothing can be a "mere" bodily movement in that sense that the objection requires—since any determinate bodily movement must be *either* an intentional action *or*

---

[5] For an important analysis of this form of specificity, see Anton Ford's paper "Action and Generality." I'm grateful to Benj Hellie and Jessica Wilson for helping me think through some of the metaphysical issues at play here.

[6] Thanks to Beri Marušić for pressing me on this point.

a movement of some other sort. On this view, to call something a "mere" bodily movement is *already* to say something about the determinate kind of movement that it is—something that rules out its being part of an intentional action.[7]

Let us consider the conclusion of Section 19 once more in light of this discussion, with bracketed numbers added for ease of reference:

> in describing intentional actions as such, it will be a mistake to [1] look for *the* fundamental description of what occurs—such as the movements of muscles or molecules—and then [2] think of intention as something, perhaps very complicated, which qualifies this. [3] The only events to consider are intentional actions themselves, and [4] to call an action intentional is to say it is intentional under some description that we give (or could give) of it. (§19, 29:2)

I have suggested that we read [1] looking for a fundamental description of what occurs, which [2] intention is supposed to qualify, as equivalent to [1*] treating "what occurs" when a person acts as an event of the same sort that may occur in *mere* (non-actional) physical movement, and [2*] thinking that this event will amount to (or be part of) an intentional action when it takes place *along with* something *further* that can also exist in such a standalone fashion. (Thus there is a parallel with treating "*X*'s being colored" as picking out a *state of affairs* to which *X*'s having a particular color could be "added" as something further.) By contrast, the position that Anscombe argues for in Section 19 is that [3] all *determinate* events are either actions or events that are not actions. If this is correct, then [4] to say that someone did something intentionally is not to say both (i) that something happened and (ii) that this was joined by the *further* feature(s) necessary for it to qualify as an intentional action, but rather that what happened was the particular kind of event, intentional action, that is the interest of our inquiry.

Notice how modest this conclusion turns out to be. On my reading, Anscombe is not saying that intentional actions can't be identified by their psychological characteristics—indeed, we have already seen her propose some such characteristics, such as the possession of non-observational knowledge, in discussing when her "Why?"-question is given application.

---

[7] On this point compare Hornsby, who writes of the mistake in "supposing that the bodily movements that there are when there are actions might be located in a world bereft of beings who do things for reasons—a world where so-called 'mere movements of bodies' belong. The supposition prevents one from treating movements in such a way that they can be rightly related to the agents who produce them" ("Dualism in Action," p. 393).

Nor does her position entail that we cannot apply many of the same (e.g., neurochemical, physiological) concepts in describing both intentional actions and events of other kinds. The conclusion of Section 19 is only that an allegedly "fundamental" description of certain muscular, molecular, etc., movements that is neutral between, or captures something common to, actional and non-actional cases alike cannot be a *determinate* description of what occurs "in the world," which when something *else* occurs (or is present) in the mind of an agent amounts to (or is part of) an intentional action. It is instead a perfectly legitimate but *indeterminate* description of an occurrence, which leaves open whether that occurrence was an intentional action or not. And this latter question is not to be settled by discerning the presence or absence of some other feature that may have been *missing* from the original description. How it is to be settled instead is a question that Anscombe does not answer here: thus "For the moment, I will not ask *why* this question 'Why?' should be applicable to some events and not to others" (§19, 28:3).

3.2 Further intention (§§20–21)

Recall the three headings under which Anscombe introduced her topic at the start of Section 1. Briefly:

(1)   A person *expresses* an intention by saying, e.g., "I am going to do such-and-such," where this is not a mere estimate of the future;

(2)   An *action* is intentional when it is not accidental, involuntary, a mere reflex, etc.; and

(3)   We describe a person's *further* intention, or the intention *with which* a person acts, by characterizing her reason or purpose in acting.

As we saw, Anscombe proposed to to begin her inquiry by considering heading (2), in order to use what was learned there to shed light on the other ways that our concept of intention is employed. Sections 5–18 completed the first stage, working out an initial characterization of intentional action in terms of the conditions in which "Why?"-questions are granted or refused application. Having done this, in Section 20 she reintroduces the other two headings and begins to consider how they relate to one another. To do this, she raises the following question (see *I*, §20, 30:2):

Could we have a concept of *doing something intentionally* without the ability to *express intention for the future* and describe the *further intentions with which* we act?

This question may seem like an unlikely place to begin. Remember, however, that Anscombe has just argued in Section 17 that it is possible for an action to be intentional even if it is done for no reason. She also argued in Sections 12–14 that a "Why?"-question can be answered in a way that gives a reason for acting but does not identify any further intention or aim of an action—for this answer may instead explain the action through what she called an interpretative or backward-looking motive. In posing this question, Anscombe is asking whether we could have a concept of intentional action as something about which we ask "Why?" in her special sense even if these were the *only* sorts of answer that "Why?"-questions could receive. Could we have this concept, embodied in the practice of seeking and giving our reasons for acting, if we did not also express intentions to do certain things in the future and explain our actions in terms of our further intentions? If not, then we will have our first clear evidence of what connects the three headings we began with.

In order to address her question, Anscombe asks us to imagine according to "two rather curious suppositions":

(*a*) Suppose that "intention" only occurred as it occurs in "intentional action," and (*b*) suppose that the only answer to the question "Why are you X-ing?," granted that the question is not refused application, were "I just am, that's all." (§20, 30:2)

The purpose of each supposition is to isolate a concept of intentional action that is set off from one or the other of our original three headings.[8] That is:

- Supposition (*a*) invites us to imagine that we have a concept of intentional action without the possibility of expressing intention for the future, though there is such a thing as identifying one's further intention in acting.[9] On this supposition "Why?"-questions will have their special

---

[8] My interpretation of this argument is indebted to that of Candace Vogler in *Reasonably Vicious*, pp. 205–212. However, an important difference is that Vogler treats Anscombe's two suppositions as applying both at once, whereas I take them to be independent. In support of my reading, see fns. 9 and 10.

[9] The latter thing becomes clear when, as Anscombe explores the consequences of supposition (*a*), she allows the possibility that a person doing X may have the further intention of doing Y

sense, but they can be answered *only* by giving a further description of something that one is already doing, and not by describing something else that one is going to do later on. This supposition gives us practices corresponding to headings (2) and (3) in the original division, in the absence of anything corresponding to heading (1).

- And on supposition (*b*) we are to imagine that although there *is* such a thing as expressing intention for the future,[10] no such expression, nor one describing something a person is presently doing *in* acting a certain way, could be a way of identifying the intention *with which* a person acts, or is going to act. According to this second supposition a person can talk about what she is doing, and also say what she is going to do, but "the only answer to the question 'Why?' is 'I just am' " (§20, 32:2). There are, in other words, practices corresponding to headings (1) and (2) in the original division, but nothing corresponding to (3).

If neither supposition turns out to make sense, that will be evidence that the three headings are conceptually unified—that is, that the concept of intentional action is not "*formally independent* of those other occurrences of the concept of intention" (§20, 30:2; emphasis added).

Supposition (*a*): No expression of intention for the future

The first thing we are to suppose is there is no such thing as explaining what one is doing by citing a future action one intends to perform, or future state of affairs one intends to bring about. This supposition allows, however, for a question like "Why are you out walking?" to receive positive answers like the following:

(1)   (Because) I felt the need to get out

(2)   (Because) I enjoy it

and

(3)   (Because) I am taking in the local scenery.

"so long as it is reasonable to say that he is doing Y in, and at the same time as, doing X" (§20, 31:2)—thus doing Y will be the person's *further* intention in acting, but one directed toward another present action rather than a future one.

[10] That is, on this supposition "intention is supposed to occur both in present intentional action and in expression for the future" (§20, 32:2).

Each of these answers describes a *reason for acting* rather than a mere cause of one's behavior: in the terminology introduced in Sections 12 and 13, an answer like (1) gives a *backward-looking* motive, (2) is *interpretative*, and (3) describes the *further intention* with which one acts. This supposition will also permit answering "Why?"-questions with statements like "I don't know why" and "I just thought I would," though the upshot of allowing these answers will be explored when we consider supposition (*b*). By contrast, the sorts of statement that supposition (*a*) rules out as possible answers to a "Why?"-question are ones like:

(4)   To get to the store

and

(5)   (Because) I am going to buy some new pants.

What is taken to be impossible according to the present supposition is any answer to a "Why?"-question that describes the point or purpose of an action by relating it to something in the future. Instead, the only way to answer a "Why?"-question positively is by appeal to "the intention of doing whatever one is [already] doing" (*I*, §20, 32:1).

Having explained this supposition, Anscombe then says that the concept of intentional action it leaves over is "a very thin one" (§20, 32:1), and that because of this it undermines "a great deal of the point" of the way we "argue against motives—i.e. criticise a man for having acted on such a motive" (§20, 31:3). We saw earlier what this sort of *argument* against a person's account of her motives is supposed to be like:

> not as when one says "Noises should not make you jump like that: hadn't you better see a doctor?" but in such a way as to link it up with motives and intentions: "You did it because he told you to? But why do what he says?" (§15, 24:2)

The idea seems to be that since the point of such argument is not just to cast aspersions or induce sentiments of regret or inadequacy, but rather to persuade people *to change* what they do in the future, this practice of criticism would lose its rationale on supposition (*a*). And this is because it would be impossible on this supposition to respond to a question like "Why do what he says?" by saying, e.g.,

(6)   You're right—I'll be more independent from now on

—for a statement like (6) expresses the intention *to do* something in the future, and this possibility is just what supposition (*a*) rules out. Even if criticism of a person's motives could *result* in their going on to act differently, the terms of supposition (*a*) would make it impossible to represent such changes as *rational* responses to *understood* criticism, i.e., ways of *taking someone's advice* about what to do in the future, as opposed to *brute* changes in one's behavior that happen to be prompted by another person's words.[11] This shows that the possibility of expressing intention for the future is required for our concept of intentional action to undergird the distinctively rational form of give-and-take that "Why?"-questions usually invite.

Supposition *(b)*: No expression of further intention in acting

According to supposition (*b*), although there is such a thing as expressing intention for the future, no such statement, nor one expressing the intention of doing something that one already did or is already doing, can be used to answer a "Why?"-question. That is, while statements like

(7)   I was taking a walk
(8)   I am taking a walk

and

(9)   I am going to take a walk

are possible according to the present supposition, such statements cannot be given as *answers* to questions like "Why did you go outside?," "Why are you putting on your shoes?," and "Why are you going to be unavailable this evening?" Instead, according to supposition (*b*) the only possible way to answer a "Why?"-question without refusing its application is with statements like

(10)   I just did
(11)   I just am

and

(12)   For no particular reason.

---

[11] I owe this last point, and some of the phrasing I use to make it, to Kim Frost.

Supposition (*b*) allows that intentions for the present and the future can both be expressed, but never as a way to *explain* what one did, is doing, or is going to do. It thus rules out any appeal to a person's "reasons and aims" (*I*, §20, 33:3) in the description of why she acted, is acting, or is going to act in a certain way.

What is left of our concept of intentional action if we suppose that action *cannot be explained by describing one's further intention?* According to Anscombe, the trouble is that "a question whose only answer is a statement that one *is* doing the thing cannot be identified with our question 'Why?,'" and thus "on the present hypothesis there would be no distinction between such things as starts and gasps and, quite generally, *voluntary* actions" (§20, 32:2). The point here is that statements like (10), (11), and (12) can all be given as answers to "Why?"-questions concerning involuntary motions like a shudder or a gasp, and so if these were the *only* ways to answer a "Why?"-question without refusing its application then there would be no way to distinguish between intentional actions and involuntary behaviors. Without the possibility of answering "Why?"-questions positively by stating our further intentions in acting, there would be no way to make this important distinction.

One might object, however, that this argument overlooks two other ways of answering "Why?"-question positively without expressing a further intention, namely with the description of a backward-looking or interpretative motive. That is, supposition (*b*) seems to leave open the possibility of answering a question like "Why are you out walking?," not only with a dismissive answer like (10), (11), or (12), but also with our original statements (1) and (2):

(1)   (Because) I felt the need to get out
(2)   (Because) I enjoy it.

If the possibility of answers like (10), (11), and (12) is not enough to distinguish a concept of intentional action, what if answers (1) and (2) are allowed as well? Here we should recall that Anscombe has already argued in Section 14 that what distinguishes answers like (1) and (2) as explanations of *intentional* action is bound up with the concept of a reason for acting: for example, a backward-looking explanation will characterize an action as one of revenge only if the intended action is conceived as a way *of doing harm*. Applied to the present case, the point to see is that in order for statements like (1) and (2) to count as giving a different *sort* of answer to the question "Why are you out walking?" than statements like

(13)   (Because) I saw a face at the window

and

(14)   (Because) I was startled

give to "Why did you knock the cup off the table?" (cf. §5, 9:4), the statement in (1) must be taken to represent getting out, and that in (2) to represent doing what is enjoyable, as *goods that are to be obtained* by going for a walk. This is what Anscombe means in saying that "the difference between bases of prediction" for an involuntary action (e.g., jumping at a face in the window) and a voluntary one (e.g., killing someone because he killed your father) "is just the difference between evidence and a reason for acting" (§20, 32:3). Supposition (*b*) leaves us unable to mark this latter difference, and thus with no way to represent the difference between statements like "He killed my father, so I killed him" and "I saw the face at the window, so I jumped."

This last point is also illustrated in Anscombe's discussion at the end of Section 20 of what it is to do something in obedience to a command. This is, she says, more than just doing something that *is* commanded, nor is it just doing something *because* of a command to do it: for "If someone says 'Tremble' and I tremble I am not *obeying* him—even if I tremble because he says it in a terrible voice" (§20, 33:2). The idea here is that in order for the concepts of command and obedience to get off the ground we must have the concept of *taking a command as a reason* for acting in the way commanded, in contrast to doing a commanded thing in such a way that the command was, not one's reason for acting, but *merely* a cause of what one did. This shows, again, that the concept of a further intention in acting is required for us to draw a robust distinction between intentional and involuntary behavior.

Especially given the opacity of her presentation, it is easy to miss the importance of the argument of Section 20 for Anscombe's overall project in *Intention*. In fact the argument is *extremely* important, for several reasons.

First, it improves on the tentative suggestion at the end of Section 14 that the concept of intention has something to do with the concepts of "good and harm" (§14, 22:4), by clarifying what is distinctive in the sort of explanation that is provided in a statement of one's reasons for acting.

Second, it allows Anscombe to affirm a qualified version of the classical doctrine that action is always carried out *sub specie boni*, i.e., "under the appearance of the good."[12] This is not, she says, necessarily because there is "some *one* purpose that has an intrinsic finality about it" and so is "one and

---

[12] I will have much more to say on this topic in chapter 5.

the same for all actions" (§21, 34:1), nor even because every intentional action has a reason or purpose behind it. The point is rather that concepts of acting with a further purpose or in pursuit of a future end are *essential* to any rich concept of intentional action as something to which "Why?"-questions can be given application.

Finally, the argument of Section 20 is important because it is the first place where the three intention-concepts introduced in Section 1 are shown to be interrelated. The concept of intentional *action*, as something about which we can ask "Why?" in a sense that seeks the agent's reason for acting, depends on the possibility of expressing intention for the future, since only in this way can one represent what she intends *to do* by way of what she is presently doing. And it depends as well on the concept of further intention or intention *with which* a person acts, since it is only through this concept that we can represent the difference between voluntary and involuntary behavior—a distinction that presupposes a concept of action as potentially *rationalized*, as opposed to merely caused, by the circumstances that make sense of it. Though it is possible to act intentionally without a reason or purpose, still "the concept of voluntary or intentional action would not exist, if the question 'Why?', with answers that give reasons for acting, did not" (§21, 34:2). Among these possible answers must be ones that characterize the agent's "reason or purpose" (§21, 34:1), i.e., the intention of doing something *else* in the future or *further* in acting as one already is.

3.3 The A–D order (§§22–23, 26)

Section 22 begins a "closer examination" of statements that describe "the intention *with which* a man does what he does" (*I*, §22, 34:3). As we have seen, these statements can have either of two forms. First, one may answer a "Why?"-question concerning a present action by giving "a description of some future state of affairs" (§22, 34:3), as, e.g., "if you say 'Why are you crossing the road' and I reply 'I am going to look in that shop window' " (§22, 35:2). The second possibility is to give instead "a wider description of *what* [one] is doing" already:

> For example, someone comes into a room, sees me lying on a bed and asks "What are you doing?" ... an answer like "Resting" or "Doing Yoga," which would be a description of what I am doing in lying on my bed, would be an expression of intention. (§22, 34:3–35:1)

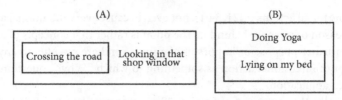

Figure 3.1 Forward-looking (A) and outward-looking (B) explanation of action.

For ease of reference, let us call these the *forward-* and *outward*-looking forms of explanation, respectively: an expression of intention looks *forward* when it describes some future thing one is going to do or bring about, and *outward* when it says what one is doing already *in* acting as one is. A schematic way of representing each form of explanation is supplied in Figure 3.1. Our task now is to gain a better understanding of what these forms of explanation involve and how they relate to one another.

The first thing that Anscombe considers in Section 22 is the distinctive nexus of dependency that is implicated in forward-looking explanation. A statement that one is doing P because she is going to do Q, e.g., that I am *crossing the road because I am going to look in that shop window* (§22, 35:2) or *going upstairs to get my camera* (§22, 35:5), implies that there is some *connection* between the two things described. What sort of connection is this, however? Anscombe describes it as a form of dependency: "the future state of affairs mentioned must be such that we can understand the agent's thinking it will or may be brought about by the action about which he is being questioned" (§22, 35:4); and thus "to make sense of 'I do P with a view to Q,' we must see how the future state of affairs Q is supposed to be a possible later stage in proceedings of which the action P is an earlier stage" (§22, 36:2). But she adds further that what grounds this dependency, connecting P and Q as stages in a single proceeding, is not something that can be understood simply from the outside—for it is only on the assumption that *the agent herself* sees P and Q as connected that an explanation of this sort makes sense. For example:

> My going upstairs is not a cause from which anyone could deduce the effect that I get my camera. And yet isn't it a future state of affairs which *is going to be* brought about by my going upstairs? But who can say that it is going to be brought about? Only I myself, in this case. It is not that going upstairs usually produces the fetching of cameras, even if there is a camera upstairs—unless indeed the context includes an order given to me, "Fetch

your camera," or my own statement "I am going to get my camera." (§22, 35:5–36:1)

The forward-looking statement that I am going upstairs to get my camera presupposes that these two events are connected: it says that my doing the first thing will lead somehow to my doing the second. But the connection that is postulated here is not a merely natural necessity—not, that is, the sort of connection in virtue of which someone could *predict* the latter event on the basis of the former, at least without knowledge of my intention. To clarify what sort of connection it is instead, we have to bring outward-looking explanation into the picture.

The discussion of outward-looking explanation begins in earnest in Section 23. To illustrate this concept, Anscombe considers an example of a man involved in a criminal plot. This man is pumping drinking water into the cistern of a house, and the source from which he is pumping has been contaminated with a deadly poison. The inhabitants of the house whose cistern he is filling include a group of Nazi leaders, and the person who contaminated the water—a different person from the man pumping—has calculated that by killing these Nazis he will get into power some people "who will govern well, or even institute the Kingdom of Heaven on earth and secure a good life for all the people" (§23, 37:1). All this information has been shared with the man at the pump: so he understands the nature of the scheme he is involved in, though of course there are lots of things that may happen, e.g., that the Nazis' friends or descendants will receive legacies if these men are killed, that he and the person behind the scheme likely know nothing about. Concerning this example, Anscombe asks: "What is this man doing? What is *the* description of his action?" (§23, 37:3).

These questions are puzzling. It is hard to know what they ask or what would be the significance of answering them correctly. Nor does it help much when Anscombe asks further: "Are we to say that the man who (intentionally) moves his arm, operates the pump, replenishes the water supply, poisons the inhabitants, is performing *four* actions? Or only one?" (§26, 45:6; and cf. §23, 40:3–41:1). Her eventual answers to these questions, which were echoed by Donald Davidson in his influential paper "Agency," are usually taken to be contributions to a metaphysical debate about the individuation of events—that is, a debate about the conditions under which descriptions like "pumping water" and "killing off the Nazi leaders" pick out one and the same event. But Anscombe indicates in a later paper that this was not the way she meant for her arguments to be understood:

I have always balked at the question "What is your theory of event-identity?" or "What theory of event-identity lies behind saying that (in [an] imagined case) putting the book down on the table and putting it down on an ink puddle were the same action?" Any "theory of event-identity" had better yield this result: it itself is not a theory or part of one.[13]

According to Anscombe, the position she works out beginning in Section 23 is "something that isn't a philosophical thesis at all, and which no one denies" ("UD," p. 211). It can, however, be hard to see how that can be, simply because the questions themselves seem to concern matters of metaphysics. This makes it difficult to identify what non-philosophical questions, whose answers "no one denies" in the course of ordinary life, the questions she has raised are supposed to correspond to. We cannot work out her position unless we overcome this barrier.

I propose that the way forward is, first, to treat Anscombe's question

(Q1)   What is *the* description of the man's action?

as equivalent to an ordinary question like "What are you (/is he or she) *doing*?," with the same emphasis on "doing" that culminates an exchange like the following:

> *Officer:* Sir, what are you doing?
> *Man:* Well, I'm operating this pump here, and—
> *Officer:* I can see very well that you're operating the pump. What are you *doing*?

The appropriate answer to the officer's final question, asked with this peculiar emphasis, will give what Anscombe calls *the* description of the man's action: that is, the description of his action in terms of which his action in its other descriptions makes sense. Second, I suggest treating the question

(Q2)   How many actions are there?

as equivalent to questions like "*How many times* did so-and-so do X?" and "Is there *anything else* that you are (/he or she is) doing?"—anything else, that is, other than the action for which *the* description is given in answer to

[13] "UD," p. 210.

a question like the one just posed. These questions are ordinary enough, and our answers to them will usually be straightforward—though at times there may be "obscure or borderline cases" ("UD," p. 210) where we do not know quite what to say, and we should not expect Anscombe's account to sort them more neatly than this.

Anscombe's discussion of these questions runs through the end of Section 26, and in the course of this discussion she introduces several key claims about the distinctive form of *unity* that is embodied in human action. These claims are as follows:

Unity   In a case like the one under consideration the agent is doing only *one* thing—that is, there is *only one action* picked out by all the many descriptions that can be given of what the person is up to.

Finality   *The* description of a person's action will be the one giving the *intention with which* she acts, where this is the last description in a progressively outward-looking series that takes us from "more immediate descriptions" of her action (cf. *I*, §48, 87:3) to the "wider" descriptions of what she is doing *in* or *by* acting in these ways.

Teleology   The *unity* of such an action, in virtue of which all the many descriptions of it pick just one action out, is a *teleological* unity of means and ends.

The presentation of these claims in Sections 23–26 is only provisional, and the thesis of Teleology in particular will receive a sustained treatment only later on. Nevertheless, the discussion here plays an essential role in setting the stage for what follows.

To begin, Anscombe says in answer to (Q1) that in the case she describes the man will be doing *all* of the things which can truly be said to be "going on, with him as subject": "E.g. he is earning wages, he is supporting a family, he is wearing away his shoe-soles, he is generating [certain] substances in his nerve-fibres" (§23, 37:4). She then notes, however, that among these descriptions the only ones that pick out things the man is doing *intentionally*, which of course is what interests us when we seek "*the* description" of his action in an exchange like the one I imagined earlier, are those that meet the conditions on the applicability of a "Why?"-question that were introduced earlier.[14] And in the present case there will be many descriptions of the man's

---

[14] These are the conditions (C1) to (C4), as discussed in sections 2.2 and 2.3.

action to which such questions do apply, such that the man could answer them positively by stating his further intentions. For example (cf. §23, 38:1):

"Why are you moving your arm up and down like that?" —"I'm pumping."
"Why are you pumping?" —"I'm filling the water-supply of that house."
"Why are you filling the water-supply?" —"To poison the inhabitants."

This dialogue supplies us with four descriptions of what the man is intentionally doing: he is moving his arm (call this "A"), he is pumping ("B"), he is filling the house water-supply ("C"), and he is poisoning the inhabitants of the house ("D"). The alphabetic shorthand is a reminder that these are not merely a *bunch* of descriptions of the man's action, but a *series* of descriptions of it, where *the order of this series is no accident*.[15] The man is not just moving his arm *and* pumping *and* filling the water-supply *and* poisoning the inhabitants, but doing each thing in the series *because* he is doing the next: that is, "each description is introduced as dependent on the previous one, though independent of the following one" (§26, 45:6). These relations of asymmetric dependency mean that the series A–B–C–D will have the following structure:

- First, the order of the series is irreflexive, since to say that the man is doing A (in order) to do B, or because he is doing B, is to say that his doing A *depends* in some way on his doing B, and that the converse relation does not hold—for doing A cannot depend on doing B if doing B depends in the same way on it.

- Second, there will be a converse form of dependency that holds between a later term in the series and an earlier one. This converse form is the dependency appealed to in answering what we may call a "How?"-question, i.e., a question that asks *how* one is doing a certain thing, where a positive answer gives the *means by which* one is doing it (cf. §26, 46:2). Thus if the man we have considered could answer the question "Why are you operating that pump?" with the statement that it is *because* he is poisoning the Nazis, then by the same token he could answer the question "How are you poisoning the Nazis?" with the statement that he is doing this *by* operating the pump.

---

[15] Thus a numerical shorthand would be better in a way—for the order of the alphabet *is* accidental.

- Third, the relations of dependency elicited through these "Why?"- and "How?"-questions are transitive: if a person is doing A because she is doing B and B because she is doing C, then she is also doing A because she is doing C; and if she is doing C by doing B and B by doing A, then she is doing C by doing A as well.

- Finally, in virtue of this transitivity the last item that can be given in an A–D series will have a special status relative to the others, since it will be "the intention (so far discovered) *with* which the act in its other descriptions was done" (§26, 46:2).[16] That is, where D is the last description in such a series, the answer "To do D" or "Because I am doing D" can be given in answer to the "Why?"-question asked about *any* of the earlier members, and so the person's action under *each* of these other descriptions, as well as any others that might be interposed between them (see §26, 47:3), will be explicable in relation to this last one.

Anscombe calls this final feature the "swallowing up" (§26, 46:2) of the earlier items in the series by the last, and says that this final description of the intention with which a person is acting—the description giving the *last* or *final* thing that a person can be said to be doing in acting as she presently is—should be counted as *the* description of her intentional action, since it is in relation to her action in this last description that the other descriptions of a person's action can all be understood. And it is because of the way this description "swallows up" the others that it, in a way the others do not, gives *the* description of what the man of Section 23 is intentionally doing: for it is when someone (such as a police officer) brings the man's action under this description that he finally *understands* the situation, by making sense of *what the man is up to* in acting as he evidently is. This yields the thesis that I called Finality: *the* description of an action is the description of the action that explains it in all its other descriptions, and is not explained by any of them, but only by something on the far side of the "break" separating outward-looking description of what the person *is doing* from forward-looking description of what she is *going to do*. (We will discuss this last concept further in what follows.)

---

[16] The emphasis in this sentence is unfortunate. It makes it seem as if "intention *with* which" is going to be used as a technical term for the intention given in this final description, but this is not a convention Anscombe follows. It would be better to say that this description gives *the* intention with which the person acts, i.e., *the* intention in relation to which the act in its other descriptions can be understood.

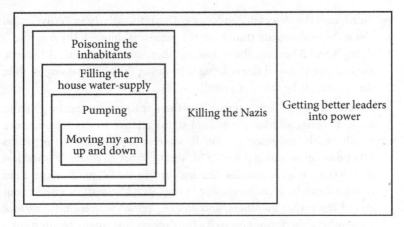

Figure 3.2 Representing the action of the man at the pump.

Using the schema introduced earlier in this section, we can represent the action of the man at the pump as shown in Figure 3.2, with the series of outward-looking descriptions that takes us from his arm movements to the poisoning shown in the vertical boxes on the left and the forward-looking explanation in terms of his further aims shown in the further progression rightward. According to the thesis of Finality, *the* description of an action is the last description in the outward-looking series, i.e., the last description that can be given in an explanatory order that moves from immediate descriptions of the action to wider descriptions in terms of the agent's further intentions. But here it is important to notice that, as Anscombe herself emphasizes, this "break" between outward-looking explanations and forward-looking ones is usually not sharp:

> E.g. is there much to choose between "She is making tea" and "She is putting on the kettle in order to make tea"—i.e. "She is going to make tea"? Obviously not. And hence the common use of the present to describe a future action which is by no means just a later stage in an activity which has a name as a single whole. E.g. "I am seeing my dentist," "He is demonstrating in Trafalgar Square" (either might be said when someone is at the moment e.g. travelling in a train). But the less normal it would be to take the achievement of the objective as a matter of course, the more the objective gets expressed *only* by "in order to." (§23, 40:1)

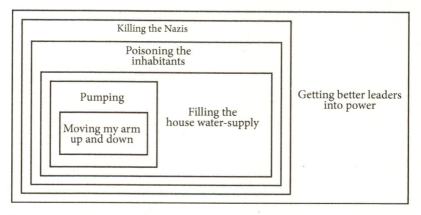

Figure 3.3 Another way of representing the action of the man at the pump.

These examples show us that outward- and forward-looking explanations of an action lie on a spectrum, and that where on this spectrum we draw the line between the two will obviously depend on context—for *how normal it is* to treat something as a matter of course will depend on such things as what is assumed in the context, or what is at stake in the truth of our judgments. And the schema for representing action that was introduced previously accounts for this, since a vertical series can be redrawn as a horizontal one, and vice versa, without any further change in what is represented: thus the series shown in Figure 3.2 could also be represented as in Figure 3.3 if, say, there were some question as to whether the man's pumping was actually filling the water-supply right now, but no real doubt that if he is indeed doing that, then the inhabitants of the house are drinking this water and thereby being poisoned.

However, even as Anscombe treats the distinction between outward- and forward-looking explanations as both flexible and dependent on context, it is also quite clear that she takes this distinction to have real philosophical importance.[17] For example, in introducing the concept of the A–D series in Section 23 she writes that only *sometimes* is it correct, when a person gives a description Y in answer to a question like "Why are you doing X?," "to say not merely: the man is X-ing, but also: 'the man is Y-ing'" (§23, 38:2). Such a statement will be correct only if "nothing falsifying the statement 'He is Y-ing' can be observed" (§23, 38:2)—and what *falsifies* a statement of what a person

---

[17] I am grateful to Eric Marcus for pressing me to develop this point.

is doing will depend on whether that statement has an outward-looking sense or a forward-looking one, as an example in Section 23 makes clear:

> Sometimes, jokingly, we are pleased to say of a man "He is doing such-and-such" when he manifestly is not. E.g. "He is replenishing the water-supply," when this is not happening because, as we can see but he cannot, the water is pouring out of a hole in the pipe on the way to the cistern. (§23, 39:3)

This example will come up again several times, but the thing to notice here is that it is *only* if the statement that

(1)   The man is replenishing the water-supply

gives an outward-looking description that the observation that there is a hole in the pipe will count against it. For if the sense of (1) is forward-looking instead, as if, e.g., today's pumping is only for practice and the poison won't be placed at the source until tomorrow, then this statement *won't* be falsified just because the pipe has a hole in it right now—for someone might be coming by this afternoon to do repairs. The same goes in turn for the evaluation of a person's claim to *knowledge* of what she does: e.g., it is only if the man's knowledge that he is replenishing the water-supply is knowledge of his *present* action under "a wider description of *what* he is doing" (§22, 34:3–35:1), that in knowing this he knows something about what is happening in the world—namely, that the water-supply is filling up, and that this is due in the right way to his present movements.[18] And this, as we will discuss at length beginning in the next chapter, is just what Anscombe says about the non-observational knowledge of one's intentional actions: it is knowledge of what "is actually taking place" in the world (§28, 50:3), including under descriptions "beyond that of bodily movements" (§28, 50:2). Erasing the distinction between outward- and forward-looking descriptions would render this position much less interesting than Anscombe clearly means for it to be.

One further thing we should observe about the thesis of Finality, which likewise helps to guard against interpreting it as a metaphysical thesis about the individuation of events, is that Anscombe gives this primacy to the last description in the A–D series only in relation to a particular set of explanatory

---

[18] Due "in the right way," since "an intended effect just occasionally comes about by accident" (§23, 39:1)—as if, unbeknownst to the man pumping, someone were to observe his movements and take them as a signal to fill up the water-supply in another way.

interests, namely those that concern a person's *point* or *purpose* in acting. And as we saw already, the sense of "Why?" that gives voice to these interests, and is answered positively by outward- or forward-looking redescription of an action, is mirrored by a corresponding sense of the question "How?"—and the answers to the latter sort of question will move *inward* and *backward* from more remote descriptions of an action to more immediate ones.[19] Suppose, for example, that the man at the pump calls up a friend to tell him that he is killing off a group of Nazi officials, and the following exchange ensues:

> "How are you poisoning those people?"—"I'm poisoning their water-supply."
> "How are you poisoning the water-supply?"—"I'm pumping."
> "How are you pumping?"—"I'm moving my arm up and down."

This sense of "How?" given voice in these questions is a *special* sense of that word, similar to the sense of "Why?" that has been our focus so far. When the question "How?" is asked in this sense, a positive answer to it will give the *means* by which one does something rather than the *manner* in which she does it: thus "How are you poisoning the inhabitants?," asked in this sense, could not be seriously answered by "Quickly." Since the interests by which "How?"-questions move our understanding inward and backward is no less legitimate than those by which "Why?"-questions take us outward and forward, there is no reason to deny that the last item given in an inward-looking series of the form D–A, i.e., the description of the movements *by means of which* the agent acts in pursuit of her further ends, could just as well be counted as "the" description of the action, in the context of the relevant explanatory interests.[20]

It is helpful to have this last point in the background in considering the thesis of *Unity*, according to which there is only one action picked out by all of the descriptions that form a series of the form A–D:

> Are we to say that the man who (intentionally) moves his arm, operates the pump, replenishes the water supply, poisons the inhabitants, is performing

---

[19] In "The Representation of Action," Anton Ford makes a powerful case that it is this question "How?," rather than the Anscombean "Why?," that should be given pride of place in the theory of action.

[20] This last description in a D–A series might be taken to characterize the agent's "basic" action—that is, the thing she is doing most "immediately," such that there is not something else *by which* she is doing this thing. For discussion of the concept of basic action within an Anscombean framework, see Douglas Lavin, "Must There Be Basic Action?," and Jennifer Hornsby, "Basic Activity."

four actions? Or only one? ... if we say there are four actions, we shall find that the only *action* that B consists in here is A; and so on. Only, more circumstances are required for A to be B than for A just to be A. And far more circumstances for A to be D, than for A to be B. ... In short, the only distinct action of his that is in question is this one, A. For moving his arm up and down with his fingers round the pump handle *is*, in these circumstances, operating the pump; and, in these circumstances, it *is* replenishing the house water-supply; and, in these circumstances, it *is* poisoning the household. (§26, 45:6–46:1)

The unity that Anscombe describes here is the unity of the series A–D, and thus a unity that shows up in light of the interests that we express in asking her question "Why?" This makes it is different from the unity that might be the concern of a physiologist, whose interest might be in the complexity of human behavior and so the great number of things that could be said to be "going on, with [a given agent] as subject, which are in fact true" (§23, 37:4).[21] It might also be different from the concern of a metaphysician who is formulating a general criterion of action- or event-individuation, or a linguist giving a general criterion for co-reference of descriptions. And, finally, it is different from the unity we would explore in asking "How?" instead of "Why?"—that is, the unity or disunity that would be our interest in considering what the man does *in* filling the cistern with poison. (If, e.g., the operation of the pump required pushing a pedal with his foot in addition to moving the handle with his arm, then if our interest were in identifying the *means* by which the man acts we might say that he was doing two things at once, both of them in pursuit of a single aim.) The claim of Unity says that insofar as the description D is the common *terminus* to the series of "Why?"-questions asked about A, B, and C, in doing A, B, C, and D the man is performing only one action. This unity appears from the perspective of one who seeks to *make sense* of what a person does, i.e., to understand *why*

---

[21] Consider as well the complexity that is contained even in our bodily movements as they unfold over time: the man moves his arm up *and* down, then up *and* down again, and so on. Or again, he might (a) fill the cistern of one house with poisoned water from morning to noon and then fill the cistern of a different house with unpoisoned water from noon until the day is done; (b) fill and then refill the same cistern with poison twice in a day; or (c) complete a single process of filling the cistern that is interrupted "by a fit of coughing" ("UD," p. 216). From the perspective of, say, the physiologist there may be no relevant difference between (a) and (b), whereas (c) might be viewed as a pair of separate acts. But from the perspective of the police officer he will have been doing two quite different things in each of (a) and (b), whereas the interruption in (c) will not make a relevant difference. There is, once again, no reason to read Anscombe as treating either set of answers as better approximating some sort of God's-eye view of the metaphysical situation.

he is doing all the "many" things corresponding to true descriptions of his action.[22]

This brings us in turn to the last claim, that the unity of an action in its various descriptions is a *teleological* unity of means and ends. The centrality of this point can be obscured by some of what Anscombe says about the man at the pump. For example, when she says in the passage just quoted that it is the *circumstances* of the man's action that make the movement of his arm identical to the operation of the pump, and this identical in turn to the replenishment of the water-supply, and so on,[23] it can seem as if she is claiming that the unity in what these descriptions pick out is settled by facts about the material environment—i.e., that it is simply because the man's movements of his arm *bring about* these other things that his moving his arm is also his doing them. But there are several reasons to resist this reading of the text. First, not in every case where a person is doing one thing *by* or *as a means of* doing another will there be such a straightforwardly "productive" relationship between the events picked out by these descriptions: e.g., in the case of making tea by putting on a kettle (cf. §23, 40:1), if one's doing the latter thing *is* her doing the former, this cannot be because boiling water tends to result in pots of tea.[24] Second, even in cases where there is a straightforwardly "productive" relationship between an immediate description of an action as doing X and a more remote description of it as doing Y, on Anscombe's view it is only when the agent herself *knows without observation* that she is acting in these ways, and is able to link them *herself* in a series of questions "Why?" or "How?," that they constitute a series of descriptions of her intentional action. Finally, recall once again that the interests in relation to which a person is said to be doing one thing rather than many are interests in her reasons for acting—and the sense of "Why?" that gives voice to these interests, and so

---

[22] A similar point applies to what we might call *branches* in action: if, e.g., the man beats out the rhythm of "God Save the King" in the way he moves the pump (cf. §26, 47:2), and is doing this intentionally, then his action under *this* description will not be rationalized by the intention to poison the inhabitants of the house (unless, perhaps, it is by moving the pump in this rhythm that he gets the water to flow properly). Is is therefore a separate act? As Anscombe says about cases at the border between reasons and causes (see §15, 24:1), it is hard to see what would be the point of the distinction. But if, say, beating out this rhythm were a way to signal to some further group of conspirators that now was the time to …, then we would be more inclined to speak of the man as doing two different things at once. Thanks to Eric Wiland for some discussion of this.

[23] For these remarks see §26, 45:6–46:1.

[24] Anscombe also gives the example of "a man doing things with an array of wires and plugs and so on," but where "not enough has gone on" for it to be evident what he is up to (§23, 39:2). Perhaps the man is building a radio—but the circumstances that make it the case that his doing these things *is* his building a radio will not be that movements of this sort, even in circumstances like those he is in, tend to give rise to radios.

brings to light the unity of the series A–D, is different from the sense in which we ask why, e.g., a vase fell off the shelf. The unity of an action is not merely a unity in which one event brings about some others: it is the unity of something that is *done as a means to an end*.

3.4 Intention and foresight (§§24–25, 27)

The previous section explored two ways that the various descriptions of what a person is doing—that is, the various "description[s] of what is going on, with [a certain person] as subject" (*I*, §23, 37:4)—can be placed into relations of explanatory dependence. First, a description B of a person's action explains another thing A that she is doing in an *outward-looking* way when B describes a further thing that the person is doing *in* acting in doing A—as when, e.g., a person explains why she is lying on a bed by saying that she is resting (§22, 35:1). Second, a person's doing B explains her doing A in a *forward-looking* way when A describes a present happening and B something further that she is going to do, which her doing A is supposed to help bring about—as when a person says that she is going upstairs (because she is going) to get her camera (§22, 35:5–36:2). This distinction between outward- and forward-looking explanation is not always sharp, and where we draw the line in any given case will be sensitive to various contextual factors: thus whether we say that the man working at the pump *is killing* the Nazis (an outward-looking description) rather than that he *is going to kill* them (a forward-looking one) can depend on such things as how "normal it would be to take the achievement of the objective as a matter of course" (§23, 40:1)—and this in turn may be influenced by what is at stake, and so on. Despite this porousness and flexibility, the distinction between outward- and forward-looking explanations is important to our understanding of what is to act for a reason.

With all this in the background, in Section 25 Anscombe introduces a "further difficulty" that comes up in connection with her example of the man operating the pump, namely that in a close variant of the case she has described "the man's intention might not be to poison [the party leaders] but only to earn his pay" (§25, 41:3). This will come out if in answer to a question like

(W)   Why did you poison the water-supply?

his answer is something like,

(J)   I didn't care about that, I wanted my pay and just did my usual job.[25]

According to Anscombe, in this variant on her original case

> although [the man] knows concerning an intentional act of his—for it, namely replenishing the house water-supply, is intentional by our criteria—that it is *also* an act of replenishing the house water-supply with *poisoned* water, it would be incorrect, by our criteria, to say that his act of replenishing the house supply with poisoned water was intentional. And I do not doubt the correctness of the conclusion; it seems to shew that our criteria are rather good. (§25, 42:1)

Several interpretive questions arise here. First, more must be said in order to understand how a statement like (J) could be a way of refusing application of the "Why?"-question asked in (W). Second, it is not really clear that the criteria introduced so far in *Intention* are enough to account for why this would be. Third, the conclusion Anscombe draws here may seem to invite the very sort of idea that she has set herself against, i.e., that some special "interior movement" (§25, 42:1) or other psychological episode occurring within an agent is essential to determining the descriptions under which an action is intentional. And finally, it may not be evident what the wider upshot is of Anscombe's discussion of this variant on her original case. In what follows I will consider each point in turn.

(1) Let's use *Work* to name the situation in which the man is pumping poison because operating the pump is part of his usual job, and *Conspiracy* to name the situation in which he's pumping poison because he's part of a plot to kill the Nazi party leaders. What are the differences between these situations that are supposed to make it legitimate for the man in *Work*, but not the man in *Conspiracy*, to reject the applicability of a question like (W)?

A good place to begin is by reflecting on the difference between the forms of explanation offered in statements like the following:

(1)   I'm lying on the bed because I am resting.
(2)   I'm going upstairs because I am getting my camera.
(3)   I'm disturbing the cat because I am sitting down on the couch.

Each of (1), (2), and (3) relates a pair of descriptions of one's action in an order of causal dependency. In (1), this dependency is of the sort expressed

---

[25] For (W) and (J), see §25, 42:1.

in outward-looking explanation: the statement describes a further thing (namely, resting) that one is doing *in* acting as she is (that is, in lying on the bed), offering the latter as an explanation of the former. By contrast, in (2) the dependency represented is forward-looking: it explains what is happening immediately (one's going upstairs) in terms of a future thing one intends to do (namely, get her camera). The statement in (3), however, is different from both of these: whereas (1) and (2) offer *teleological* explanations that treat what happens as standing in an order of means to end, (3) does no such thing, but rather represents the disturbance of the cat as a *mere effect* of what one does. We can bring this out by noticing that while (1) and (2) are each equivalent, respectively, to the following:

(1*)   I'm lying on the bed in order to rest
(2*)   I'm going upstairs in order to get my camera

the statement in (3), by contrast, is not equivalent to

(3*)   I'm disturbing the cat in order to sit down on the couch.

To be clear, (3) *would* be equivalent to (3*) if, say, the cat was sleeping where one needed to sit, and disturbing the cat were a way to get it to move. But the most natural reading of (3) is as saying that the cat has been resting on or near the couch and it's *simply a fact* that one's sitting down is startling her—in which case disturbing the cat is something one does *in* sitting on the couch, but not something one does *in order to* sit down. Put simply, not everything that a person does *because* she is doing something else falls within the teleologically unified means–end order that we explored earlier.

The difference between these two sorts of dependency can be represented with the schema shown in Figure 3.4. In (A), the dependency is of the same sort that grounds the teleological unity that we have explored: the action-descriptions "sitting down" and "disturbing the cat" are shown to be related in an outward-looking manner, as in the reason-giving statement (3*). This is just the sort of dependency expressed in the man's description of his action in Anscombe's original case of *Conspiracy*:

(4)   I'm pumping the water because I'm poisoning the inhabitants of that house.

By contrast, in (B) the descriptions are related in a different way, now with one treated as a *side-effect* of the other. And *this* is the sort of explanation that Anscombe's man gives of his poisoning in the newly introduced case of *Work*:

(5)   I'm poisoning the inhabitants because I'm doing my usual job.

The description in (4), like those in (1), (2), and (3*), represents two things the man is doing as standing in a relation of means to end—thus (4) is equivalent to the statement that he is pumping the water *in order to* poison the inhabitants, or that doing the latter thing is his *purpose* in doing the former. But (5) says something quite different from this. Rather, in saying (5) the man in *Work* describes the poisoning as an effect or *consequence* of doing his job—just as a cat may be disturbed when one sits down, or one's movements in pumping may *happen* to cast a shadow that looks strangely like a face (cf. §23, 37:2). This statement invites us to understand the man's action, not as represented in Figure 3.2 (p. 70), which presents the original situation in *Conspiracy*, but rather as shown in Figure 3.5, where the description "poisoning the inhabitants" is represented as a side-effect of what the man is doing intentionally, namely operating the pump to fill the water-supply as demanded by his usual job.

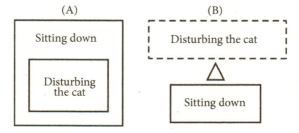

Figure 3.4 Two ways to understand (3): "I'm disturbing the cat because I am sitting down on the couch." In (A) the relationship between these descriptions is that of means to end, as in (3*). (B) represents the more natural reading, in which the disturbance is treated as a side-effect of one's sitting. Here, the triangle represents causal dependency and the description "disturbing the cat" is bordered in a dashed line to show that it does not pick out something one *intentionally* does. (Thanks to Kim Frost for the last suggestion.)

Understood in this way, the difference between *Work* and *Conspiracy* is that only in the latter case does the description "poisoning the inhabitants" (and "killing the Nazi leaders," etc.) give a *reason for acting*, since only in this case does this description fall within the means–end order that constitutes the unity of the man's intentional activity. And so Anscombe's claim at the start of Section 25 is that when we treat a description of an action in this way, as falling outside this means–end order, we thereby refuse the application of

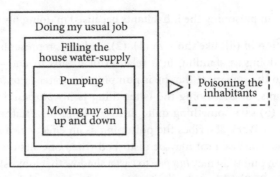

Figure 3.5 Representing the action of the man who is just doing his usual job, as in *Work*.

"Why?"-questions to the action under this description. In *Work*, the man's statement that he is only doing his usual job provides a positive answer to *a* sense of the question "Why are you poisoning those people?," but it fails to answer the sense of this question that asks for his *reasons* for acting in this way. According to the hypothesis introduced at the start of Section 5, a consequence of this is that his action is not intentional under that description.

(2) Our next question was whether Anscombe is right in saying that if indeed the man is just doing his usual job then it would not be "correct, *by our criteria*, to say that his act of replenishing the house supply with poisoned water was intentional" (*I*, §25, 42:1; emphasis added). For even if we accept that, in *Work*, the man's statement that he is only doing his usual job is a way of refusing application of the "Why?"-question to his action under the description "poisoning the inhabitants," nevertheless his action under this description seems to satisfy all of the conditions on intentional action that Anscombe has advanced so far. For whatever the man cares about, whatever motivates him, whatever is his usual job, and so on, he does not seem to require observation in order to know that he is poisoning the water-supply, and nor does he need observation to know *why* he is doing this—which will not just be a matter of his having reacted to a mental cause. Because this, if a statement like

(J)   I didn't care about that, I wanted my pay and just did my usual job

really is a way of rejecting the "Why?"-question in

(W)   Why did you poison the water-supply?

then it seems that there must be some further condition on the applicability of such a question than the ones captured by the criteria discussed so far. What Anscombe says in Section 25 about the case of *Work* seems to entail that *merely* knowing, even without observation, both *that* and *why* one is doing something that is not merely the effect of a mental cause, does not suffice for doing this thing intentionally.

There is room for some resistance here.[26] For won't it be only because the man was *told* that the water in the cistern is poisoned, etc., that he knows he is poisoning the water-supply? And if so, then doesn't this show that his knowledge that he is doing this is a kind of knowledge by observation? But notice that the same could be said for the man in *Conspiracy* who is poisoning the Nazis intentionally: he knows that he's poisoning them only because he knows that the water he's pumping is poisoned, and *this* is something he knows only by observation or testimony, etc.[27] Nor does the man in *Work* have any greater need than the man in *Conspiracy* to rely on observation for knowledge of what happens "downstream" of his pumping, such as whether the poison is actually getting into the water-supply of the house. Because of this, if the original man's knowledge of the poisoning counts as non-observational knowledge—a matter we will consider much more closely beginning in the next chapter—then so it seems will the knowledge of the man who is doing his usual job. At the very least, we need to know more about the relevant concept of non-observational knowledge before we can say confidently that the man who is doing his usual job doesn't know without observation that he is poisoning the house's inhabitants.[28]

If this is right, then even if it is true that the man in *Conspiracy* is not poisoning the inhabitants of the house intentionally, still this is not explained *by the criteria* introduced so far—i.e, by Anscombe's conditions (C1) to (C4). To address this deficiency we need to add a further condition to these:

(C5) A person does something intentionally only if her doing this is not merely a side-effect of something else that she is doing.

---

[26] Thanks to Beri Marušić for pressing me to add this clarification.

[27] Indeed, this is part of how Anscombe describes her original case: "The man who contaminated the source has calculated that if these people are destroyed some good men will get into power ... and he has revealed the calculation, together with the facts about the poison, to the man who is pumping" (§23, 37:1).

[28] According to the analysis I offer in chapter 6 we will be able to say: only the original man in *Work* has *practical* knowledge of his poisoning, since only he knows this action in light of his practical reasoning. But these concepts of practical knowledge and practical reasoning are not yet on the table at this point.

The force of "merely" here, and the concept of efficacy in question, are similar to those discussed earlier in connection with condition (C4). And as we saw in discussing that condition, it is surely possible for there to be borderline cases here, or ones where this talk of mere effects in contrast to relations of means to end will "have no point" (cf. §15, 24:1). It remains to be considered whether this added condition has some problematic consequences that should lead us to reject it.

(3) Our third concern was that what Anscombe says about the case of *Work* seems to suggest that the scope of a person's intentional activity is determined by the person's thoughts and feelings—for aren't these the things that decide between what one does as a means to an end and what are the "mere effects" of her actions? And this sounds very much like the view that Anscombe cautions against in Section 24, where she writes that what makes "the man's present pumping an intentional act of poisoning" is "a matter of circumstances, not of anything that is going on *then*" (*I*, §24, 41:2).[29] Her point there was that what makes the man's action of moving his arm *also* an action of poisoning the inhabitants of the household is not what he is thinking or saying to himself, but rather the *context* of his action. The man is doing these things insofar as his fingers are wrapped around the pump handle, the water being pumped is poisoned, and the pipe from the pump runs without interruption to the supply of water that the party leaders drink. Yet now we are supposed to accept that all this context could obtain even when the man is *not* poisoning the party leaders intentionally after all. What then is there to mark the difference between these cases, except for a difference in the state of the agent's mind? "It is really not at all to be wondered that very many people have thought of intention as a special interior movement" (§25, 42:1)—but as we have seen, this is just the sort of view that Anscombe is out to reject.

To resolve this difficulty, we need to return to the point I made earlier about the difference between *knowing* what one does, which on Anscombe's view is among the criteria of intentional action, and *consciously thinking* about an action as one performs it. I argued in section 2.2 that it is compatible with Anscombe's condition (C1) that a person can do something intentionally while something other than her action is "on her mind"—for what matters is not what the person thinks about as she acts but rather whether she *knows*, perhaps in the non-occurrent way one knows her name or the city

---

[29] And cf. the conclusion of Section 19: there may be nothing to find "in the action, or in the man himself at the moment of acting" (§19, 29:3–30:1) that decides what a person is intentionally doing.

she is in, what she is doing as she does it. And the point needed in the present case is similar to this. The difference between *Work* and *Conspiracy* reveals that *how a person understands her action* can make a difference to what she intentionally does—a point we encountered already in considering Section 22, where Anscombe showed how an agent's self-understanding will be part of what makes it the case that, e.g., her going upstairs *is* her getting her camera (see §22, 35:5–36:2, as discussed in section 3.3). Yet this self-understanding does not consist in *thinking* to oneself as one walks that, e.g., "My camera is upstairs, so I am going upstairs to get it"—for a person may *understand* her action in this way even as she is thinking about something quite different, or perhaps about nothing at all. Moreover, even when a person *does* think something to herself as she acts, this might fail to reflect her actual understanding of what she does. For example:

> I suppose that the man I imagined, who said "I was only doing my usual job," might find this formula and administer it to himself in the present tense at some stage of his activities. However, if he does this, we notice that the question immediately arises: with what intention does he do it? This question would always arise about anything which was deliberately performed as an "act of intending." The answer in this case might be "So that I don't have to consider whose side I am on." Thus the interior performance has not secured what you might have thought, namely that the man's action in pumping the water *is* just doing his usual job; it [*viz.,* the interior performance] is itself a new action. ... It is in fact only if the thought "I'm only doing my job" is spontaneous rather than deliberate that its occurrence has some face-value relevance to the question what the man's intentions really are. (§27, 47:4)

Anscombe is making several points here. The first is that intention, like understanding, is not itself a kind of act. That is, intending is not *itself* an act that a person performs; it is only other things that a person may do intentionally or *with* a given intention. Her second point is that anything that *is* an act, such as an instance of inner speech, is such that there may be a further intention with which *it* is performed. Because of this, if the man says to himself "I was only doing my job," it is entirely possible that the intention with which he says this is different from the intention with which he operates the pump. That is why the only way that such an inner saying can have any face-value relevance is if there is no intention behind it at all.

Anscombe's final point in this passage is that the bearing of an "interior performance" on the content of a person's intention will *never* be decisive, since any interior act, or other conscious mental episode, will only be one of the many factors that are relevant to this.[30] This is especially clear when the agent's thoughts, feelings, etc., are characterized neutrally with respect to their sincerity, the motivation for them, and so on—for there may be nothing evident in the content or "phenomenal character" of such a mental item that reveals whether it is insincere or questionably motivated. Moreover, even when a thought, say to the effect that one is only doing her usual job, *is* meant sincerely, and does not arise from a questionable motive, this may not be enough for the thought to be *true*—that is, any such thought will still be subject to the same "tests for truthfulness" (§27, 47:4) that would apply to a corresponding verbal statement (or signed or written one, etc.):

For example, in the case of the man who didn't care tuppence, part of the account we imagined him giving was that he just went on doing his usual job. It is therefore necessary that it should be his usual job if his answer is to be acceptable; and he must not do anything, out of the usual course of his job, that assists the poisoning and of which he cannot give an acceptable account. E.g. suppose he distracts the attention of one of the inhabitants from something about the water source that might suggest the truth; the question "Why did you call him from over there?" must have a credible answer other than "to prevent him from seeing"; and a multiplication of such points needing explanation would cast doubt on his claim not to have done anything with a view to facilitating the poisoning. (§25, 43:2)[31]

---

[30] According to Anscombe, among the other relevant factors will be such things as "the nuances in relationships with others in the plot that you will expect the man to have later; the atmosphere between him and them, and similar things" (§27, 48:1).

[31] Cf. as well the discussion of the possible techniques of "psychological detectives" (§27, 48:1) in bringing out pretense and insincerity: for example, to find out whether the man in *Work* really is only doing his usual job, we might see what happens if we tell him "such things as (to give crude examples): 'Well, then you won't be much interested to hear that the poison is old and won't work'; or 'Then you won't be claiming a share in a great sum with which someone wishes to reward the conspirators'" (§27, 48:1). The first example recalls her remark in Section 22 that if someone says she is doing P so that Q, then "to say, in one form or another: 'But Q won't happen, even if you do P' ... is, in some way, to contradict the intention" (§22, 36:3). By contrast, no such thing happens if Q is envisioned just as a side-effect of doing P: in that case the news that Q is not happening may be surprising, but won't necessarily affect the agent's sense that she is carrying out her plan. (Not *necessarily*—though in some situations it could. E.g., if doing P is an intended means to bringing about R and Q a predicted side-effect of doing P, the fact that Q is not happening could be evidence that one is not doing P or bringing about R, either.)

As Anscombe acknowledges, the check on truthfulness provided by tests like these will not be decisive either, since what a person does or says in response to such queries may be ambiguous or insincere.[32] This does mean that occasionally "there comes a time when a man can say 'This is my intention,' and no one else can contribute anything to settle the matter" (§27, 48:1). However, it simply does not follow that what a person says, either "inwardly" or aloud, will always be *accurate*, nor does a person's being able to *say* this sort of thing in a way that no one else can mean that a person always *knows* exactly what the scope of her intention is—for she may be unwittingly insincere, or perhaps even claiming sincerely to lack an intention which, in fact, she has.[33]

So there is *a* sense in which accepting condition (C5) requires us to introduce a "criterion by thoughts" into the concept of intentional action. Indeed, some such criterion was implicit already in the four conditions given earlier, since these say it is partly a person's *knowledge* of what she is doing that determines what a person does and why. It determines this only *partly*, however, because the scope of a person's intentional activity will depend as well on what she actually *is* doing, as determined by the circumstances in which she acts—e.g., whether the pipe from this pump runs to the proper cistern, whether the water being pumped really is poisonous, whether this really is the person's usual job, etc. *Against this background* a person's own understanding of what she is doing, and why she is doing it, will play an essential her role in delineating the scope of what she intentionally does. If this is a criterion by thoughts, it is not the problematic kind according to which "one can determine one's intentions by making ... a little speech to oneself" (§25, 42:1—"obvious bosh," Anscombe says), and moreover the criterion is such that, in many cases, it is not only the agent's self-understanding but also her "outward acts" (§27, 49:1) that are relevant to determining what she intentionally does.

(4) The final thing to consider is how we should understand the broader significance of Anscombe's discussion of the distinction between intention and foresight. As I explained in the Introduction, the failure to distinguish

---

[32] For the possibility of ambiguity see §25, 43:2, where Anscombe imagines that the man might distract an inhabitant's attention away from the poison not because he cares about the scheme, but rather to help keep himself out of trouble. And for insincerity see §27, 48:1, where she considers the possibility of pretense, together with some stock ways of bringing it out. Another possibility that she does not consider directly is that asking certain questions might lead to a *change* in a person's intentions from what they were before the question was asked.

[33] On this last suggestion see §27, 48:1, where Anscombe considers it briefly but is apparently unsure whether it is really possible. The discussion of self-ignorance in Section 17 is obviously relevant here: see section 2.4, pp. 44–46.

intention from foresight is one of the primary grounds on which Anscombe faults modern moral philosophers, arguing that their conception of intention makes it impossible for them to avoid justifying atrocious courses of action. It was in just this context that Anscombe saw the need for "a sound philosophy of psychology" which will, among other things, give an account of "what a human action is at all, and how its description as 'doing such-and-such' is affected by its motive and by the intention or intentions in it" ("MMP," p. 174). Yet now, as soon as she has introduced this allegedly crucial distinction, she immediately says that in the case of *Work* our interest in drawing it "is certainly not an ethical or legal interest; if what [the man] said was true, *that* will not absolve him from guilt of murder!" (*I*, §25, 45:3). What, then, is the interest of the distinction instead?

A preliminary point that may need some clarification is why Anscombe says that the man in *Work*, even if he is not poisoning anyone intentionally, is nevertheless a *murderer* in the legal sense—a position that will be unintelligible on its face if we assume that murder equates to intentional killing. But while criminal law is complex on this matter, and the details vary between jurisdictions, in fact *any* criminal code will classify a case like *Work*, no less than *Conspiracy*, as one where the man is guilty of murdering the inhabitants of the house. In some jurisdictions this is achieved by identifying murder with intentional killing but defining the category of intention in the way Anscombe opposes, so that a person counts as *intending* all the side-effects that she foresees her action will bring about—an analysis that has prevailed in English law at least since the early 1960s.[34] In others, however, murder is defined in the way that she recommends, so that it includes causing the death of a human being *either* intentionally *or* with a combination of foresight and reckless indifference to the foreseen deaths. But this just reminds us again that the relevance of this distinction, at least in the context we are considering, is not to define what a person can reasonably be blamed or punished for. So we must ask again: what *is* its relevance, and why does Anscombe introduce the distinction in such a seemingly roundabout way?

Concerning the latter question, a likely purpose of considering the distinction between intended and foreseen consequences in a context where this distinction has no ethical or legal interest is to help us theorize these concepts in the way that Anscombe recommends in "Modern Moral Philosophy," namely by "*banishing ethics totally* from our minds" and so

---

[34] Anscombe criticizes this analysis in "WM," pp. 54–55. For further discussion, with reference to case law and relevant legal codes, see M. Cathleen Kaveny, "Inferring Intention from Foresight."

treating these concepts "simply as part of the philosophy of psychology" ("MMP," p. 188).[35] For if we were to take it for granted that, for example, the scope of a person's guilt is no broader than the scope of her intention, then our account of the latter concept would likely turn out to reflect our ethical presuppositions. By contrast, if we can see how to distinguish intended and foreseen consequences in a case like *Work* even when the agent's *responsibility* for these consequences is not at all in question, we may be able to develop a psychological account of this concept which we then can reapply in other contexts where more is at stake.

What are those other contexts like, and how is this account of the intention/foresight distinction supposed to help us to think more clearly about them? We encountered one contemporary example in the Introduction, where I noted that according to Anscombe a robust concept of intention is required to make sense of the traditional prohibition against the deliberate killing of innocents: the notions of *deliberate* killing and of someone who is *innocent* from the perspective of a warring power both require distinguishing what a person intentionally does from what her actions foreseeably bring about. Anscombe gives a couple of other examples in her unpublished review of the legal scholar Glanville Williams's 1957 book *The Sanctity of Life and the Criminal Law*, arguing that we must apply this distinction in order to understand how there can be a morally relevant difference between "the destruction of an ectopic fetus" and "the killing of [a] child in the womb," or between the decision "to give a man drugs to ease his pain, knowing that their cumulative effect may kill him before the disease does" and the decision "to poison [a man] intentionally" ("GW," p. 248). As I explained in the Introduction, the upshot of admitting these distinctions is not to guarantee that these traditional prohibitions will be upheld, nor to ensure that they can be applied in every controversial case in such a way that those prohibitions turn out to be coherent. Rather, the distinction between intention and foresight is necessary for us at least to *make sense* of these prohibitions and other like them, as they all presuppose the possibility of distinguishing what is intentionally done from what is knowingly brought about. Without a way to draw this distinction, we are *guaranteed* in advance that we cannot "avoid a course of reasoning which will justify anything at all, however atrocious" ("GW," p. 247).

---

[35] The initial list of concepts that are to be investigated in this way includes: "'action,' 'intention,' 'pleasure,' 'wanting'" ("MMP," p. 108).

This last point deserves further emphasis. Williams's book, of which Anscombe wrote a truly scathing review that the commissioning journal then declined to publish, criticizes at length a conception of the distinction between intention and foresight whereby it allows a person to remove responsibility for what she does just by the suitable direction of her thoughts. And Anscombe notes in her review that this conception does indeed have some adherents among influential moral theologians:[36]

> ever since the seventeenth century a false and absurd conception of intention has prevailed, which derives from Cartesian psychology; according to this conception an intention is a secret mental act which is producible at will. In the event, theologians often treated the "direction of intention" as something that could be accomplished by telling oneself at the time of action "What I really mean to be doing is ...." [...] a typical suggestion was that a servant could go and hold the ladder for his burglarious master, so long as he "directed his intention" purely to the earning of his pay; and at the present day the conception produced the doctrine of *coitus reservatus*, which is equivalent to the practice of withdrawal accompanied by an "intention" not to ejaculate; the ejaculation that then took place would be "accidental." ("GW," p. 248)[37]

---

[36] For further discussion of these tendencies in Catholic moral theology, see Anscombe's unpublished manuscript "On Being in Good Faith," which dates from the late 1950s or early 1960s.

[37] It is important to understand that for Anscombe, the case of the servant holding the ladder while his master commits a burglary is *not* structurally equivalent to that of the man pumping poison in *Work*. For the defense of the latter man is not that he was "following orders" but rather that he was *doing his usual job*. And on Anscombe's view, if this man was not doing his usual job after all, but rather "was hired by the poisoner to pump the water, knowing it was poisoned, the case is different" (*I*, §25, 44:2), as then the man *couldn't* do the job intentionally without intentionally poisoning the inhabitants of the house. That is, in this further variant the man

> can *say* he doesn't care tuppence, and that he only wants the money; but the commission by the acceptance and performance of which he gets the money is—however implicit this is allowed to be—to pump poisoned water. Therefore unless he takes steps to cheat his hirer (he might, e.g., put what he mistakenly thought was an antidote into the water), it is not an acceptable account if he says "I wasn't intending to pump poisoned water, only to pump water and get my hire." (§25, 44:2; emphasis added)

The point here is that if someone accepts a commission to pump poisoned water, then it is *by* doing the thing that is commissioned that this person intends to get paid, and so the fact that he is pumping poisoned water cannot be a mere side-effect of what he intentionally does. In this context, the *only* reason such a person could have for thinking, e.g., "Let me just do the pumping in order to get paid; the poisoning will be only a side-effect" would be that he doesn't

In the hands of the moral theologians whom Anscombe is criticizing here, the distinction between intention and foresight becomes a tool for moral absolution, a way for a person to avoid responsibility for what she does just by *thinking* about things in the right way. Such an understanding of intention can be especially attractive, and especially hard to resist, when our point of departure is a concept of intention as something "purely in the sphere of the mind," with "what physically takes place, i.e., what a man actually does" as something that will be considered only later on (*I*, §4, 9:2). (Did Truman really intend the deaths of the citizens of Hiroshima and Nagasaki? Well, he certainly *felt* no desire to see them dead, and his *objective* was only to end the war quickly and with the minimum loss of human life, so though the deaths surely *took place* in consequence of his choice they may not have been part of his intention in the strict sense.) It is in this context that a view of intention as "interior act" (§27, 47:4) is most likely to seem attractive, and that we are most likely to endorse "the absurd thesis which is sometimes maintained: that a man's intended action is only described by describing his *objective*" (§25, 45:2).

In contrast to this, the starting-point for Anscombe's inquiry is the way that the concept of intention is put to work in our description of intentional *action*. The first question that she wants us to ask of an agent is not "What does he intend?" but rather "What is this man *doing*?" (cf. §23, 37:3)—and then the concept of intention is deployed as a way to describe *what is happening* in a way that displays the particular form of unity found in human action, and the means–end order embodied in the series of descriptions we can give of it. In this context we use the concept of intention to make *sense* of an action, to understand what connects a person's behavior in its immediate descriptions to the further ends that her movements are meant to serve. And we cannot

---

want to be a murderer, or to be troubled by feelings of guilt. And these considerations bear on what he wishes to *intend* rather than what he chooses to *do*: for whether the man cares about the poisoning or not, and however he feels about the plot he is engaged in, in accepting this commission the man has chosen to *pump the poisoned water in order to earn the pay*—which, if he carries the commission out, will be the description of what he intentionally does. By contrast, someone who pumps water as part of his regular job *might* choose to do his job despite the badness involved in it today, since the description "doing this job" is not an arbitrary one that he has invented in order to assuage a guilty conscience, but rather a description under which he regularly acts. *If* this is true, then by describing his action in this way the man will reveal "something about [*himself*]," which goes beyond what happened at the time" (§25, 45:4; quoting Wittgenstein, *PI*, §659)—not something which absolves him from guilt of murder, but something which is relevant nevertheless to our understanding of what he is up to. In neither case, however, does the crucial difference lie in a mental act by which the man directs *his intention* in one way or another. The difference is rather in the "direction" (that is, aim or end) of his *act*.

do this successfully without representing the action as intentional under those descriptions that give the *means* by which the agent's movements are intelligibly related to her ends. Thus, for example, in explaining why Truman agreed to the bombing of Hiroshima it is not enough to say that he did this in order to end the war—for this explanation is silent concerning *how* the bombing was supposed to achieve this, and in the case at issue the death of innocent civilians was no mere side-effect, but rather an essential stage in the path from the bombing to the war's eventual end. (Things might be different if Hiroshima had been home to an important store of weapons, or if the bombing were meant as a way to call down help from the gods—in these circumstances the civilian deaths would have been outside Truman's intent, though still he would have been guilty of reckless indifference to them.) The upshot of Anscombe's analysis is that this *alone* is enough to show that Truman brought about those deaths intentionally, even if he himself would have denied this—indeed even if he accepted those deaths only as something that "had to happen," and shed great tears when he learned that the deed had been done. For no matter the state of a person's inner feelings, and no matter the privilege we give to an agent's self-understanding in determining his intent, the bearing of these things is necessarily "limited by this: [a person] cannot profess not to have had the intention of doing the thing that was a means to an end of his" (§25, 44:2).[38]

3.5 Summary discussion

At this point in Anscombe's inquiry, the originally piecemeal discussion of answers that give her "Why?"-question application has begun to round into a coherent account of intentional activity. Specifically:

- Section 19 argued that in order to understand intentional action our focus should not be on the internal state of the agent, but rather on the appropriate description of those events that are "intentional actions themselves" (*I*, §19, 29:2).

---

[38] And cf. a few lines later, where Anscombe writes that "against the background of the qualifications we have introduced, we can epitomize the point by saying 'Roughly speaking, a man intends to do what he does'" (§25, 45:2). The qualifications are emphasized right away—"that is *very* roughly speaking" (§25, 45:2), since the preceding discussion has shown us how a person can do many things, even knowingly, without intending to do them. But these qualifications have to do with the way an agent *knows* or *understands* what she is up to, rather than with her interior thoughts, feelings, and ultimate objectives.

- Sections 20 and 21 took a major step toward unifying the three headings introduced at the start of Section 1, arguing that our concept of *doing something intentionally*, as an event to which a special sense of the question "Why?" can be given application, presupposes the possibility of giving answer to "Why?"-questions by *expressing intention for the future* and characterizing the *further intentions* with which a person acts.

- Section 22 invited us to account for what is involved in such answers, showing how they constitute a form of rationalizing explanation that moves *outward* to wider descriptions of what a person is doing and *forward* to descriptions of things she will do in the future.

- Finally, we saw that these descriptions form a *series* whose structure characterizes the means–end order of a person's intentional activity, revealing the underlying unity in what they describe—a unity that distinguishes a person's intentional activity from those further happenings that are merely its side-effects.

In sum, the position developed so far holds that intentional action is a teleological unity that can be represented by a series of descriptions that relate to one another in an order of means to ends. Knowledge of one's intentional action is knowledge of the unity that this series of descriptions picks out. The next thing for us to consider is whether it is true, as Anscombe claimed early on, that this knowledge is knowledge *without observation* of what a person does when she acts.

Suggestions for further reading

- Anscombe discusses the ethical significance of the intention/foresight distinction at greater length in her 1982 address to the American Catholic Philosophical Association, published as "Action, Intention and 'Double Effect.'"

- On the difference between Anscombe and Donald Davidson over the unity and individuation of action, see Julia Annas, "Davidson and Anscombe on 'the Same Action,'" and Jennifer Hornsby, "Actions in Their Circumstances."

- For careful discussion of the intention/foresight distinction within an Anscombean framework, see Jennifer Frey, "Intention and Double Effect."

- For opposition to the view that intentional action comprises mere bodily movement together with a mental event that is its cause, see Adrian Haddock, "At One with Our Actions, but at Two with Our Bodies," and Anton Ford, "Action and Generality" and "The Province of Human Agency."

- Douglas Lavin develops an Anscombean view of the unity of action in "Action as a Form of Temporal Unity."

- On the teleological structure of action explanation, see Michael Thompson, *Life and Action*, Part II, and Eric Marcus, *Rational Causation*, chapter 2.

- For careful interpretation and defense of the arguments in Sections 19 and 20 of *Intention*, see Candace Vogler, *Reasonably Vicious*, Appendix A (pp. 205–212), and "Nothing Added."

4

Knowledge without Observation

Anscombe introduced the concept of *knowledge without observation* in Section 8 as a distinguishing characteristic of intentional action. In discussing that passage earlier (see section 2.2, p. 24 and following), I argued that we should understand this position as a way of characterizing the knowledge of one's own intentional actions as a kind of *self*-knowledge, i.e., a way of knowing oneself "as subject" that is different from our ways of knowing about our non-intentional actions and the actions of other people. On this account, the reason why the self-knowledge of an agent cannot be based in such things as observation, inference, and testimony is that all these are routes to knowledge of persons and things other than oneself, and therefore depend on an *identification* of the object that is known. By contrast, concerning one's own actions a statement like "Good heavens! I didn't know *I* was doing that!" (cf. *I*, §28, 51:1) has the implication that the action in question, under that description, was not intentional. The knowledge of what one is intentionally doing cannot rest on an identification of oneself as the person who acts in the manner in question, and thus it cannot be knowledge that is based in observation.

As I noted in section 2.2, this interpretation of Anscombe's position is in keeping with the approach in her 1974 paper "The First Person," where concerning "such thoughts as 'I am sitting,' 'I am writing,' 'I am going to stay still,' [and] 'I twitched' " Anscombe raises the question:

> in happenings, events, etc. concerning what object are these verified or falsified? The answer is ordinarily easy to give because I can observe, or point to, my body; I can also feel one part of it with another. "This body is my body" then means "My idea that I am standing up is verified by this body, if it is standing up." And so on. *But observation does not show me which body is the one. Nothing shows me that.* ("FP," pp. 33–34; emphasis added)

Here, the denial that it is through observation that one ordinarily knows, e.g., that she is sitting or standing is situated within a broader discussion of how it is possible to have what Anscombe calls *unmediated* conceptions of the "states, motions, etc.," of one's own body ("FP," p. 34). What makes these conceptions unmediated is that they do not depend on *identifying* or *singling out* one's body from manifold others. And it is central to Anscombe's position in that essay that the scope of this unmediated self-consciousness is not limited to one's inner psychological states, and therefore the *object* of this self-consciousness is not anything like a Cartesian soul or ego. Thus she writes that "Self-knowledge is knowledge of the object that one is, of the human animal that one is" (p. 34). It is knowledge of the *same* object, under many of the very same descriptions, that others can also know by observing one's body from the outside.

But there is a difficulty for this position that needs to be addressed directly. According to Anscombe, when a person knows what she is intentionally doing, *what* she knows is the same thing that can be known by an outside observer, e.g., that she (*viz.*, the human animal that she is) is "sitting in a chair writing" (*I*, §4, 8:2). Despite this, the agent's *route* to this knowledge is entirely different from the observer's route to it: in doing something intentionally a person knows "from within" the very same thing that a witness to her action may know just by observing it. Section 28 of *Intention* identifies some of the difficulties that arise in trying to uphold both of these theses at once. Anscombe's further explication and defense of her position from Sections 29–32 is provisional but important, and leads to the introduction of the concept of *practical knowledge* as the key to solving the difficulties she has raised.

4.1 Raising difficulties (§28)

Recall the first two *epistemic conditions* on intentional action that were introduced in section 2.2:

(C1) A person is doing something intentionally only if she knows that she is doing this.

(C2) A person is doing something intentionally only if she knows without observation that she is doing this.

While Anscombe appeals frequently to these conditions in the subsequent pages, it is only in Section 28 that she turns to "look more closely" (*I*, §28, 49:2) at the philosophical difficulties that they present. Her focus is on condition (C2) in particular. Anscombe notes that while the concept of non-observational knowledge was first introduced by considering the way a person usually knows the state of her own body, since then this concept has been "used ... quite generally" in connection with *all* the descriptions under which a person's actions are intentional (§28, 50:2). Thus she anticipates that "the following objection will very likely have occurred to a reader":

> "Known without observation" may very well be a justifiable formula for knowledge of the position and movements of one's limbs, but you have spoken of all intentional action as falling under this concept. Now it may be e.g. that one paints a wall yellow, meaning to do so. But is it reasonable to say that one "knows without observation" that one is painting a wall yellow? And similarly for all sorts of actions: any actions that is, that are described under any aspect beyond that of bodily movements. (§28, 50:2)

As Anscombe indicates at the end of the quoted passage, this objection seems especially pressing, and condition (C2) especially difficult to uphold, in connection with what I will call *distal* descriptions of an action—that is, descriptions of an action in terms of what is happening at a distance from the agent and her immediate bodily movements. As she points out later on (see §41, 79:1), this "distance" can take several forms, the most relevant of which for our purposes are the *spatial* and *temporal* distance represented in outward- and forward-looking rationalizations, respectively: thus alongside the description "painting a wall yellow," which is spatially distant from a person's movements but temporally proximate to them, we could also consider a description like "surprising my daughter," where this refers to something that will take place only later on, when one's daughter arrives home. In each case the worry arises: since one could be moving around just as one is without actually doing these further things, how can the *knowledge* that one is doing them be grounded in just the same way as the knowledge of one's bodily movements? And a natural response is to concede the objection, saying that the scope of an agent's non-observational self-knowledge is restricted to something more "immediate," i.e., to her present state of mind or the spatially and temporally proximate descriptions of her act. It is precisely this conclusion that Anscombe wants to help us resist.

We can make the difficulty clearer by distinguishing four different ways that a person who is doing something intentionally might lack non-observational knowledge of her action under a certain description, "doing X," under which her action is intentional:

1. First, the person might believe that she is doing X, but fail to be sufficiently *confident* in this belief for it to qualify as knowledge—as in Donald Davidson's well-known example of a man making a stack of carbon copies even as he does not "believe with any confidence" that he is succeeding.[1]

2. Second, the person's belief that she is doing X might be *unsafe* in the sense that she could easily have held this belief even if she were not doing X at all. For example, imagine that one means to paint a wall yellow, and believes that she is doing this, but because of the color of the lighting one would have this same belief even if she were using white paint instead.

3. Third, the person might be *confident* in her belief that she is doing X only because of what she observes of her action—as if Davidson's clerk were confident that he was making all ten copies only because he had peeked at the bottom sheet in his stack.

4. Finally, the person's belief that she is doing X might be *safe* only because she observes that she is doing this—as when, e.g., the illumination of the room puts one in a position to see that she is indeed using yellow paint.

Each of these cases turns on the real or imagined possibility of what Anscombe earlier called a "mistake of performance," as "when e.g. I write something other than I think I am writing" (§2, 5:1). On its own the possibility of such a mistake is not enough to challenge either (C1) or (C2), since when a performance is mistaken a person *does not act* in the way she intends, whereas (C1) and (C2) concern only what must be the case when a person *does* act intentionally. However, the cases just described suggest that even in circumstances where such a mistake is merely *possible*, so long as this possibility is sufficiently likely or subjectively salient, then even if a person *is* acting as she intends to, and doing this intentionally, still she may not know that she is doing this, or may know it only through observation.

We can, then, formalize this *argument from possible failure* as follows:

---

[1] Donald Davidson, "Intending," p. 92.

(P1) It is possible to do something intentionally and either (i) lack a confident and safe belief that one is doing this or (ii) believe confidently and safely that one is doing this only because this belief is based in observation.

(P2) Knowledge requires belief that is confident and safe from error.

(C) So it is possible to do something intentionally either (i) without knowing that one does this or (ii) without non-observational knowledge that one does this.

Part (i) of the conclusion in (C) contradicts Anscombe's condition (C1), and part (ii) contradicts what condition (C2) adds to it. The argument is valid. In order to resist it we must reject one or the other of its premises.

Having raised this difficulty, Anscombe begins her reply in Section 28 by drawing an important distinction that helps to clarify her position. She writes:

> the topic of an intention may be a matter on which there is knowledge or opinion based on observation, inference, hearsay, superstition or anything that knowledge or opinion ever are based on; or again matter on which an opinion is held without any foundation at all. When knowledge or opinion are present concerning what is the case, and what can happen—say Z—if one does certain things, say ABC, then it is possible to have the intention of doing Z in doing ABC; and if the case is one of knowledge or if the opinion is correct, then doing or causing Z is an intentional action, and it is not by observation that one knows one is doing Z; or in so far as one is observing, inferring etc. that Z is actually taking place, one's knowledge is not the knowledge a man has of his intentional actions. (§28, 50:3)

By saying that observation (or inference, hearsay, superstition, etc.) may be the basis of knowledge or opinion *pertaining to the topic* of an intention, Anscombe means that it may be in one of these ways that a person knows or believes various matters of fact that are presupposed in her intelligent activity, such as the following:

- That this is a brush (A), that the paint in this container is yellow (B), that this is the way to use my brush to apply paint to the wall (C), and so if I do that with this paint I will be painting the wall yellow (Z).

- That this is a pump (A), that the water at the pump is poisoned (B), that the pipe runs to the party leaders' house (C), and so if I operate this pump I will poison that house's water-supply (Z).

- That this is a pen (A) and this is a stack of ten sheets of carbon paper (B), that pressing down hard while writing on the top sheet of a stack of n sheets of carbon paper is a way to make n legible carbon copies (C), and so that if I press down hard (etc.) (Z).

The structure A–B–C—Z should be familiar: it is the order of the "A–D series" that represents *why* a person is acting in a given way and *how* her action is supposed to be effective. We saw earlier that this is a series relating descriptions of an action as *means to ends* rather than as events to their mere effects.[2] What these examples remind us, however, is that it is only against a background of knowledge or belief about the world and its causal structure that it is possible even to *have* the intention of achieving a certain end through such-and-such means, let alone to realize that intention in purposeful action. And Anscombe's claim here is that this sort of background knowledge *about* what we do can certainly be based in observation, inference, hearsay, etc. But, she says, this does not show that the knowledge that we have *of* our intentional actions ever has such a basis.

While the ideas that are in the background to this paragraph will become very important in Anscombe's argument later on, clearly they are not enough on their own to resolve the difficulties we are concerned with. This is because the cases at issue are ones where a person *does* have the background belief or knowledge necessary to undertake a course of action that will serve her ends—and the difficulties concerned the possibility that this background grasp of the *circumstances* of one's action would be insufficient to guarantee non-observational knowledge of one's action itself. That difficulty is especially pressing if, as on Anscombe's view, the action that is known in this way is supposed to be something "actually taking place" (§28, 50:3) in the outwardly observable world. As she writes:

Say I go over to the window and open it. Someone who hears me moving calls out: What are you doing making that noise? I reply "Opening the window." I have called such a statement knowledge all along; and precisely because in such a case what I say is true—I do open the window; and that means that the window is getting opened by the movements of the body out of whose mouth those words come. But I don't say the words like this: "Let me see, what is this body bringing about? Ah yes! the opening of the window." Or even like this "Let me see, what are my movements bringing

---

[2] For discussion of this point, see sections 3.3 and 3.4.

about? The opening of the window." To see this, if it is not already plain, contrast this case with the following one: I open the window and it focuses a spot of light on the wall. Someone who cannot see me but can see the wall, says "What are you doing making that light come on the wall?" and I say "Ah yes, it's opening the window that does it," or "That always happens when one opens that window at midday if the sun is shining." (§28, 51:2)

The first part of this quotation emphasizes what later, in parallel with my earlier discussion of the expression of intention for the future, I will call Anscombe's *factualist* understanding of the content of an agent's non-observational knowledge. For Anscombe, what one knows in knowing what one does is nothing other than what is happening in the world, namely that the movements of one's body are bringing about certain effects (here, the opening of a window). And the second part of the quotation reminds us that the *character* of an agent's self-knowledge is different from that of the corresponding knowledge of things that one is doing non-intentionally or bringing about as mere side-effects of an intentional action. The example of the window is supposed to show how knowledge of one's intentional actions is a kind of *self*-knowledge, even as the *scope* of this knowledge extends beyond one's bodily movements, encompassing things that happen in the world beyond one's body. The challenge, however, is to see how we can uphold this position in the face of the evident difficulties with it.

4.2 False avenues of escape (§§29–30)

I have framed the difficulty in understanding how we can have non-observational knowledge of action in terms of a tension between two of Anscombe's central commitments. First, knowledge of one's own actions is non-observational because it is *self-specific*: the basis of this knowledge is different from the basis of our knowledge of the actions of others. Second, Anscombe's *factualism* is the thesis that in knowing our actions, *what* we know is the same sort of thing that others can also know by observation, namely that a certain event is taking place in the material world. Here is how she puts the difficulty at the start of Section 29:

> What can opening the window be except making such-and-such movements with such-and-such results? And in that case what can *knowing* one is opening the window be except knowing that that is taking place?

Now if there are two *ways* of knowing here, one of which I call knowledge of one's intentional action and the other of which I call knowledge by observation of what takes place, then must there not be two *objects* of knowledge? How can one speak of two different knowledges of *exactly* the same thing? (*I*, §29, 51:3)

The concern that different "ways" of knowing will entail different objects of knowledge may seem strange or outmoded, but the underlying idea is straightforward. In general, our knowledge of what a person is doing will be knowledge through observation, inference, testimony, or one of our other usual ways of knowing what happens in the world around us. But the factualist conception of agential knowledge says that what one knows, in a distinctively first-personal way, in knowing what she intentionally does, is the *very same* sort of thing that one may also know, now in a third-personal way, in knowing such a thing about someone else. Yet how can it be that just because a certain body is *my* body, I can know in a special way which such occurrences I am involved in—especially if these are "described under any aspect beyond that of bodily movements" (§28, 50:2)? Even if we often *seem* to have a special sort of knowledge of our actions, this won't amount to much if we can't explain how this is possible and account for the cases that seem to raise difficulties for it.

It isn't until the final sections of *Intention*, when Anscombe has worked out the idea that the knowledge of what one is intentionally doing is distinctive in being a form of *practical* knowledge, that her response to this challenge is fully in view. Before this, in Sections 29–30 she argues against what she sees as three unsatisfactory responses to the difficulties that she has raised. These responses hold:

1. That the content of an agent's non-observational knowledge encompasses only what she *wills* or *tries* or *intends* to do (see §29, 51:4–52:1);
2. That the content of an agent's non-observational knowledge encompasses only her *immediate bodily movements* (see §30, 53:2–54:2); and
3. That an agent's judgments of what she is intentionally doing are *infallible* or self-constituting (see §29, 52:2–53:1).

Common to all three responses is the idea that intentional action should be partitioned into an "interior" component and an "exterior" one, with the scope of an agent's non-observational knowledge limited to the first component and the latter "known by observation to be the *result*, which was also willed in the intention" (§29, 51:4–52:1).[3] Anscombe's arguments against these positions are brief and somewhat sketchy, but together they help to bring out a deeper motivation for her uncompromising view. Let us consider each in turn.

First response: Knowing what I will

According to the first response to the difficulties raised in Section 28, the domain of an agent's non-observational knowledge is limited to something psychological, e.g., what she *wills* or *tries* or *intends* to do, while observation is an essential part of how she knows her action itself. Anscombe's objection to this position has a familiar Wittgensteinian flavor: she says that it is "a mad account; for the only sense I can give to 'willing' is that in which I might stare at something and will it to move" (*I*, §29, 52:1)—and from here she moves on immediately to consider the next possibility.

This objection is unpersuasive as it stands, since surely there are ordinary phenomena of willing, trying, or intending to do something that nevertheless one does not do, and also of *knowing* in such a case what one wills, tries, or intends. But Anscombe does not mean to rule these things out—indeed, we saw earlier that on her view there *is* such a thing as intention that is "complete" though "fully interior" (§4, 9:2). The target of her objection is the idea that the scope of the distinctively first-personal *knowledge* that a person has in acting is limited to something internal to her mind, while "the rest is known by observation to be the *result*" (§29, 51:4). That is, Anscombe is arguing against the idea that we know our intentional actions only as "external" events, i.e., by observing (or inferring, being told, etc.) what takes place, while an agent's non-observational self-knowledge is limited to her inner psychological condition. There is, however, an undeniable appeal in that idea: for knowledge of one's mental states is usually more secure than knowledge of one's bodily actions, and one's actions *can* be known directly by an outside observer in a way that one's mental states perhaps cannot. So what is wrong with supposing that the self-knowledge of an agent is circumscribed by this boundary?

A better way to undermine this position than by challenging the meaning of concepts like "willing" is to ask what sense we can give to talk of *observing*

---

[3] Kevin Falvey ("Knowledge in Intention," p. 21) calls this the "two-factor thesis."

or *inferring* what happens when one acts. To illustrate the difficulty here, consider a position in the philosophy of perception that parallels the one Anscombe is challenging, namely that

(P)   What we *really* know in virtue of our perceptual experience is what our perceptual sensations are like, while the rest is known by inference to be the cause of those sensations.

The trouble with (P) is that while it seems undeniable that *sometimes* the causes of our sensations are known only by inference (for example, I may feel pressure on my back and take this as a "clue" that I am sitting against one of my children's toys), the idea that sensory knowledge is like this *in general* seems to stretch the concept of "inference" beyond its proper limits. We need *some* way of marking the difference between things known immediately through perception and those known through a combination of inner sensation and an inference like the one above, and (P) threatens to erase that distinction altogether.

Consider now a parallel case in which the object of observation or inference is one's own action:

I open the window and it focuses a spot of light on the wall. Someone who cannot see me but can see the wall, says "What are you doing making that light come on the wall?" and I say "Ah yes, it's opening the window that does it," or "That always happens when one opens that window at midday if the sun is shining." (§28, 51:2)

In the case just described, the fact that I am shining the spot of light on the wall is something that I "know[...] by observation to be the *result*" (§29, 51:4) of my movements, and it is not in the *same* way as this that I know I am opening the window. We need a way of marking the distinction between these two ways of knowing what one does, and the view in question threatens to erase it altogether. While this counterargument does not challenge the more modest position that *sometimes* the possibility of failure means that an agent's non-observational knowledge is limited to what she wills or intends, it does seem sufficient to block a fallacious, but tempting, route to a more dramatic conclusion.

Second response: Knowing how I move

According to the second response (see *I*, §30, 53:2), an agent's non-observational knowledge of her intentional actions extends beyond her psychological states but is limited to her bodily movements or muscular contractions. This position is vulnerable to the objection just raised: to sustain it, we would need to explain the sense of "observe" in which a person opening a window depends on *observation* (or inference, etc.) to know that she is doing this. If, however, we accept Anscombe's earlier arguments that bodily awareness is non-observational, then this position may look like an attractive way around the difficulties at issue here. It concedes the conclusion that we cannot always have non-observational knowledge of our actions "described under any aspect beyond that of bodily movements" (§28, 50:2), while preserving the intuition that we have a self-specific way of knowing *some* of the outwardly observable things that happen when we act, namely the ways we move our bodies. But Anscombe rejects this attempt to circumscribe the domain of an agent's self-knowledge:

> The only description that I clearly know of what I am doing may be of something that is at a distance from me. It is not the case that I clearly know the movements I make, and the intention is just a result which I calculate and hope will follow on these movements. (§30, 53:2)

We should note carefully what Anscombe says here. In contrast to the first response, where it seems incontestable that in general we *do* have privileged and non-observational knowledge of what we will or intend, here she claims that in general we *do not* "clearly know" our bodily movements even as well as we know our actions under their distal descriptions. In order to show this, she imagines learning to operate a mechanism in which, by moving a handle upward and downward in a certain pattern, she can keep a certain device level:

> Now my instruction is: Keep it level, and with a bit of practice I learn to do so. My account of what I am doing is that I am keeping the thing level; I don't consider the movement of my arm at all. I am able to give a much more exact account of what I am doing at a distance than of what my arm is doing. So my keeping the thing level is not at all something which I calculate as the effect of what I really and immediately am doing, and therefore directly know in my "knowledge of my own action." In general, as Aristotle says, one does not deliberate about an acquired skill; the description of what one is doing, which one completely understands, is at a distance from the details of one's movements, which one does not consider at all. (§30, 54:2)

Anscombe's claim is that in a case like this she will have *better* knowledge of her action under a distal description—here, that she is keeping the device level—than of her bodily movements described independently of the achievement of these further ends. That is, to the extent that one can say how she is moving her body it will only be in terms of these more distal effects: e.g., she will say that she is moving her arm (or the mechanism) *in the way that keeps the thing level.* Anscombe's position here parallels the one she advanced earlier concerning the relationship between bodily self-knowledge and kinesthetic or proprioceptive sensations (see §8, 13:4–14:1), where she argued that these sensations can't be described separately from our description of the actual position of our bodies, and thus that we can't come to know our bodily position by way of an independent knowledge of our bodily sensations. Similarly, in the present case her idea is that much of the knowledge we have of our bodily movements proceeds *through* our understanding of what we are doing "at a distance" from our bodies, and not the other way round. If what Anscombe says here is correct, it seems to show that bodily self-knowledge isn't privileged, relative to the knowledge of our distal actions, in the way that this position assumes.

Third response: Doing what I think

The final response says that beliefs about one's intentional actions are infallible or self-constituting, because "I really 'do' in the intentional sense whatever I think I am doing" (*I*, §29, 52:2). This position may be hard at first to find appealing, especially when Anscombe glosses it by appeal to the Schopenhauerian view of action that Wittgenstein advanced in the *Tractatus* (see §29, 52:3). But in fact the Oxford philosopher H.A. Prichard had also advanced such a view in his 1945 paper "Acting, Willing, Desiring":

> An action, i.e. a human action, instead of being the originating or causing of some change, *is* an activity of willing some change, this usually causing some change, and in some cases a physical change, its doing or not doing this depending on the physical conditions of which the agent is largely ignorant.[4]

However bizarre this position may strike us at first, Anscombe's response to it turns out to be quite illuminating. She tells us that "formerly" in considering

---

[4] Prichard, "Acting, Willing, Desiring," p. 277; emphasis added.

the problems with thinking of intention as an internal movement she "came out with the formula: I *do* what *happens*":

> That is to say, when the description of what happens is the very thing which I should say I was doing, then there is no distinction between my doing and the thing's happening. (*I*, §29, 52:6–53:1)

While Anscombe admits that "everyone who heard this formula found it extremely paradoxical and obscure" (§29, 53:1), the arguments we have just considered will help us to see what the formula amounts to, as well as how to situate it in relation to some contemporary action-theoretic debates. Opposed to the claim that acting is *doing* what happens is the alternative analysis of acting as *causing* what happens (or, on Prichard's view, merely *willing* to cause such a change), where the agent's contribution is merely to *initiate* a process whose unfolding is not itself an exercise of her agency, but only a downstream effect of it. In certain cases this latter analysis does seem apt: e.g., when a golfer strikes a ball which then travels down the fairway, the agent's contribution is complete once the club has struck the ball, and what happens thereafter is the *result* of what the golfer herself does. And here it might be natural to say that it is *through observation* that the golfer knows how the ball is traveling, and where it will end up. But not every case fits this mold. Consider once more the example of opening a window (or moving a matchbox: here see §29, 52:1):

> I do open the window; and that means that the window is getting opened by the movements of the body out of whose mouth those words come. But I don't say the words like this: "Let me see, what is this body bringing about? Ah yes! the opening of the window." Or even like this "Let me see, what are my movements bringing about? The opening of the window." (§28, 51:2)

The window is getting opened *by* the movements of Anscombe's body, and this means that there is a connection between the two: the window would not be opening if her body were not moving in this way. But that is not because the opening of the window is something *produced* by Anscombe's bodily movements, such that there are two separate happenings here one of which *results* from the other. In the case at issue, Anscombe's bodily movement simply *is* her opening the window, just as a golfer's movement of her arms simply *is* her swinging of the club (cf. §26, 46:1)—and thus there is in this case no distinction to be drawn "between [her] doing and the thing's happening" (§29, 53:1).[5] And as we have seen, a central thesis of *Intention* is that this indistinction between *doing* and *happening* is mirrored in the agent's epistemic relation to these events. Thus it is that the window's rising, no less than her bodily movement in raising it, is something that a person opening a window by raising it up will know, not by *observing* how things unfold as an effect of what she does, but rather as an aspect of her action itself. The significance of saying that in acting we *do* what happens is to remind us of how, at least in ordinary situations, we *know* what happens simply in knowing what we do.[6] This is Anscombe's position, and we have seen how determined she is to uphold it. We should also now be able to appreciate its intuitive appeal. But still we do not have a proper explanation of how it could be correct. How, that is, can there be such a thing as non-observational knowledge of what happens in the world outside of one's own mind or body?

4.3 Beginning to sketch a solution (§§31–32)

"Having raised enough difficulties" in the preceding sections, Anscombe says at the start of Section 31 that now she will "try to sketch a solution" to them (*I*, §31, 54:3). She opens this attempt with a strange-sounding question:

> What is the contradictory of a description of one's own intentional action? Is it "You aren't, in fact"?—E.g. "You aren't replenishing the house water supply, because the water is running out of a hole in the pipe"? I suggest that it is not. To see this, consider the following story, which appeared

---

[5] That is, it's a case of what Jennifer Hornsby, in "Actions in Their Circumstances," calls doing something *non-mediately*.

[6] Having admitted that her formula was found "extremely paradoxical and obscure" (§29, 53:1), Anscombe then *seems* to take it all back in the final paragraph of Section 29, in connection with a case in which "I shut my eyes and write something" (for all of the following see 53:1). This passage is easy to misread! It can look as if it is all written in Anscombe's voice, so that she is the one saying, e.g., that in writing "the essential thing [one] does, namely to write such-and-such, is done without the eyes," and therefore "without the eyes one knows what he writes." But that is precisely the opposite of her position—it is rather the position of the *Tractatus* that she has just been arguing against. And if we look more closely we can see that this entire discussion is in the voice of her imagined interlocutor: thus the passage begins by saying that "what happens must be given by observation," and concludes that "If there are two ways of knowing there must be two different things known"—yet all of this is opposed to the view Anscombe has just staked out. We should, then, take all of this as expressive of a natural thought that Anscombe wants us to resist, rather than a statement of her own position. (On the role of Anscombe's interlocutor in her writing, see Rachael Wiseman, *Guidebook to Anscombe's* Intention, pp. 69–72, and Eylem Özaltun, "Practical Knowledge of What Happens," pp. 55–56 and *passim*.) I am grateful to Samantha Berthelette for help in analyzing this passage. I discuss it further in the final paragraphs of section 6.5, pp. 197–198.

for the pleasure of the readers of the *New Statesman*'s "This England" column. A certain soldier was court-martialled (or something of the sort) for insubordinate behaviour. He had, it seems been "abusive" at his medical examination. The examining doctor told him to clench his teeth; whereupon he took them out, handed them to the doctor and said "You clench them." (§31, 54:3–55:1)

This passage invites us to draw a parallel between two situations. In one, a person's description of what he intends to be doing (here, the statement "I'm replenishing the house water-supply") is confronted with another statement that opposes it in some way (in this case, one like "You aren't, because the water is running out of a hole"). In the other, a similar relation holds between an *order* given by one person (here, the examining doctor's instruction "Clench your teeth") and what is said or implied by the recipient of the order (here, the soldier's indication that he can't clench his teeth at all, since they are false). And Anscombe's claim is that in neither case is the second statement the *contradictory* of the first. Rather, she says, in order for there to be a contradiction in the second case the soldier would have to *refuse* to obey the order, while in the first case the statement "Oh, no, you aren't pumping water through that pipe" would have to come from someone who "sets out e.g. to make a hole in the pipe with a pick-axe" (§31, 55:2).

The first step toward understanding this passage is to systematize what Anscombe says about her three cases, as shown in Table 4.1. The statements in rows *(a)* and *(c)* are all either *commands* or *expression of intentions*, with the command or expression of intention in *(c)* opposed in each case to the corresponding one in *(a)*. Meanwhile, the statements in *(b)* share some descriptive content with those in *(c)* but differ from them in being mere *estimates* of what is happening or is going to happen.[7] That is, the one who says these things makes a claim about the world (that she won't clench her teeth, that the water-supply isn't being filled, that someone won't go to bed at a certain time) that is independent of any *intention* of her own concerning the matter in question. Anscombe's claim, then, is that in each of these cases the statement in *(a)* is contradicted by the one in *(c)* rather than *(b)*—that is, that a command or expression of intention is not *contradicted* by an opposing estimate, but only by an opposing command or expression of intention. But now what is the deeper significance of these distinctions, and how are they supposed to bear on our problem?

---

[7] For this terminology see §2, 2:1 and 2:4–3:1, as discussed in section 1.2.

Table 4.1 The three cases discussed in Section 31.

	Case 1	Case 2	Case 3
(a)	"Clench your teeth."	"I'm replenishing the house water-supply."	"I am going to bed at midnight."
(b)	"My teeth are false (and so I cannot clench them)."	"The water is running out of a pipe round the corner (and so you aren't replenishing the water-supply)."	"You aren't going to bed at midnight, for you never keep such resolutions."
(c)	"Do not clench your teeth."	"Oh, no, you aren't" (said by someone who sets out to make a hole in the pipe).	"You aren't going to bed at midnight, for I am going to stop you."

There is one *very* tempting interpretation of this claim that turns out to be both philosophically problematic and ultimately ruled out by what Anscombe herself says in these sections.[8] On that reading, when Anscombe says that a statement like "I'm replenishing the house water-supply" is not *contradicted* by saying, e.g., that the water is running out of a hole in the pipe, she means that the original statement will be *true* even if the pipe has a hole in it. This reading makes sense of the text in a simple way and suggests a tidy resolution to the difficulties raised in Section 28, since on this analysis an agent will have a *true belief* about what she is doing even in a case where she fails in performance. If this were Anscombe's view, then she could reject premise (P1) of the argument from possible failure: any case presented to show the lack of safety in beliefs about what one is doing would fail to serve that purpose, and any lack of confidence in what one is intentionally doing would be misplaced.

---

[8] For such a reading see Graham Hubbs, "Anscombe on Intentions and Commands."

This cannot, however, be the conclusion that Anscombe wants us to draw. It is rather just a variant of what she earlier called the "false avenue of escape" of supposing that "I really 'do' in the intentional sense whatever I think I am doing" (§29, 52:2)—the very position that she argued against in Section 29. And Anscombe rejects this position quite directly in what she goes on to say about the case where there is a hole in the pipe, namely that in this situation what the agent says "*is not true*," since "something is not the case which would have to be the case in order for his statement to be true" (§32, 56:3; emphasis mine).[9] This remark echoes what she said in Section 28 concerning the case of opening a window, namely that in this case Anscombe's description of her action expresses knowledge "*precisely because in such a case what I say is true*—I do open the window; and that means that the window is getting opened by the movements of the body out of whose mouth those words come" (§28, 51:2; emphasis mine).[10] All this is enough to rule out a reading of Section 31 as trying to show how a person can *know* what she is doing even if, in the ordinary sense, she is not doing this at all, on the grounds that a mere "description" of her as failing to do this will not genuinely contradict the agent's claim to knowledge. But then what is Anscombe saying instead?

I believe that the key to a better interpretation is to read Anscombe's talk of "contradiction" in these passages as picking out a *distinctive kind* of opposition between statements, similar to Aristotle's canonical distinction between contraries and contradictories. In Aristotelian logic, a pair of statements are *contradictories* just in case the truth of each entails the falsehood of the other and vice versa; and *contraries* just in case the truth of each entails the falsehood of the other, but the falsehood of neither entails the other's truth.[11] Because of this, there is a sense in which Aristotelian contradictories are opposed in a more *exact*—or, as Anscombe puts it later, "head-on" (§52, 92:3)—way than contraries are: each member

---

[9] Consider also the entry for Section 31 in the Table of Contents: "Attempt at a solution by comparing the facts which may *falsify* a statement of intentional action to the facts which may make an order fall to the ground" (*I*, p. vii; emphasis mine).

[10] Cf. as well her earlier remark that "there is a point in speaking of knowledge only where a contrast exists between 'he knows' and 'he (merely) *thinks* he knows' " (§8, 14:1). The position under consideration would do away with this contrast for judgments of one's own actions. (Thanks here to Kim Frost.)

[11] For example, the universal proposition "Every man is mortal" and the particular "Some men are not mortal" are contradictories because they are both exclusive and exhaustive; there is no middle ground between them. By contrast, the universal propositions "Every man is mortal" and "No men are mortal" are contraries: they exclude one another but leave open a third possibility, namely that some men are mortal and others are not.

of a contradictory pair says *precisely* that the other member is false. But Aristotelian contraries are opposed as well, as each member of a pair of contraries is such that its truth would entail the falsity of the other—which is just how Anscombe characterizes the relation between an expression of intention and an opposing estimative statement in Section 32:

> The case that we now want to consider is that of an agent who says what he is at present doing. Now suppose what he says is not true. It may be untrue because, unknown to the agent, something is not the case which would have to be the case in order for his statement to be true; as when, unknown to the man pumping, there was a hole in the pipe round the corner. But as I said, this relates to his statement that he is replenishing the water-supply as does the fact that the man has no teeth of his own to the order "Clench your teeth"; that is, we may say that in the face of it his statement falls to the ground, as in that case the order falls to the ground, but it is not a direct contradiction. (§32, 56:3–57:1)

My suggestion, then, is that in each of the three cases Anscombe presents in Section 31, the statements labeled *(a)* and *(c)* in Table 4.1 are supposed to be related as practical *contradictories*, while those in *(a)* and *(b)* are related as practical *contraries* instead. On this reading, the members of a pair of practical contraries are mutually opposed to this extent: if one member of the pair is true, then the other one necessarily is not. But this constitutes a different kind of opposition from the direct or "head-on" way that practical contradictories are opposed, as each member of a pair of practical contradictories says *exactly* the opposite of the other. Unlike the tempting but mistaken interpretation considered earlier, this reading squares with Anscombe's repeated insistence that if a person says that she is doing something, then what she says *is not true* if, in fact, she is not doing what she says—a claim that she repeats later on about the case of intention for the future (see §52, 91:7–92:5).[12] She insists this even though she holds that a statement of the form "I am doing X," where this expresses the speaker's intention to do what she says, is not *just* an estimate of what is taking place—which is why the "*direct* contradiction" of such a statement is found in the expression of an opposing intention rather than an estimate, made on the grounds, e.g., of observation, that things are not happening as the agent says.

---

[12] I discuss this important passage in chapter 7.

This reading of Sections 31 and 32 makes sense of the text without saddling Anscombe with a view that she clearly wishes to reject. And while it also leaves us without a clear view of how the contrast between orders and expressions of intention is supposed to help resolve the difficulties at issue, in fact that is just where Anscombe herself comes down at this point, writing at the close of Section 31 that though this comparison "is interesting and illuminates the periphery of the problem, it fails at the centre and leaves that in the darkness that we have found ourselves in" (§31, 55:3).

Section 32 introduces a further element to this analysis: Anscombe's famous example of the shopper and detective. We are to imagine a man going around town with a list that says what he is to buy, while a detective follows him and makes a list of the man's purchases. Concerning this case, Anscombe says that the relation of the shopper's list to what he purchases—that is, the relation of this list to *what happens*, or to *what the shopper does*—is different from the relation of the detective's list to this. What is that difference?

> It is precisely this: if the list and the things that the man actually buys do not agree, and if this and this alone constitutes a *mistake*, then the mistake is not in the list but in the man's performance (if his wife were to say "Look, it says butter and you have bought margarine," he would hardly reply: "What a mistake! we must put that right" and alter the word on the list to "margarine"); whereas if the detective's record and what the man actually buys do not agree, then the mistake is in the record. (§32, 56:1)

This passage recalls the distinction from Section 2 that was attributed to Theophrastus: when, e.g., "I write something other than I think I am writing ... the mistake here is one of performance, not of judgment"—and thus "the facts are, so to speak, impugned for not being in accordance with the words, rather than *vice versa*" (§2, 4:5–5:1).[13] And Anscombe's claim now is that a person's statement of what she is intentionally doing stands in the same relation to her action as the shopper's list, rather than the detective's, stands in to his purchases. The relevant difference between these relations is a not a difference in the *content* of the respective descriptions, nor a difference in how likely they are to be correct, but rather a difference that determines what sort of *mistake* any instance of non-correspondence amounts to. Since the detective's list is supposed to be a *record* of what the man buys, its relation to the man's purchases is that of an accurate recording, and so if there is

[13] See my earlier discussion in section 1.2, pp. 11–12.

a discrepancy between those things and what is on the list, then the list is inaccurate. And while the shopper's list is also a description of what he will purchase, in contrast to the detective's list it is a description that is meant to *direct* the man's purchases. Because of this, the relation of the shopper's list to the things that he buys is the same as that of an order, and so if he does not buy these things this might show that the shopper made a mistake in what he *did*, not that there was any mistake *in the list* that required correction.

Such divergence *might* show that the shopper made a mistake—this qualification is important because not every case of divergence between the shopper's list and what he buys will show that there was any mistake on his part. There are several possibilities here:

- First, the shopper might not buy everything on the list because "some of the things [on it] were not to be had, and ... one might have known they were not to be had" (§32, 56:2). Here, Anscombe says, "we might speak of a mistake (an error of judgment) in constructing the list" (§32, 56:2)—that is, we might say that there was a mistake in *telling* the man *to buy* those things, and no mistake in his failing to buy them. This parallels the cases discussed in Section 31 where an order or expression of intention "falls to the ground" because "something is not the case which would have to be the case" in order for it to be fulfilled: "as when, unknown to the man pumping, there was a hole in the pipe round the corner" (§32, 56:3).

- Second, the shopper's purchases might diverge from the list simply "because he changed his mind and decided to buy something else instead" (§32, 56:2). Here there is no mistake either in the list or in what the shopper does—except in the sense that we might question whether the shopper "made a mistake" in going against what the list said to buy, or that he might judge the list to be mistaken in saying that he should buy such-and-such, even though this was there to be had. And this in turn parallels the examples in Section 31 of "direct contradiction" of an order or expression of intention: it is a case of *choosing to act* in opposition to what was said, not merely *happening* to do something out of accordance with it.

- Finally, what Anscombe calls a "mistake in performance" is different from either of these first two cases: it is one where the shopper *simply* does not buy what is on the list, perhaps because he overlooks an item or mistakenly picks up the wrong thing.

Table 4.2 Three possibilities for divergence between what happens in the world and what is described in an order or expression of intention (compare *I*, §32, 56:1–57:2).

	order	expression of intention
falls to the ground	It is shown that the order cannot be followed, since the necessary background facts do not obtain.	It is shown that the person cannot act (or be acting) as expressed, since the necessary background facts do not obtain.
contradicted	The order is refused; or an opposing order is given.	An opposing intention is expressed.
directly falsified	The recipient simply fails to act as ordered.	The person simply fails (or is failing) to do what she says.

Having drawn these distinctions, Anscombe says of the last possibility that it parallels a case where a person expresses the intention to do something, but "is *simply* not doing what he says":

> As when I say to myself "Now I press Button A"—pressing Button B—a thing which can certainly happen. This I will call the *direct* falsification of what I say. And here, to use Theophrastus' expression again, the mistake is not one of judgment but of performance. That is, we do *not* say: What you *said* was a mistake, because it was supposed to describe what you did and did not describe it, but: What you *did* was a mistake, because it was not in accordance with what you said. (§32, 57:1)

This leaves us with three possibilities for divergence between what happens in the world and what is described in an order or expression of intention, which are summarized in Table 4.2. The first and second possibilities correspond to rows *(c)* and *(b)*, respectively, in Table 4.1, while the third adds a new possibility, namely that of a mere mistake in performance. According to Anscombe, noting these differences should help us to see how "a discrepancy between . . . language and that of which the language is a description" (§32, 57:2) will come to something different when that language has the role of an order or expression of intention rather than that of a record or report. And she suggests in the closing paragraph of Section 32 that the failure to make this sort of distinction is at the root of our inability to see how the knowledge of what one is intentionally doing can be knowledge without observation:

> Can it be that there is something that modern philosophy has blankly misunderstood: namely what ancient and medieval philosophers meant by *practical knowledge*? Certainly in modern philosophy we have an incorrigibly contemplative conception of knowledge. Knowledge must be something that is judged as such by being in accordance with the facts. The facts, reality, are prior, and dictate what is to be said, if it is knowledge. And this is the explanation of the utter darkness in which we found ourselves. For if there are two knowledges—one by observation and the other in intention—then it looks as if there must be two objects of knowledge; but if one says the objects are the same, one looks hopelessly for the different *mode of contemplative knowledge* in acting, as if there were a very queer and special sort of seeing eye in the middle of acting. (§32, 57:3)

This passage ends Section 32. It is not yet any kind of solution to the difficulties that Anscombe has raised, but only an indication of what such a solution will require. Specifically, it identifies four ideas that all need to be explained further and brought into connection with the others in order for a true solution to emerge. These ideas are:

- That the knowledge of one's intentional actions is knowledge *without observation*.
- That the *relation* of this knowledge to what it is knowledge of is different from that of knowledge that is supposed to be an accurate record or representation of its object, as a discrepancy between a person's actions and what she takes herself to be doing may involve a "mistake in performance" rather than an "error of judgment."
- That a person's knowledge of her actions has a kind of *priority* with respect to the reality that it is knowledge of.
- And that this knowledge is *practical* rather than "contemplative"—a distinction which, Anscombe tells us at the start of Section 33, "can only be understood if we first understand 'practical reasoning'" (§33, 57:4).

Explaining the nature of practical reasoning is the task of Sections 33–44. Following this we will return to the other items in the list and see what work they can do in addressing the difficulty at hand.

4.4 Summary discussion

Section 28 of *Intention* gives expression to a worry that for many readers will have come to mind right away when Anscombe's conditions (C1) and (C2) were first advanced. How is it possible to have non-observational knowledge of what we intentionally do—especially under descriptions that concern what happens at a spatial or temporal distance from our immediate bodily movements? In rejecting the various interiorizing responses that she considers in Sections 29 and 30, Anscombe clarifies her uncompromising commitment to a *factualist* analysis of an agent's knowledge of her act. On this analysis, which parallels what she argued earlier about the expression of intention for the future, the content of an agent's self-knowledge is nothing short of *what is happening* when she acts.

Having clarified her position in this way, in Sections 31 and 32 Anscombe begins her defense of it by drawing a few important distinctions. These are:

- The distinction between (i) *contradicting* an expression of intention with a statement that gives an opposing order or expresses an intention to oppose it, and (ii) opposing such a statement in a less direct or "head-on" way with a conflicting statement of fact.

- The distinction between several ways that a statement of the form "I am doing X," where this expresses the intention of acting in the manner described, can be untrue:

  (i)   such a statement *falls to the ground* if "something is not the case which would have to be the case in order for [it] to be true" (*I*, §32, 56:3–57:1);

  (ii) it is *directly falsified* if due to a "mistake in performance" the speaker "is *simply* not doing what he says" (§32, 57:1); and

  (iii) it is *contradicted* by the action of one who says, e.g., "You won't, for I am going to stop you" (§31, 55:2), and then begins to do just this.

- And the distinction between *practical* and *contemplative* knowledge.

To appreciate this last distinction, we need first to understand the concept of practical reasoning. This will be our task in the next chapter.

Suggestions for further reading

- For accounts that are congenial to Anscombe's of the relation between action, bodily movement, and its further effects, see Ursula Coope, "Aristotle on Action," Rowland Stout, "What Are You Causing in Acting?," and Jennifer Hornsby, "Actions in Their Circumstances." For an opposing view, see Maria Alvarez and John Hyman, "Agents and Their Actions."

- For an early objection to Anscombe's thesis that actions are known without observation, see Keith Donnellan, "Knowing What I Am Doing." For a more recent discussion that has largely set the agenda for contemporary work on this topic, see Kieran Setiya, "Practical Knowledge."

- For close and critical exegesis of Anscombe's essay "The First Person," see Part II of James Doyle's *No Morality, No Self*. Rachael Wiseman explores connections between that essay and the argument of *Intention* in "What Am I and What Am I Doing?"

- Anscombe's case of the shopper and the detective is frequently said to have introduced the concept of "direction of fit" into contemporary philosophy of mind. For critical discussion of this concept see Kim Frost, "On the Very Idea of Direction of Fit."

5

Practical Reasoning

The final paragraph of Section 32 introduced the concept of *practical knowledge* as "the key to the utter darkness in which we found ourselves" (*I*, §32, 57:3) in trying to understand the possibility of non-observational knowledge of action. At the start of Section 33 we are told that this concept "can only be understood if we first understand 'practical reasoning'" (§33, 57:4).[1] What Anscombe says in discussing this concept is therefore central to the argument of *Intention*—and as we will see, it bears not only on the understanding and defense of conditions (C1) and (C2) but also on her account of what I have called the *teleological unity* of action. It is, however, also a *very* difficult discussion to make sense of. While various specific points are clear and of obvious importance, the motivation for some of Anscombe's arguments, and the overall trajectory in what she says, are mostly left implicit. So in this chapter I will first work to provide some essential context and then proceed piecemeal through the text, focusing in on some of the central ideas while trying also to show what they reveal when taken together.

5.1 A difference in form (§33)

What is the difference between practical reasoning, or the reasoning through which a person decides what to do, and theoretical reasoning, or reasoning about ordinary matters of fact? One common answer is that practical reasoning is distinguished by the *normative or evaluative content* of the considerations at stake in it. On this view, in reasoning practically a person considers what she *should* do, or what she *ought* to do, or what she has *most reason* or *sufficient reason* to do; whereas in theoretical reasoning a person

---

[1] Anscombe says that "practical reasoning" is equivalent to Aristotle's "practical syllogism" (§33, 57:4–58:1). I will also speak at times of practical *thinking* or practical *thought*, which in my use mean the same as these.

considers only what is "factually" the case. By contrast, the position that Anscombe advances in Section 33 is that the difference between practical and theoretical reasoning is a *formal* difference, i.e., a difference in the way that the conclusion of a practical inference *relates* to its premises, rather than a difference in the subject-matter or *content* that practical reasoning concerns. In what follows I will discuss how we should understand the difference between these views.

(1) According to Anscombe, the idea that there is a single *form* that is shared by practical and theoretical reasoning alike is reflected in the common assumption that both kinds of reasoning are supposed to provide a *proof* of their conclusion. In theoretical reasoning this conclusion is taken to be factual or descriptive: it says only what is (or was, will be, could be, etc.) the case, and the premises relied on in the reasoning are supposed to prove that this is so. Since the conclusion of practical reasoning is taken to be normative or evaluative instead, so are the premises one reasons from: in the canonical case these will include a "universal" premise stating some general norm that is to be followed in certain circumstances, plus a "particular" premise bringing the reasoner's circumstances under that description, from which it is supposed to follow that the reasoner *should act* in the manner described. Among Anscombe's contemporaries, one who held a view like this was her Oxford colleague R.M. Hare, who in *The Language of Morals* (1952) presents practical reasoning as a matter of drawing an imperative conclusion whose truth is supported by some more general imperatives or practical principles. In the best case this relation will be that of entailment, as in one of Hare's examples (see *LM*, p. 27):

Take all the boxes to the station.
This is one of the boxes.
∴ Take this to the station.

According to Hare, the validity of this inference lies in the fact that a person who accepts the premises but rejects the conclusion must, on pain of irrationality, have "misunderstood one or another of the sentences" (*LM*, p. 25)—thus the possibility of reasoning in this way shows that "there must be entailment-relations between commands" (p. 25) just like those which govern our inference to indicative judgments about what is or will be the case. Although Hare gets only one rather offhand reference in the text of *Intention* (see *I*, §33, 59:fn), Anscombe likely expected her readers to call his position to mind in considering the example she gives at the start of Section 33:

> "Everyone with money ought to give to a beggar who asks him; this man asking me for money is a beggar; I have money; so I ought to give him some." Here the conclusion is entailed by the premises. So it is proved by them, unless they are doubtful. Perhaps such premises never can be certain. (§33, 58:1)

Anscombe's remark here about the possibility of doubt or lack of certainty also mirrors a central thesis of Hare's book: he argues that "a Cartesian procedure, either in science or in morals, is doomed from the start" (*LM*, p. 38), on the ground that there are not in general any self-evident first principles from which our moral judgments can be derived. Because of this, Hare says, sometimes we must make "decisions of principle" when our standing principles are "no longer adequate" to our current situation (p. 72), or when we lack the antecedent principles necessary to guide us in a given case. As Hare sees it, in cases like this the "crucial decisions" we must make concerning "which principles to keep, which to modify, and which to abandon" (p. 73) can only be determined by weighing the *effects* of acting according to one principle rather than another: so what makes it "no longer adequate" to (say) refrain altogether from slaughtering civilians may be that "conditions have changed (e.g. through a protracted war or an industrial revolution)" so that war can no longer be conducted effectively in this way (p. 72), and therefore the principles that worked well enough for older generations can no longer do the same for us. This, of course, is precisely the *consequentialism* that Anscombe argued against in "Modern Moral Philosophy"—it is a position on which "'the right action' means the one which produces the best possible consequences" ("MMP," p. 33), and therefore there can be no such thing as "the prohibition of certain things simply in virtue of their description as such-and-such identifiable kinds of action, regardless of any further consequences" (p. 34).[2]

---

[2] Hare's views are referenced directly in "MMP" at pp. 33–34 and 42, and obliquely (though not by name) in the final paragraphs of her 1957 radio address, "Does Oxford Moral Philosophy Corrupt Youth?" This led to a heated exchange between Hare and Anscombe in the pages of the magazine where her address was first published: see *The Listener*, issues of Feb. 21, Feb. 28, March 28, and April 4, 1957. (Thanks to Rachael Wiseman for providing me with these letters.) For further discussion of Anscombe's opposition to Hare's moral philosophy, see the Introduction to this volume.

Surprisingly, perhaps, the place where Anscombe sets her sights on Hare's account of practical reasoning is not on his utilitarianism or his rejection of exceptionless moral principles, but rather on his assumption that the cases of "science and morals" should be treated in parallel at all. That is, her objection is to the more basic assumption that *what it is* for a practical conclusion to be drawn appropriately from an imperative premise in "an argument about what to do"[3] is the same as what it is for a factual conclusion to be proven by evidence. As she writes, on a view like Hare's the reasoning in both cases is taken to be "reasoning towards the truth of a proposition, which is supposedly shewn to be true by the premises" (*I*, §33, 58:1). This is revealed in the fact that both of the "practical" inferences imagined earlier could be mirrored by inferences about ordinary matters of fact: thus Hare's inference is parallel to "All the boxes are going to the station; this is one of the boxes; so this is going to the station," and Anscombe's to "Everyone with a job must have some money; this man here has a job; so he must have some money." If this is all that there is to practical reasoning, then it is no more a special *sort* of reasoning than is reasoning reasoning about mince pies (cf. §33, 58:2): in each case the very same sort of inferential process is applied to a distinctive domain. But what is supposed to make this conception of practical reasoning so problematic?

For ease of reference, let us call the thesis that practical and theoretical reasoning share a common form, and are distinguished only by their content or subject matter, the thesis of *Parallelism* about practical reasoning. The argument of Section 33 is supposed to show that assuming this thesis makes it impossible to account for the way that the conclusion of practical reasoning is, as I will put it, something *actionable*—that is, something of a sort that the person who reaches this conclusion can *do*. In what follows I will explain further what this means.

(2) Anscombe frames her objection to Parallelism by appealing to Aristotle's thesis that the conclusion of practical reasoning *is an action*, and not merely a judgment about what ought to be done. Here is Aristotle:

> for example, whenever one thinks that every man ought to walk, and that one is a man oneself, straightaway one walks; or that, in this case, no man should walk, one is a man: straightaway one remains at rest. And so one acts in the two cases provided there is nothing to compel or prevent. Again, I

---

[3] For this phrase, see *LM*, p. 57.

ought to create a good, a house is good: straightaway he makes a house. I need a covering, a coat is a covering: I need a coat. What I need I ought to make, I need a coat: I make a coat. And the conclusion "I must make a coat" is an action. (*De Motu Animalium* 7, 701a12–20)

According to Anscombe, whereas Aristotle "appears to envisage an action as following" (*I*, §33, 59:1) from the premises appealed to in practical reasoning, a judgment of the form "I ought to do such-and-such" is not itself an action, nor indeed does *anything* about actually doing anything follow from a judgment about what one ought (or has most reason, etc.) to do. But why is this consequence so problematic? And what reason is there, beyond mere fidelity to Aristotle, to assume that practical reasoning must *conclude in action*?

We can address the second question by distinguishing two ways of understanding this Aristotelian view. An *ambitious* interpretation of Aristotle's doctrine holds that, at least in the paradigmatic case, a person's practical reasoning is not fully concluded until she actually does what she decides to do, i.e., *executes* the action that her practical reasoning settles on. By contrast, a comparatively unambitious interpretation says only that the conclusion of practical reasoning must be the sort of thing that a person *can* do, i.e., something *actionable* in the sense suggested earlier, even if in fact she never actually does it. While Anscombe clearly prefers the ambitious thesis, an immediate difficulty with appealing to it as a premise in her argument is that this makes her argument turn on a controversial claim that many philosophers would reject, and that in any case needs its own defense. Things are more straightforward if we take the unambitious starting-point, however: for it is hard to see how practical reasoning can be a way of deciding *what to do* unless its conclusion is something that can *be done*. The challenge, then, is to explain why the assumption of Parallelism would rule out this last possibility.

To see why Anscombe thinks that Parallelism has this problematic consequence, let us begin by comparing the following two statements, each of which might be justified by a process of reasoning aimed at deciding what to do:

(1)   I will give money to beggars.
(2)   I will give money to this beggar.

As I intend these statements to be read, (1) represents a general principle or policy, something that is realized in action over the course of a person's life or some stretch of it—as we might say of someone that *during her college years she studied hard, after she married she cared for her husband, throughout her life she kept her promises*, and so on.[4] Statement (2), by contrast, should be read as representing a commitment to do something quite specific—something, that is, of a sort that can be done on a particular occasion. If the difference I have in mind is not already clear, it might be brought out further by considering the present-tense counterparts of these two statements. For (2) as I mean it to be read, this counterpart will be a sentence whose verb phrase has imperfective aspect, describing a particular action one is in the midst of performing, i.e.:

(2P)   I am giving money to this beggar.

By contrast, the present-tense counterpart of (1) will have *habitual* aspect instead, describing a standing practice or routine rather than anything specific that one does on a certain occasion:

(1P)   I give money to beggars.

While the truth of (1P) clearly depends on that of (2P) insofar as a person cannot give money to beggars without sometimes giving a particular beggar some money, nevertheless (1P) does not itself contain a description of any specific act: for it may (now) be true that I (now) *give money* to beggars even if I am not (now) *giving money* to anyone at all. This means that even if someone committed to (1) is thereby committed to *sometimes* reaching conclusions like (2) as well, and so putting her policy or principle into action, doing so requires taking on a further commitment than (1) itself contains. This is what I mean by saying that the conclusion in (1) is not *actionable* in the sense defined previously: being generous to beggars is not *itself* something one can do, and so one who has committed herself only to this general principle has not really answered the question of how to act.[5]

---

[4] I believe that it was John O'Callaghan who first helped me to see that positive moral precepts necessarily have the form represented in (1).

[5] Notice that this argument does not presuppose that an actionable conclusion must represent what one will do in all its particular details—for then the conclusion in (2) would also fail this test, pending further specification of how much money to give, what hand to extend it with, etc. The crucial difference is in the *sort* of generality that is instanced in each conclusion. If, e.g., I decide to go to San Francisco next week, then on this account I have made an *actionable* judgment about what I will do then, even as many details remain to be filled in (will I fly or drive? on which airline? and so on). This is because in deciding to go to San Francisco I have decided on something that I can do *on* a particular occasion—a condition that is not satisfied if, say, I decide that in retirement I will travel. For discussion of the way that practical reasoning can "particularize" a plan of action, and the essential role of perception in this process, see Anton Ford, "Praktische Wahrnehmung" and "On What Is in Front of Your Nose."

It seems fair to demand that a philosophical account of practical reasoning must explain how such reasoning sometimes issues in conclusions that are *actionable* in the manner of (2). One reason for this is descriptive: people *do* very often reason in a way that settles on specific actions, e.g., giving some money to a beggar, that they perform in light of the considerations from which they reason. That is, the word "so" in a statement of one's reasoning like "Everyone with money ought to give to a beggar who asks him; this man asking me for money is a beggar; I have money; so I ought to give him some" (§33, 58:1) represents what follows it as a *conclusion* that is drawn from the preceding considerations[6]—and it is a task of philosophy to explain how it is possible to reason cogently in this way. Another reason to accept this constraint is that if practical reasoning could not yield actionable conclusions then it is not clear what *use* this reasoning would be: for while doubtless it is good to know that one should repay one's debts, keep one's promises, give money to beggars, and so on, these general principles are entirely idle without a way of determining how to put them into action. And presumably this is part of what practical reasoning is supposed to provide:[7] thus knowing, e.g., that one ought to give money to beggars, that this man here is a beggar, and that I have some money, I may decide that ("so") I will now give some money to this man—something which I may now do at once.

(3) Why, though, should we think that practical reasoning cannot yield actionable conclusions if all such reasoning has the form described by Hare? That form is supposed to parallel that of ordinary reasoning about factual matters: at least in the best case, it is reasoning to a conclusion that is "necessitated" (*I*, §33, 59:1) or "shewn to be true" (§33, 58:1) by the considerations adduced in its favor. And it might be hard to see why such reasoning cannot be reasoning to action in the sense I have defined: for just as the premises "This is Socrates" and "Socrates is a man" can take us from the judgment that all men are mortal to a corresponding judgment about the mortality of a particular individual, so the premise "This man is a beggar" is the only thing required to move us from the general principle in (1) above to an actionable conclusion like (2). This is, in fact, just the sort of inference that Anscombe imagines in introducing the example of the beggar, and it is

---

[6] Jonathan Dancy helpfully calls this the "practical 'so'" (*Practical Shape*, p. 15).

[7] Cf. Hare's claim that "the function of moral principles is to guide conduct. ... And this is what makes ethics worth studying: for the question 'What shall I do?' is one that we cannot long evade" (*LM*, p. 1).

also the form that Hare employs in his example of moving the boxes. What is supposed to be inadequate in this proposal?

Anscombe begins her objection by modifying an example of Aristotle's, imagining a person who reasons from the following considerations, which going forward I'll refer to as the *bank of premises* (see §33, 60:3):

(BP)   Vitamin X is good for all men over 60.
          Pigs' tripes are full of Vitamin X.
          I'm a man over 60.
          Here's some pig's tripes.

It seems possible to reason from the premises in (BP) to an actionable conclusion, such as the decision *to eat* the tripes that are before one—but can we explain this possibility on the assumption of Parallelism? Anscombe's argument (here see §33, 59:1) has the form of a dilemma. Either (i) practical reasoning proceeds from universal principles that state what one is *always* to do in certain circumstances, or (ii) it does not. If (i), then the view is unrealistic, appealing either to premises "which no one could accept for a moment" (§33, 59:1) or to premises too detailed to be attributed to ordinary reasoners. And if (ii), then on the assumption of Parallelism the premises will not necessitate an actionable conclusion. I will present this argument in more detail in what follows.

Consider the second horn (ii) first. Anscombe's argument here is that if the starting point of a person's practical reasoning included only considerations like those listed in (BP), then the only conclusions whose truth could be *shown* by the considerations this person reasons from are ones like the following (cf. §33, 61:2[8]):

(a)   So it'd be a good thing for me to have some.
(b)   So I have some good reason to have some.
(c)   So perhaps I ought to have some.

While all these judgments are obviously relevant to the question of what to do, none of them gets us to the genuinely actionable conclusion we are after, as nothing follows from any of them about *actually* doing anything at all. This is because a person can decide, on general grounds about nutrition and so on, that eating a certain food would suit her very well, without its following that she can be accused of any kind of any kind of inconsistency if she does

---

[8] My conclusion (a) is the same as (c) in Anscombe's list, while my conclusion (d) in the second list is the same as her (a) and my (e) the same as her (b).

not thereupon go in and eat it, even if there are no impediments to doing so—for she may decide instead to eat some other nutritious food.[9] Examples like this show that if practical reasoning proceeds only from premises that do not state what one is *always* to do, at least in certain circumstances, then such reasoning cannot yield an actionable conclusion—at least on the assumption of Parallelism, i.e. the assumption that the conclusion of practical reasoning must be proved or *shown true* by the premises that one reasons from.

This brings us to horn (i). We have seen that in order for practical reasoning to yield a genuinely actionable conclusion, the form of this conclusion would have to be like one of the following:

(d)   So I'll have some.
(e)   So I'd better have some.
(f)   So I ought to have some.
(g)   So I have definitive reason to have some.

Unlike the conclusions in (a) to (c), a person who reaches a conclusion like one of these, but then does not act in the way described, might be regarded as guilty of a kind of rational inconsistency—at least given certain assumptions about the rationality of failing to act in the way one judges to be best. Now, however, the trouble is that none of these conclusions, nor any others like them, can be *shown* to be true by appeal only to the considerations in our bank of premises. To reach them, we would need to add to (BP) a further premise like the following (here see §33, 61:6):

(NEC)   It is necessary for all men over 60 to eat any food containing Vitamin X that they ever come across.

And while the addition of (NEC) to our bank of premises might be enough for them to yield an actionable conclusion, this principle has the disadvantage of being obviously false (Anscombe says "insane": §33, 61:7). That was the first horn in the dilemma: if according to Parallelism it is possible to reason to an actionable conclusion *only* by appeal to a premise like (NEC), then Parallelism has the absurd consequence that conclusive practical reasoning requires the endorsement of premises "which no one could accept for a moment" (§33, 59:1).[10]

---

[9] This diagnosis mirrors what Anscombe says about the example of buying a dress: see §33, 59:1.

[10] Anscombe notes that things could be different with "negative general premises" (like "Don't ever procure the judicial condemnation of the innocent," etc.), but the problem is that "these, even if accepted as practical premises, don't lead to any particular actions ... but only to not doing certain things" (§33, 61:10).

This last argument might seem too quick. First, we might think that Anscombe's objection to (NEC) as a general principle of action could be resisted just by allowing this principle to contain some implicit escape clauses (see §33, 62:1): e.g., the principle might state that such a person should eat food with Vitamin X *unless* he is full, *unless* he is driving, *unless* the food is too expensive or belongs to someone else, etc.[11] Moreover, it might appear that in the example of the beggar that we considered just earlier, premise (1) illustrated the possibility of a universal principle from which an actionable conclusion like (2) could follow as a specific instance. However, as we saw already the generality of (1) is not of the required form: the principle in (1) describes something that is to be done *habitually* or *in general*, and there is no irrationality at all in accepting such a principle while not also, even at a moment when one accepts it, giving a particular beggar any money. What would be needed, then, is a restatement of (1) as a universal principle along the lines of (NEC) above, e.g.:

(1N)   I will give money to every beggar that I ever come across (*unless* I am a beggar myself and down to my last dime, or the beggar in question is trying assault me, or there is a child drowning in a pond across the street, ...).

Together with premises stating that *S* is a beggar I have come across and the escape clauses are not met, (1N) yields the conclusion that I will give money to *S*, and if I accept this conclusion then I will be guilty of a kind of inconsistency if this is not what I go on to do. But the problem with this reply is that most people simply *do not accept* any—or at least very many—universal practical principles along the lines of (1N), i.e., principles of the form "In *C*, I shall always do *F* (unless *a*, *b*, *c*, ...)," and nevertheless they seem to *reason perfectly well* to actionable conclusions about what they are going to do. That is, in the ordinary case a person who reasons to the decision to give money to a beggar will do so, not from a universal premise like (1N), but rather from a much less committal premise like one of the following:

(1*a*)   Beggars deserve our charity.
(1*b*)   Beggars need money for food and shelter.
(1*c*)   A person like myself should give money to those in need.

---

[11] How about a saving clause that is more general, e.g., that something should be done "if the circumstances don't include something that would make it foolish" (see §33, 62:1)? The problem is that this clause makes the principle totally uninformative: absent some specification of the foolish-making circumstances, it is equivalent to saying that one should do something ... unless she should not.

At least on its face, our ordinary conception of practical reasoning allows that person who accepts a principle like one of those just listed, and sees that a certain person is a beggar, *may* then decide *on these grounds alone* to give money to that person, with nothing *lacking* in her reasoning compared to that of someone who reached the same conclusion on the basis of a stricter premise like (1N) instead. Assuming that it is indeed *possible* to reason to a decision to do something from a general premise like one of these, and that there is nothing practically *irrational* in reasoning in this way, a philosophical account of practical reasoning that cannot accommodate this possibility must be rejected. And this is exactly the situation for any account on which the conclusion of a practical syllogism must be a claim that is shown true by the considerations adduced in its favor.

(4) A natural way to respond to this argument is by pointing out cases of quite good reasoning about ordinary matters of fact in which the premises from which we reason fall short of *proving* the conclusion we go on to draw.[12] Jonathan Dancy gives a nice example of this.[13] Suppose you are a detective investigating a murder, and your investigation turns up the following facts:

> The murder weapon was found in the butler's cupboard.
> There was no sign of its having been planted there.
> Your investigation was conducted with great care.
> There are no other serious suspects.
> The butler had something (but not much) of a motive.

Taken together, the facts turned up in your investigation are clearly insufficient to *prove* that the butler did the deed, but they do seem like enough to justify you in drawing the conclusion that this is what happened. And the same might appear true in cases of practical reasoning like those considered earlier. If, for example, one accepts the considerations in the bank of premises while also, perhaps, believing such reasonable things as that the tripes haven't been poisoned, they don't belong to anyone else, this isn't an inappropriate time or place to eat them, there isn't any preferable food in the vicinity that is also nutritious, and so on, can't she then decide on this basis to eat them, in just the same way that Dancy's detective can conclude that the butler did it?

---

[12] I think that Sarah Buss, Jennifer Daigle, Jonathan Dancy, and Beri Marušić have each pressed me on this point at one time or another.
[13] Jonathan Dancy, *Practical Shape*, p. 75.

But this reply overlooks a deeper disanalogy between the two cases. In Dancy's case, the conclusion that you express by saying "The butler did it" will not be an *outright* belief that this is what happened, but only the belief that this happened *unless*, e.g., the butler was set up by a very skilled framer.[14] By contrast, nothing similar is required if you are reasoning from the considerations in (BP) to a decision you'd express by saying "I'll eat some tripes." For the knowledge that Vitamin X is good for a person like oneself, these tripes contain Vitamin X, etc., is *all* that one could possibly need to decide, *outright* and yet entirely reasonably, that one *will eat* the tripes that one sees—*even if* another vitamin-rich food happens to be present as well. If, say, you were also to learn that the tripes had been lovingly prepared by your mother, this might give you *more* reason to eat them than if you only thought them healthy, but your judgment of what you'll do does not have to be "hedged" according to the extent of your reasons for acting in the way that theoretical beliefs are required to reflect the extent of the evidence supporting them.

Another way of responding to this argument is to claim that practical reasoning proceeds from universal premises similar to (NEC), though at a broader level of generality.[15] Consider, for example, the following two principles:

(MAX)   One should always do what one has most reason to do.

(SAT)   One should always do what one has sufficient reason to do.

A person who accepts a principle like (MAX) or (SAT) might then take considerations like those represented in (BP) as evidence that eating some tripes falls under the description that this principle contains—that is, as considerations that show this action to be the one most favored by her reasons, or at least one that is favored sufficiently by them to go ahead and do it. Couldn't such a person then reach an actionable conclusion like those in (d) to (g)—that is, a judgment to the effect that not only would it be *good* to eat some tripes, but that she actually *should* go ahead and do this?

The response gets this much right: contrary to my suggestion earlier, there are *some* defensible practical principles by means of which a person could reason to an actionable conclusion even on the assumption of Parallelism. The trouble, however, is that it is entirely unrealistic to suppose

---

[14] I owe this point to Marshall Thompson.

[15] Here again I am grateful to Marshall Thompson, for both raising the objection and helping me to see how to address it.

that ordinary practical reasoning always proceeds in this way.[16] That is, even if one or the other of these principles is part of a correct normative theory of rational decision-making, this does not require that ordinary people make rational decisions by *applying* these principles as premises in practical reasoning—even if, perhaps, they might endorse some such principles upon reflection. A similar point would hold if a principle in the vein of (MAX) or (SAT) were part of a correct *descriptive* theory of how human beings make decisions: even if this were so, it would not show that it is by applying such principles that anyone ever decides what to do. On the contrary, in ordinary situations the *only* considerations that a person will usually call to mind in reaching a decision, or appeal to in explaining her decision to someone else, will have to do with first-order facts like those in (BP). It is only when we look at things through a lens colored by prior philosophical commitments that it will seem as if those considerations are not in themselves sufficient to justify the action of eating some tripes. And even if what *explains* this sufficiency is something that the considerations reveal about the expected utility of this action (or the strength of the reasons in favor of it, etc.), *that fact* does not need to be appreciated by a person who decides, entirely rationally, to do this on their basis.

A yet further response might be that ordinary reasoning from evidence to a factual conclusion can be *permissive* in a way that Anscombe's arguments assume it is not. To say that reasoning is permissive is to say that it is possible reasonably to draw any of several incompatible conclusions from a given body of evidence—something that will be possible on, e.g., a subjective Bayesian view of reasoning, where different assignment of prior probabilities will make for differences in which conclusions one can rationally draw.[17] If practical reasoning is permissive, this might explain why one who accepts certain premises about, e.g., the nutritional benefits of pigs' tripes might then decide either to eat them *or not*: the premises would then *permit* drawing either conclusion rationally, without determining the *unique* decision that should be made in light of them. But in fact this does not resolve the difficulty, since even if ordinary reasoning is permissive the permissible differences will be only *between* different reasoners, or between different "stages" of a single person

---

[16] A further problem is that a person who reasons only from (SAT) is going to need a way of deciding between what will usually be a lot of different things that she has sufficient reason to do on any given occasion. (For more on this, see my discussion of "picking" at the end of this section.) And while (MAX) avoids this problem, it has to deal with the opposite one: it fails to provide guidance in any case where there isn't a single course of action that one's reasons uniquely favor.

[17] For an important criticism of permissive epistemologies, see Roger White, "Epistemic Permissiveness."

whose priors or evidential standards differ across their life. No one holds that it can be reasonable to think: "X and Y, which means Z could either be true or not, but I'll go with Z"[18]—yet as Anscombe points out, this is *exactly* what happens in "what is by far the most common situation for anyone pursuing an objective" by reasoning practically about what to do:

> Let someone be building a house, for example; his plan may not determine whether he has sash or casement windows; but he must decide which kind of window to have, at least when he comes to it, or the house will not get finished. And his calculation "if I choose this, this will be the result, if that, that; so I'll have this" is calculation with a view to an end—namely, the completed house; even though both alternatives would have fitted his plan. He is choosing *an* alternative that fits, even though it is not the only one that would. (*I*, §44, 81:4)

Clearly the decision to choose a certain kind of window is not *proven* to be correct (or uniquely reasonable, obligatory, etc.) by the considerations exhibited here, but this is no strike against it: for in a case like this *all* that matters is that the man chooses *an* option from among those that his considerations reveal as fitting. Even if the most that he could conclude, even "permissively," through theoretical reasoning is that he should choose *either* A *or* B, this does not mean there is anything irrational or extra-rational in deciding on one or the other—indeed, what *would* be irrational would be for the man to suspend judgment in the way that theoretical reasoning sometimes requires us to. But reasoning to action is not so constrained, and this reveals a fundamental difference between it and the kind of reasoning that takes us from premises to a conclusion they show to be (even only probably) true.

A final way one might resist this argument is by suggesting that valid practical reasoning assumes a general principle to the effect that, if multiple different specific acts are equally (or comparably) favored by one's situation, one is rationally obliged to "pick" from this set a specific act that one will perform.[19] So far this seems right: in the face of a range of things that one could equally well do it would clearly be irrational to stand fast, as Buridan's ass does, unable to act until some consideration is adduced so that one

---

[18] Of course this can happen if "going with Z" means something like *betting* on Z, or *acting on the assumption* that Z is true. But these are kinds of action, and so the reasoning in question would be practical reasoning.

[19] The terminology of "picking" is due to Edna Ullmann-Margalit and Sidney Morgenbesser, "Picking and Choosing."

of them is favored uniquely. But this observation does not help to rebut Anscombe's arguments. The principle envisioned says that one is rationally obliged to pick a permissible option: Yes, but which option, and in what way? Any random way will do—just pick one. Yes, but how? This leaves us back where we began, needing to close the gap between the generality of what ordinary reasoning can prove and the specificity of an actionable conclusion. To fill this gap, a different sort of reasoning will be required.

5.2 Calculation (§§33–35)

Practical reasoning does not give "an argument that something is true" (*I*, §33, 60:1)—it is therefore "another *type* of reasoning than reasoning from premises to a conclusion which they prove" (§33, 62:1). What type of reasoning is it instead?

Consider again Anscombe's modification of the Aristotelian "classroom example" (§33, 60:3):

Vitamin X is good for all men over 60.
Pigs' tripes are full of Vitamin X.
I'm a man over 60.
Here's some pig's tripes.

Imagine someone who thinks along these lines, and in light of what he thinks then begins to "take some of the dish that he sees" (§33, 60:4). If it is not a form of proof or entailment, then what is the relation to these premises that makes the man's action reasonable? Anscombe answers that *(1)* the action will be reasonable if the person's reasoning has "the form of a *calculation* what to do"—that is, if this reasoning yields a conclusion "whose *point* is shewn by the premises" (§33, 60:1; both emphases mine). She adds further that *(2)* it is a "mark" of this sort of reasoning that "the thing wanted is *at a distance* from the immediate action, and the immediate action is calculated as the way of getting or doing or securing the thing wanted" (§41, 79:1). I will discuss the role of desire or "wanting" in section 5.3. For now let us focus on the italicized terms in order to understand what Anscombe means in saying that practical reasoning has a distinctively *calculative form*.

(1) Anscombe says that practical reasoning is *calculative*: specifically, it is a calculation "of means to ends, or of ways of doing what one wants to"

(*I*, §38, 73:1). More specifically, reasoning is calculative insofar as it is aimed at identifying *how to get* something one wants to possess, *how to do* something one wants to do, or *how to become* something one wants to be. Anscombe gives a couple of examples in Section 34 of reasoning that has this form (see §34, 62:2):

> "I want a Jersey cow; there are good ones in the Hereford market, so I'll go there."
> "If I invite both X and Y, there'll be a strained atmosphere in light of what X has recently said about Y and how Y feels about it—so I'll just ask X."

The first example here is one of reasoning aimed at *getting* something: a Jersey cow is what one wants, and going to Hereford market is identified as a way to get it. In the second example one's reasoning is a way of figuring out how to *do* something one wants to do, namely host a party with a suitably pleasant atmosphere. Finally, in the case of the man thinking about pigs' tripes the presumed goal is to *become* (or remain) physically healthy, and eating tripes is identified as a suitable means to this end. In each case, the conclusion is justified insofar as it supplies an answer to the question "How shall I (get / do / become) F?," where F is something that the reasoner wants to get, do, or become.

The concept expressed by this question "How?" is worth our attention. Notice first that it is distinct from the sense of "How?" in which one asks, e.g., how an internal combustion engine works, or how a person broke her arm or leg. Rather, the sense of "How?" that is operative here is the very same as the one I introduced earlier as the mirror image of Anscombe's "Why?"-question:[20] it is the question that seeks the *means* by which to reach a given end, rather than—as with "Why?" in its special sense—the end or goal one aims at in doing something. This means that the reasoning by which an agent chooses an action is the inverse of the reasoning by which her action is usually understood by another person: an observer who asks "Why are you doing that?" (or "What are you doing?") seeks an outward- or forward-looking explanation in terms of which the agent's immediate actions can be made intelligible, while the agent who asks "How am I to do this?" (or "What shall I do?") has an end in mind already and reasons "backward" to a way to attain or realize it in what she does.[21] But as we have seen, the *order* represented in these questions is one and the same, only shown in

---

[20] See section 2.1.

[21] For illuminating discussion of this point, see Anton Ford, "The Representation of Action."

two different directions: thus the question "Why?" has application, and can be answered in a forward- or outward-looking way, "wherever there is a calculation of means to ends, or of ways of doing what one wants to do" (§38, 73:1). I will explore this point further in what follows.

(2) Anscombe says as well that the premises of a practical inference *show the point* of the action that is its conclusion. This is not to say that practical reasoning *itself* is concerned with showing an action's point or purpose: for the aim of practical reasoning is to *get things done*, not to explain an action or show the rationale behind it. This is why the *calculative* order embodied in practical reasoning is precisely the opposite of the *justificatory* order represented in a rationalizing explanation of what a person does: the series of questions "How?," which are the concern of an agent who is deciding what to do, moves in the opposite direction from the series of questions "Why?," which are the concern of someone who is trying to understand what she is up to. Thus the classroom example of Section 33 could be reimagined as follows:

"Why are you cutting up those tripes?"—"I'm going to eat them."
"Why eat tripes *(of all things)*?"—"Because they are full of Vitamin X."
"Why do you need foods rich in Vitamin X?"—"Because Vitamin X is good
     for all men over 60, like me."

Here, the final answer gives the *intention with which* the man is cutting up the tripes, and the ones in between describe the considerations that move him from a general end (being healthy) to a particular action (cutting up these tripes) that he identifies as *a* suitable way of attaining that end. And it is in relation to these considerations that the man's action has a point—that is, the *point* or *purpose* of his cutting up the tripes is shown by describing the (real or supposed) facts that this action is a response to. The man is cutting up some tripes in light of what he knows (or believes) about how tripes can be eaten, about their nutritional content, and about the nutritional needs of a man like himself, much as one might *believe* something in light of what she knows or believes about (say) the partisan affiliations of the candidates, the state of the economy, and the usual effect of economic factors on voters' decisions. But as we have seen, the *relation* between what a person thinks, and the conclusion she draws in light of it, is different between these two cases.[22] In

---

[22] Compare a remark from Section 2: "The reasons justifying an order are not ones suggesting what is probable, or likely to happen, but e.g. ones suggesting what it would be good to make

the latter case, which is one of theoretical reasoning, the considerations that a person reasons from are supposed to *demonstrate* her conclusion, or at least provide sufficient reason for endorsing it over the alternatives. By contrast, in practical reasoning one's premises are supposed to show that her action is a *suitable way to achieve* (to get, do, or become) something she wants—which, again, is not necessarily to show that her action was "the" (right, best, most reasonable) way to do this, let alone "the" thing to do *simpliciter*.[23] All that is required for an action to have a point, and thus for the practical reasoning that settles on this action to be in order as it stands, is for the action to be *a* means to *an* end of the agent's. We will return to this last idea and consider it in more detail in what follows.

(3) In practical reasoning, what one calculates is how to get or do or secure something that is "*at a distance* from the immediate action" (*I*, §42, 79:1). This is in contrast with a case where there is *no* calculation, e.g.:

> "He killed my father, so I shall kill him" is not a form of reasoning at all; nor is "I admire him so much, I shall sign the petition he is sponsoring." (§35, 65:3)

What is the difference here? Notice that the examples in this quotation are cases of action in light of, respectively, *backward-looking* and *interpretative* motives in the sense introduced earlier. And as we saw, one who acts in light of considerations like these does not have any *further* intention *with which* she acts. Rather, in the second case the role of the explanation is just "to put [the action] in a certain light" (§13, 21:2), and in the first case "revenge is not some further thing obtained by killing him, it is rather that killing him is revenge" (§13, 20:2). Thus Anscombe suggests that the latter example would be genuinely calculative if instead it were of the form: "I admire ... and the best way to express this will be to sign, so I shall sign ..."

---

happen with a view to an objective, or a view to a sound objective" (*I*, §2, 4:1). Read in light of the current discussion, Anscombe's point here is not that orders (or actions) are justified by a distinct class of considerations than those that justify beliefs: for the very same consideration might suggest both that something is probable and that it would be good to make something happen with a view to an objective. What Anscombe means is that there is a difference between *what it is* for a consideration to do each of these two things.

[23] There is a natural confusion that needs to be forestalled here. The premises of a practical syllogism *show* that doing X is a suitable way to get, do, or become something that one wants. But this fact doesn't function as an intermediary consideration by means of which one moves to the conclusion that she'll do this—since, as we saw in section 5.1, that wouldn't make a difference to the validity of the reasoning. I have more to say on this point in section 5.4.

(§35, 65:4), while the former would be calculative if revenge were "made the object" of the person's action, "as with Hamlet" (§35, 66:1)—who, of course, *figured out how* he was going to avenge his father's death. The upshot of this restriction, then, is that there is practical reasoning in the strict sense only where forward- or outward-looking explanation of an action—which, according to the argument of Section 20, are a necessary part of any rich concept of intentional action—are able to come into play.

5.3 The role of "wanting" (§§35–36)

Consider again the person who reasons: "I want a Jersey cow; there are good ones in the Hereford market, so I'll go there" (*I*, §34, 62:2). Anscombe says two things in connection with this case: *(1)* that in every case of practical reasoning it is "desire in some sense—i.e. wanting—that prompts the action" that one reasons to (§34, 62:2), and so Aristotle is right to hold that in this form of reasoning "the ἀρχή (starting point) is τό ὀρεκτόν (the thing wanted)" (§34, 63:2); and *(2)* that nevertheless "it is misleading to put 'I want' into a premise if we are giving a formal account of practical reasoning" (§35, 65:2)—that is, "[t]he *role* of 'wanting' in the practical syllogism is quite different from that of a premise" (§35, 66:2; emphasis mine). She also says *(3)* that the "primitive sign" of the sort of wanting that interests her here "is *trying to get*" (§36, 68:2,3), and thus that it "cannot be said to exist in a man who does nothing toward getting what he wants" (§36, 67:4–68:1). I will consider each point in turn.

(1) The principle or starting-point of practical reasoning is something *wanted* or *desired*. Opposed to this is the idea that practical reasoning is specifically *ethical* reasoning: thus Anscombe says that while the premises and conclusions of practical reasoning are sometimes put in terms of what one *should do*, the word "should" used in this way "is a rather light word with unlimited contexts of application" (*I*, §35, 64:1). If, for example, you tell me that you want a good Jersey cow and I say in reply that in that case you should go to Hereford market, I am not at all saying that you have any (even conditional or hypothetical) *obligation* to go there, but only that this action would be a sensible way to get what you want. Similarly for the use of "good" in "Vitamin X is good for all men over 60" (§33, 60:3): to say that something is *good for* you is to say that it will benefit your health; and so this advice means only that if good health is what you are after, it would make sense for

you to have some Vitamin X.[24] If, on the other hand, you just don't really care about your health, then these facts about the benefits of Vitamin X won't motivate you to eat foods that contain it: you will be able to reason from the given premise to the conclusion that it *would be good* (for your health) to eat some such food,[25] but in your case this conclusion will be "idle," since the premises from which you infer it are not "on active duty" (§33, 60:1).

It is important to see that in claiming that practical reasoning depends on antecedent desire, Anscombe is *not* committing herself to the thesis that reason cannot inform our ends. Indeed, she says it is *obvious* that there can be "moral general premises, such as 'People have a duty of paying their employees promptly'" (§41, 78:2)—and it is not as if the endorsement of principles like these is entirely indifferent to rational reflection. Her position is rather that the endorsement *only* of such general premises is not enough to yield action that accords with them: for a person who reasons to the conclusion that doing X would be good (in general) will turn to the task of calculating how to do X, and then decide on this basis to act in the way she settles on, *only* if she desires to do what is generally good.[26] And she may not desire this, as we will consider later: for a person may desire simply to do what is bad, in which case the goodness of doing something might be precisely what counts *against* acting in that way. It is in this way that "the reasoning leading up to an action [will] enable us to infer what the man so reasoning wanted" (§35, 66:2). For it is only if one *wants* to get, do, or become X that there can be a "point" to his acting in a way that is ordered to that end.

(2) Though practical reasoning depends on desire, it is wrong to represent it *formally* by including "I want ..." in giving the premise that represents its starting-point. Rather, this premise should "characterise[...] the thing wanted *as* desirable" (*I*, §37, 70:3): that is, it should reveal the respect in which the reasoner wants, desires, or—as we shall consider later—sees "as good" the thing that she is calculating how to get. In order to bring out this distinction and appreciate why it matters, let us consider an example discussed by Jonathan Dancy, which he credits to John Hyman:

[24] Similarly for "needs," which also appears once in this passage ("machinery needs lubrication": §35, 64:2). On this form of "necessity," see Anscombe's 1969 paper "On Promising and Its Justice."

[25] Compare what Anscombe says at §35, 66:2.

[26] That is, "moral general premises ... will only occur as premises in *practical* reasoning in people who want to do their duty" (§41, 78:2; emphasis mine). In fact an amoralist may consider these premises in practical reasoning too, say as part of a consideration of how *not* to act, or of how to act in order to thwart the plans of someone who tends to obey such premises, etc.

Someone who believes that there are pink rats living in his shoes may take that he believes this as a reason to go to the doctor or perhaps a psychoanalyst. This is quite different from the person who takes (his belief) that there are pink rats living in his shoes as a reason to call in the pest control officer. Such contrasts show that we will distort what we have been calling the light in which the agent acted, or the agent's reasons, if we insist that they are properly specified as "that he believed that p." If there is a significant difference between the explanation "that he believed that p" and the simpler "that p," the advantage is normally all on the side of the simpler version. "That I believe that p" is almost never the right way to specify the light in which I act, my reasons for doing what I do, if it is taken as significantly different from the simpler "that p."[27]

Dancy's idea here is that while both of these cases *can* be represented as an inference of the form "I believe that X, so I'll do Y," a more careful presentation of the two should lay bare the essential difference between them, namely that in Dancy's second case the person reasons *from* what he believes to something that he does in light of it, whereas in the first the person reasons *about* his belief and identifies something he can do to change it.[28] So the reasoning in Dancy's first case can be represented as follows:

(B1)   I believe that there are pink rats living in my shoes.
          So I'll call the psychoanalyst.

The clause "I believe ..." is included in the first premise of (B1) as a way of indicating that the person is thinking about his belief "as such," i.e., as a mental state he is in which the psychoanalyst might be able to assist in getting him out of. But no such thing is true of the person who is thinking only about pink rats:

(B2)   There are pink rats living in my shoes.
          So I'll call the pest control officer.

Making use of Anscombe's phrasing, we can say that in Dancy's second case the premise must *be* believed in order for it to lead to action, and so the formal presentation in (B2) characterizes it *as* believed by giving it the form of an indicative statement. Still, the *fact* of one's believing it should not be included in this representation of one's reasoning, as it is in (B1)—for otherwise we

[27] Dancy, *Practical Reality*, p. 125.

[28] For further discussion of this distinction and the forms of self-knowledge that are connected to it, see my paper with Eric Marcus, "Assertion and Transparent Self-Knowledge."

would have no way to represent the difference between how these two people reason.

It is easy to come up with parallel pairs of cases where it is desire, not belief, that is at issue. For example, reasoning "I want to eat an incredible amount of food, so I should see the nutritionist" is different from reasoning "I want to eat an incredible amount of food, so let me go to that restaurant with the all-you-can-eat buffet." This is because in the second case, one reasons *from* her desire to something that she does in light of it, whereas in the first one reasons *about* her desire to something that she can do to change it. Thus our respective formal presentations would be:

(D1)   I want to eat a lot of food.
         So I'll see the nutritionist.

and

(D2)   It's time to eat.
         So let me go to that restaurant with the all-you-can-eat buffet.

In (D2), the premise characterizes eating "*as* desirable": it shows the *point* of going to the restaurant, or *what* one is after in going there. (That would be different if the premise were "I'm too thin" or "My father is coming for dinner and he'll want to eat a lot.") The first case as represented here might need some "filling in" (see *I*, §22, 35:3), but we can guess pretty easily the desire in light of which the conclusion is drawn: it is a desire *not* to want to eat a lot of food—because this is unhealthy, or a sign of illness or depression, etc. And once again, *this* desire should not be represented formally with a premise that begins "I want . . .." Rather, a statement of the suppressed premise should reveal how *lacking this want* would be desirable.

Anscombe's claim, then, is that a person who reasons from certain considerations to an action she carries out in light of them must have desired *something*, and we need to show what she desires in order to lay bare the reasoning in light of which she acts. But what we need to show is *what* she desires, while the *fact that* she desires this is not itself something that the agent ever thinks about. This means that the reasoning of the farmer who goes to the market looking for a cow would be better represented along the following lines (cf. §37, 70:3):

Any farmer with a farm like mine could do with a cow of such-and-
    such qualities.
A Jersey has these qualities.

They have good Jerseys at the Hereford market.
So I'll go there.

In this case the premises given show the aim (end, purpose, point) of what the man is doing, by showing the respect in which the object desired—namely, a Jersey cow—is desirable—namely, for the qualities that suit it to his farm. Having shown this, there is no need to answer a further question like "What do you want 'what you could do with' for?" (§37, 70:3): for *such* a question is no longer a question about the practical reasoning in light of which he is acting, but rather one about the sensibility of what he has taken as his end. We will return to this last point in section 5.4.

(3) "The primitive sign of wanting is *trying to get*" (*I*, §36, 68:2,3). This is not a behaviorist thesis: Anscombe allows explicitly that there are forms of wanting other than the kind "that interests us" (§36, 67:4) in the analysis of practical reasoning, and some of these involve doing nothing at all toward getting what one wants. Examples of these are idle wishing, hope, or the mere prick of desire (see §36, 67:2–3): a person may want something in *these* ways without ever trying to get it, but that is only to say that they will not engage in practical reasoning to determine how to get what they want—that is, they will not engage in the sort of practical reasoning where the premises are "on active duty" (§33, 60:1).

Anscombe goes on to say that in anyone who *does* try to get something, where this agent is either a human person or a non-human animal (cf. §36, 68:3–69:1), the wanting that is made manifest in trying will have two features: "movement towards a thing and knowledge (or at least opinion) that the thing is there" (§36, 68:3). A bit later on, a third feature is added to this list: the agent must "at least suppose[...]" that its action or movement "*is of use* towards" the object of desire (§36, 70:1). Here the *movement towards* a thing is the movement by which an agent tries to get it, and it is in light of the attribution of knowledge or belief to the agent that we understand that movement as *aimed at* getting something "at a distance" from the movement itself, such as a piece of meat that the dog smells lying on the other side of a door (cf. §36, 68:3). Anscombe's point is that it is only where this minimal complexity is present that it makes sense to speak of trying, and so only an organism whose cognitive and behavioral capacities make room for such complexity can be described as acting intentionally. But clearly the "movement" she envisions need not be anything overt: one may, e.g., lie in wait for something that is going to come around the corner, and sometimes a movement in *thought* "towards a thing"—that is, a process of practical reasoning that is ordered to the end of getting it—may terminate in a judgment that the thing isn't really worth getting after all. The essential thing is to see the difference between "idle" reasoning about what one *would* do, *if* one ("really") wanted ...— a kind of counterfactual thinking that is possible in the absence of any desire of the sort that would manifest itself in trying to get the thing under consideration—and reasoning whose aim is to move one from a state of mere desire to an *action* carried out in fulfillment of it.

5.4 The guise of the good (§§37–41)

Sections 35 and 36 introduced *desire* as a central concept in the analysis of practical reasoning. A person reasons practically, in the sense that interests us here, when she reasons *to* an action, *from* a desire for something that she supposes this action to be a way to get. Desire is thus the first principle or *arché* of practical reasoning: a statement of the "first premise" from which the reasoner proceeds should represent what the person finds desirable in the object that, through her reasoning, she calculates how to get.

Section 37 raises a further question: "is not anything wantable, or at least any perhaps attainable thing?" (*I*, §37, 70:4). Anscombe's answer will be that there are no restrictions on the possible *objects* of want or desire, so long as the agent takes the wanted object to be attainable and understands her action as a way to attain it. But there is what I will call a *formal* restriction, namely that in order to desire something a person must "see what he wants *under the aspect of some good*" (§39, 75:2; emphasis added). Let us now discuss why we are to think this, and what is the point of saying that this is a restriction in *form* rather than *content*. Having done this, we can then consider how goodness can be seen as governing the form *of reasoning* through which one reasons to action.

(1) Concerning the suggestion that the possible objects of desire are entirely unrestricted, Anscombe asks us to consider what it would be "to approach someone and say: 'I want a saucer of mud' or 'I want a twig of mountain ash' ":

> [One who says such a thing] is likely to be asked what for; to which let him reply that he does not want it *for* anything, he just wants it. It is likely that the other will then perceive that a philosophical example is all that is in

question, and will pursue the matter no further; but supposing that he did not realise this, and yet did not dismiss our man as a dull babbling loon, would he not try to find out *in what aspect* the object desired is desirable? Does it serve as a symbol? Is there something delightful about it? Does the man want to have something to call his own, and no more? Now if the reply is: "Philosophers have taught that anything can be an object of desire; so there can be no need for me to characterise these objects as somehow desirable; it merely so happens that I want them," then this is fair nonsense. (*I*, §37, 70:4–71:1; emphasis added)

What is "fair nonsense" here is *not* the statement that one desires a twig or a saucer of mud. The nonsense is rather in the idea of wanting such a thing *simply*, and not *for* anything at all. Thus Anscombe continues:

cannot a man *try to get* anything gettable? He can certainly go after objects that he sees, fetch them, and keep them near him; perhaps he then vigorously protects them from removal. But then, this is already beginning to make sense: these are his possessions, he wanted to *own* them; he may be idiotic, but his "wanting" is recognisable as such. So *he* can say perhaps "I want a saucer of mud." (§37, 71:2)

The reason why the statement of desire would make sense in this wider context is that a desire to *own* things is one that we can all understand. Once a person characterizes her desire in this way we are able to appreciate *what she sees* in the thing she asks for—i.e., to appreciate the *point* of her request, or *why* she has asked for the thing in question.[29] Similarly for the possibility that someone might ask for something just "to see if we would take the trouble to give him one" (§37, 71:2): the desire to *find out* such a thing is something we can understand in the same way we understand the desire to own something, and so we can make sense of a person's action by seeing it in this light. But "to say 'I *merely* want this' without any characterisation is to deprive the word of sense; if [the speaker] insists on 'having' the thing, we want to know what 'having' amounts to" (§37, 71:3).[30]

---

[29] Notice however that what we can understand or appreciate here "is not a mere matter of what is usual in the way of wants and what is not" (§37, 71:3). For we can easily make sense of people who have quite unusual wants.

[30] Cf. §39, 75:2: "it would be an affectation to say 'One can want anything and I *happen* to want this,' and in fact a collector does not talk like that; no one talks like that except in irritation and to make an end of tedious questioning."

We saw earlier that Anscombe goes on to put this point by saying that an object of desire must be "seen under the aspect of some good" (§39, 75:2; italics modified), and in considering this slogan it will be instructive to draw out the parallel with Wittgenstein's discussion of "noticing an aspect" in *Philosophical Investigations* II.xi. Imagine someone saying that she mistook a certain drawing, say one of a duck, as picture of a rabbit. In order to make sense of such a statement we need to understand *how it is* that the person came to see things in this way—that is, we need to grasp the characteristics of the drawing in virtue of which it appeared to her in the way that it did. Thus we may observe that the duck's beak looks rather like a pair of ears, and the back of its head like a nose, and so on: once we understand all this the mistake will be intelligible, as we will have a grasp of *what* was "seen in" the drawing, in virtue of which the person mistook it for a drawing of something else. And it will not do instead to say that the person *merely* made this mistake, or else we deprive the word "mistake" of any real sense. Even if it is true that anything *can* be mistaken for, or seen as, anything at all, our ability to understand this to have happened in any specific case will depend on a grasp of the features of the stimulus in virtue of which it appeared in the way described.

In the case of a perceptual mistake or otherwise literal "sight" of an aspect, the characteristics of an object that make a mistake or attribution of perceptual aspect intelligible are *structural* characteristics of a stimulus in virtue of which it resembles, or perhaps is taken to signify or be an attempt to represent, a thing of a certain sort. And the parallel claim that Anscombe advances in Section 39 is that the characteristics of an object that make it intelligible that someone desires it are characteristics having to with its real or apparent *goodness*. Following Aristotle,[31] she identifies three *general* respects in which things can appear or be thought to be good, each corresponding to the form of a possible first premise in a practical syllogism (for these examples see §35, 64:1):

(a)   Dry food suits any man.

(b)   I should taste everything sweet.

(c)   Anything sweet is pleasant.

In (a), the premise represents a certain sort of food as suitable or *useful*: that is, as an appropriate means to a goal like that of health. In (b), eating the food is represented as obligatory or *befitting*: that is, as something one

---

[31] And Aquinas: see, e.g., *ST* I, q. 5, a. 6. On this connection, and for a careful defense of this threefold division, see Candace Vogler, *Reasonably Vicious*.

"ought" to eat, either in general or perhaps—and more likely—in a specific context, such as when one is cooking (see §35, 64:2–65:1). And in (c) the food is represented as enjoyable or *pleasant*: a concept which, Anscombe says later on, she will "leave ... in its obscurity; [as] it needs a whole inquiry into itself" (§40, 77:4). Her claim for now is that bringing an object under one of these concepts is a way to show what a person "sees" in it: these statements "are characterisations of what they apply to as desirable," and once a person has given such a characterization "no further questions 'what for?,' relating to the characteristic so occurring in a premise, require any answer" (§37, 71:4–72:1). Of course the fact that no such answer is *required* does not preclude that sometimes one *may* be given—for a person may always try to explain in more depth why she found something worth going after, just as we might attempt a further investigation of the features in virtue of which a visual stimulus appeared to someone under a certain aspect. *That* an object was desired is sufficiently explained, however, just by showing how the object was regarded under one of these aspects: for "when a man aims at [e.g.] health or pleasure, then the enquiry 'What's the good of it?' is not a sensible one" (§39, 75:2). Having characterized an object in one of these ways, a person has *already* brought it "under the aspect of some good" (§39, 75:2).

(2) I said that the concept "good" as it is used in these passages is a *formal* concept—where "formal" concepts are contrasted with material or, as Wittgenstein puts it, *proper* ones.[32] Roughly, a concept is formal if it is a concept of a *manner of representation*, whereas material or "proper" concepts are concepts of (in a very broad sense) objects or things. To bring out the difference let us consider one of Wittgenstein's examples of a formal concept, that of number: for Wittgenstein, this concept is *formal* insofar as it is part of a second-order characterization of *what it is* to use the particular numerical concepts—like "one," "two," "three" and "plus," "minus," "more," "less," "equal," and so on—that are deployed in quantitative thinking. But these first-order

---

[32] For this usage, see *Tractatus Logico-Philosophicus* §4.126. "Proper" or "material" concepts are the same as what Christopher Frey and Jennifer Frey call *referential* or *classificatory* concepts ("G.E.M. Anscombe on the Analogical Unity of Intention in Perception and Action"). They contrast these with what Anscombe, drawing on the later Wittgenstein, called *grammatical* concepts, which are those employed in "the rather special interest of getting grammatical understanding" (Anscombe, "The Intentionality of Sensation," p. 8). Notice that Anscombe argues in that essay that the question "What do you see?," asked in what the Freys call the "aspectual use" where it asks a person to describe the character of her sensations, is also "grammatical" in this sense. Thanks to Chris Frey and Jen Frey for discussion of this parallel, and to Jeremiah Carey, Justin Matchulat, and Jimmy Doyle for discussion of what follows.

concepts are the only ones that the person engaged in numerical thinking needs to apply, and so the thesis that

(N)   To count things, one must regard them under the aspect of number

does not require that a person who counts things must employ a concept of number *in addition* to particular number-concepts like "one," "two," "three," and so on. The point of (N) is to explain the *sort* of thinking involved in applying these concepts, not to identify a further concept that one who applies them must employ. Similarly for the parallel between goodness and truth that Anscombe develops in the long paragraph at the start of Section 40: the thesis that *truth is the object of judgment* (see *I*, §40, 76:2), i.e., that

(T)   To judge something, one must regard it as true

does not require that one who judges something must apply the concept "true" to it, as something over and above the concepts that make up the content of her judgment. (If that were so, then a regress would loom.) Rather, (T) tells us that to judge something *is* to regard it as true, and therein offers a formal characterization of what it is to judge something rather than, say, to deny or question or bracket it.[33]

Return now to the thesis originally under consideration:

(D)   To desire something, one must regard it under the aspect of some good.

Recognizing that "good" in (D) represents a formal concept allows us to see that this thesis does not require that one who desires something must *apply the concept* "goodness" to it, or otherwise represent the desired object in such a way that goodness is part of the *content* of this representation. (Once again, if this were the view then a regress would loom: for one could always ask what

---

[33] This parallels a point that Thomas Aquinas makes in the *Summa Theologiae*: he writes that the thesis "being cannot be apprehended except under the notion of the true" does not mean that "being cannot be apprehended unless the idea of the true be apprehended also," but rather that "being is not apprehended, unless the idea of the true follows apprehension of being" (*ST* I, q. 16, a. 3, ad. 3)—that is, that a *formal* concept of truth is part of the analysis of what it is to apprehend how things really are. It is in this way that "the intellect apprehends primarily being itself; secondly, it apprehends that it understands being" (*ST* I, q. 16, a. 4, ad. 2): thus the idea of being is prior to that of truth, which is yielded only by the analysis of what the apprehension of being *is*. Anscombe's remarks in Section 40 (76:2–77:1) about the difference between the ideas of truth and goodness also parallel Aquinas's argument in *ST* I, q. 16, a. 1c.

the point of being good is.) The force of (D) is to characterize the *manner* in which an object is represented insofar as it is desired, and not a special *property* that one who desires an object must represent it as having.[34]

That "good" in (D) represents a formal concept can also help us to see why Anscombe takes this thesis to be compatible with holding that a statement like Milton's "Evil be thou my Good" is not necessarily senseless (see §39, 75:2–76:1). This is because "evil" as used here is a material or proper concept rather than a formal one: it is used to pick out evil *things*, or evil *deeds*, or an evil *way of life*, which then are regarded as the thing one will seek or treat as her life's aim—that is, they are characterized *formally* "as good." And it is not hard to see see the sense in such a choice: if at some point a person's answer to the question "What's the good of it?" is

> "The good of it is that it's bad," this need not be unintelligible; one can go on to say "And what is the good of its being bad?" to which the answer might be the condemnation of good as impotent, slavish, and inglorious. Then the good of making evil my good is my intact liberty in the unsubmissiveness of my will. (§39, 75:2)

And this last thing is an achievement that anyone *can see* as something a person might desire, i.e., see under the aspect of some good.

(3) As desire can be characterized formally as the ascription of goodness to things, so the *reasoning* that takes us from desire to an action that is supposed to be a way of getting its object can also be characterized as reasoning that proceeds *sub specie boni*, "under the appearance of the good." Consider again the person who reasons as follows (cf. *I*, §37, 70:3):

> Any farmer with a farm like mine could do with a cow of such-and-such qualities.
> A Jersey has these qualities.
> They have good Jerseys at the Hereford market.
> So I'll go there.

Previously we raised the question how this conclusion could be drawn from the premises supporting it, since clearly it is not proved or "shewn to be true" (§33, 58:1) by them. Our initial answer was that this conclusion is reached because it is *shown good* by considerations that one reasons from. Now we

---

[34] For development of a similar position, see Sebastian Rödl, "The Form of the Will."

can add that "good" as it appears here represents a formal concept: practical reasoning is not *moral* reasoning or reasoning *about the good*, and thus "the practical syllogism as such is not an ethical topic" (§41, 78:2). If practical reasoning were what Hare supposed, i.e., "a proof about what one ought to do, which somehow naturally culminates in action" (§41, 78:2), then the first premise in the syllogism would say what one *ought to have* and the conclusion what one *ought to do*: but then either the first premise would be "insane," or nothing would follow from it about actually doing anything, or both. Things are different, however, if we understand goodness to characterize the *manner* of reasoning involved: in practical reasoning, it is not that the goodness of something is *shown to be true* by the premises, but that the premises *show the goodness of the action* one decides on. Thus Anscombe imagines a group of Nazis "caught in a trap in which they are sure to be killed," while one of them reasons in a way we might represent as follows (compare §38, 72:3):

> It befits a Nazi, if he must die, to spend his last hour killing Jews.
> I am a Nazi, and this is my last hour.
> There are some Jewish children in that compound over there.
> The best way to kill them is with a mortar.
> So I'll set one up over here.

The first premise here offers "a desirability characterization which makes an end of the questions 'What for?'" (§38, 72:3)—or, equivalently, questions like "Why?," "What's the point?," "What's the good of it?," and so on. The Nazi has *calculated* that he can do what (he thinks) befits him, i.e., kill some Jews in his dying hour, by setting up this mortar over here and then firing it into the compound. This conclusion *follows from* his premises insofar as the reasoning he engages in is the sort of reasoning where an action is brought under an aspect of some good—thereby showing it to be an "action or movement which … is of use towards" getting what he desires (§36, 70:1), and thus to be "*an* alternative that fits" with the plan to get it (§44, 81:4). And this is why the ways of "taking exception to, or dissenting from" the Nazi's reasoning may include such things as the following (see §38, 74:2):

(1)   Denying the first premise, by holding, e.g., that a dying Nazi should do something other than exterminate Jews (such as perform some Nazi sacrament), or that in fact it doesn't "befit a Nazi as such to exterminate Jews at all";

(2)   Suggesting doing something else that befits a Nazi equally;

(3)   Calling into question the good of doing what befits a Nazi; and

(4)   Suggesting that while exterminating Jews does befit a dying Nazi, still it is "not quite necessary" to do this, and so he might do other things instead.

Each of these is a way of calling into question whether the action that the Nazi has decided on really is a good thing for him to do—but not by any specially "moral dissent" (§38, 74:2) having to do with the impermissibility of murder or the opposition of doing "[w]hat a *man* ought to do" (§39, 74:3) with doing what befits a Nazi. Rather, the arguments in (1) question the goodness of the Nazi's goal from within the perspective of one who accepts the prima facie permissibility of murder and goodness of Nazism, and the other arguments grant the Nazi's first premise but challenge his reasoning in another way:[35]

- An argument like (3) "oppose[s] the desire of what it mentions, namely to do what befits a Nazi in the hour of death" (§38, 74:2); and

- So in a way does (4), since it invites him to act on some other desire than the desire to do what befits a Nazi; while

- The challenge in (2) accepts this desire but questions whether the man has chosen the *only* way to do what befits him.

If an argument like one of the latter three leads the Nazi to abandon his plan, then his "particular practical syllogism ... fails," but not in the way it would fail if it were supposed to be a *proof* of what he should do—i.e., not "on account of any falsehood in the premise, even according to him, nor on account of any fault in his practical calculation" (§38, 74:2). For all these arguments are meant to be ways of getting the Nazi to conclude that the action he's settled on isn't really worth doing, even in light of the considerations he has brought forward in favor of it.

So practical reasoning is "reasoning with a view to an end" (§44, 81:1): it is reasoning *to an action* which is shown *to be good* in relation to something one desires. In many cases this conclusion will not rest on any kind of demonstration that an action is uniquely obligatory, since usually what one chooses to do "is not determined by his end" (§44, 81:3) insofar as there may be other, equally good ways of "getting or doing or securing the thing wanted" (§41, 79:1). And the governing role of goodness in practical thought does not make this any kind of moral or ethical reasoning—not only because "goodness" and its relatives are "rather light word[s] with

---

[35] Thanks to Eric Wiland for help with the following.

unlimited contexts of application" (§35, 64:2), but because the concept "goodness" need not figure in the *content* of practical thinking at all. Its role is, rather, parallel to that of truth in the characterization of logical validity: valid theoretical reasoning is *truth-preserving* in that, given the truth of its premises, its conclusion is also true; whereas valid theoretical reasoning is *goodness-transmitting* in that, given the goodness of what one desires, there is sufficient purpose or "point" in acting as one concludes.

5.5 "... an order which is there ..." (§§42–43)

So far we have described practical reasoning as if it might be a *process* that a person runs through prior to action, beginning with desire and proceeding through a series of premises that terminate in an action that is a way of trying to satisfy it. But this *philosophical* characterization should not be confused with an account of the *psychological* processes or mechanisms from which action results. To see this, imagine going to pick an object up off the floor and put it in its proper place. You act for reasons—and these *might* be elicited by a series of questions "Why?," just as they *might* be represented in an Aristotelian practical syllogism:

> That thing is out of place.
> I should put it back where it belongs.
> So I'll go and get it.

The point to see now is that this syllogism can display the reasoning in light of which you act even if you never run through the considerations represented in it. Indeed, Anscombe writes at the start of Section 42 of the "absurd appearance when practical reasonings, and particularly when the particular units called practical syllogisms by modern commentators, are set out in full" (*I*, §42, 79:3)—a point that could apply equally well to the formal presentation of chains of theoretical reasoning, as anyone who has tried to introduce *modus ponens* or categorical logic in an introductory philosophy course can attest. Anscombe notes also that "it would be very rare for a person to go through all the steps of a piece of practical reasoning as set out in conformity with Aristotle's models," and thus that "if Aristotle's account were supposed to describe actual mental processes, it would in general be quite absurd" (§42, 79:3–80:1). She continues:

The interest of the [Aristotelian] account is that it describes an order which is there whenever actions are done with intentions; the same order as I arrived at in discussing what "the intentional action" was, when the man was pumping water. [...] In a way, my own construction is as artificial as Aristotle's; for a series of questions "Why?" such as I described, with the appropriate answers, cannot occur very often. (§42, 80:1)

In what follows I will consider several of the most important concepts that come up in the first sentence here. All this will be discussed in more detail when we turn to the argument of Sections 46–48.

(1) The Aristotelian account of the practical syllogism *describes an order*—and this is *the same order [we] arrived at in discussing what "the intentional action" was, when the man was pumping water*. So this "order" is the order of the series A—D that was introduced in connection with the example of the man at the pump. That is, it is the *order of descriptions* of an action that can be represented in the answers to a series of "Why?"-questions, e.g.:

"Why are you getting up?"—"I'm going over there."
"Why are you going over there?" —"To pick that thing up."
"Why do you want to pick that thing up?" —"I'm going to put it away."

Here the descriptions getting up, going over there, picking up the thing, and putting it away fall into a *series* whose properties I characterized in section 3.3. This series relates those descriptions in an order of means and ends, representing both *why* the agent is acting (i.e., the end she seeks) and *how* she is going about this (i.e., the means she takes to get there). Thus it is a series of the form:

Doing A **as a way of** doing B **as a way of** doing C, etc.;

... or, alternatively:

Doing D **by** doing C **by** doing B, etc.

These series of descriptions, which together represent the teleological unity in the person's activity, take their bearing from some further description lying outside that series, across what Anscombe calls the "break" separating what the agent is *doing* from what she is *going* to do (or equivalently: what she is out to do, what she is doing these things in order to do, etc.—here see *I*, §23, 39:3–40:1). So in the series of questions and answers just imagined there is an implicit reference to a further end, which might be represented as follows:

(E)   That thing belongs in such-and-such a place.

This statement (E), we can now say, supplies the characterization of what is wanted or desired, in relation to which the other descriptions are on "active service" (§33, 60:1)—that is, (E) represents the desire in virtue of which this syllogism amounts to more than an instance of "idle" practical reasoning about what one *would* do, *if* one wanted … (here see §33, 60:1 and §35, 66:2, especially). The *order* displayed in the series of descriptions A–B–C–D—E is therefore the same as the calculative order whose form we discussed in the preceding sections.

(2) This order is there *whenever actions are done with intentions.* This does not mean that it is there whenever a person *acts intentionally*—for as we have seen, Anscombe holds that it is possible to act intentionally from a motive but without any *further* intention with which one acts.[36] That is, the calculative order represented in the practical syllogism will *not* be present where there is nothing "at a distance" from a person's immediate movements which her action is supposed to be a way of getting, doing, or securing.[37] And Anscombe's point is that without some such "distance" there will be no calculation, and thus no practical reasoning, though there may be *reasons for acting* that could be given in answer to a "Why?"-question—that is, backward-looking or interpretative motives in light of which one acts. And sometimes there will not even be these: then the action will be done "for no particular reason" or "just because I thought I would." But we saw in Section 20 that it cannot always be like this.

(3) The order *is there* when a person acts. This contrasts with the idea that the order represented in the practical syllogism is always realized in mental states or psychological *processes*—whether conscious or unconscious, at the personal or subpersonal level—that precede action and give rise to it. Thinking this would involve the same sort of mistake as thinking that the order in a series of the form A–D must always be realized in *actual* answers

---

[36] On this point, see my discussion in sections 2.4, 3.2, and 5.2.

[37] On the possible forms of "distance" between a person's movement and her further ends, see my discussion of outward- and forward-looking explanation in section 3.3.

given to an *actual* series of "Why?"- or "How?"-questions (perhaps carried out *sotto voce* or in the language of thought), when in fact such answers only *represent* an order which *is there* whether or not the questions are ever asked and answered (on this point see *I*, §25, 42:2–43:1). In the same way, what realizes the order in represented a practical syllogism is not something that takes place "in the mind" of an agent, but simply *what the agent does* when she acts with an intention. Indeed, this order is of a sort that that can be revealed already in a description of an action:

> such a description as "paying his gas bill," when all [a man] is doing is handing two bits of paper to a girl, might make an enquirer say: "Description of a human action is something enormously complicated, if one were to say what is really involved in it—and yet a child can give such a report!" And similarly for "preparing a massacre," which would be a description of what our Nazi was doing when he was dragging metal objects about or taking ammunition out of a drawer. Aristotle's "practical reasoning" or my order of questions "Why?" can be looked at as a device which reveals the order that there is in this chaos. (§43, 80:2)

The order is there *in* the chaos of a person's movements and their effects. That is, in saying that someone handing a girl some paper is paying his gas bill, we are not describing something *else* that he did or is doing (like deliberating about how to pay the gas, say) in addition to moving his hand, but rather describing the sort of movement that it already *is*. When we conceive of what happens in action not just as so much chaos, but as self-conscious movement that is directed to an end, we conceive *already* what is represented more artificially in an Aristotelian practical syllogism or an Anscombean A–D series. To understand in this way what a person is doing—or, what is the same, to know the answers to a series of questions "Why?" or "How?" that could be asked about her action; to be able to construct a syllogism that displays the point of what she does, i.e., what she wants and is "trying to get" in acting as she is—*already is* to understand her action as embodying the order of practical reasoning. This accounts for a point that Anscombe made early on (see §4, 8:1–9:1, as discussed in section 1.3), namely that usually we can know a person's intentions simply through the observation of what she is intentionally doing—for what we thereby know is not an inner state for which her outward behavior serves as evidence, but a form of movement that *itself* embodies the means–end order that has been our interest. We understand a person's practical reasoning whenever we see her behavior as more than just a "chaos" of bodily movements and their effects, but rather as the sort of movement, informed by reason, that is ordered to the attainment of an end.

This analysis puts us in a position to see how, for Anscombe as for Aristotle, a person's intentional action can itself be the conclusion of her practical reasoning. This does not mean that there is no such thing as practical reasoning that does not culminate in successful action: for as we have seen, and will consider again later, it is possible to reason badly in a way that fails to identify a suitable action, and also to reason well but then fail to act as one decides to, whether because one makes a mistake or because one is prevented. And of course it is possible also to reason to an action that one is going to perform only in the future[38]—a decision that one may not follow through on, either because one forgets or changes one's mind. And, finally, it is possible as well to change one's mind midway through the execution of an action and so decide not *to do* what one *has been doing* (cf. §23, 39:2)—as the dying Nazi might, if one of our opposing arguments were to succeed. The point is only that when one *does* act in the way we have described, with an understanding that embodies the calculative order that has been our interest, there is only a notional distinction between the understanding-that-is-her-practical-reasoning and the acting-under-descriptions whose order is grounded in this understanding. To describe what a person intentionally does, in a way that privileges "*the* description" giving the intention with which she acts and relates the other descriptions of what she does to this one, *is already* to display the order of her practical reasoning and show her as acting in light of it. It is thus that the three divisions introduced in Anscombe's first paragraph are shown to be equivalent, such that, e.g., "the answers 'I am going to fetch my camera,' 'I am fetching my camera,' and 'in order to fetch my camera'"—respectively, an expression of intention for the future, a description of one's intentional action, and a statement of the further intention with which one acts—"are interchangeable as answers to the question 'Why?' asked when I go upstairs" (§23, 40:2). For in the case that interests us, where actions are done with intentions, all three concepts can be used to describe a person as acting-with-an-intention-ordered-to-an-end.

---

[38] Though such reasoning could be understood as concluding in the act of *waiting until then* to do such-and-such.

5.6 Summary discussion

The central thesis advanced in Sections 33–43 of *Intention* is that practical reasoning—that is, reasoning *to action*, which is not the same as reasoning *about* what it is good or reasonable to do—consists in the *calculation* of means to an end. In characterizing this form of reasoning, and distinguishing it from reasoning in which a judgment of what to do is proved or "shewn to be true" (*I*, §33, 58:1) by the premises one reasons from, Anscombe makes several more important claims. These include the following:

- That the first principle or *arché* of practical reasoning—and, therefore, of the intentional activity that is its conclusion—is something wanted or desired. While a person who does not want or desire something might consider what she *would* do *if* she were going to go after it, it is only with desire in the background that such reasoning can be reasoning *to action*.

- That in order to rationalize action in the way that a positive answer to a "Why?"-question is meant to, this desire must be intelligible as a way of "see[ing] what [one] wants under the aspect of some good" (§39, 75:2). But "good" as it appears here is not a moral or ethical concept. It is rather a *formal* characterization of the sort of representation involved in seeing something as pleasant, useful, or befitting—a characterization that continues to apply even when what makes an object appear in one of these ways is precisely the fact that it is somehow bad.

- That the "validity" of practical reasoning, in virtue of which a person who reasons "A, B, C, so I'll do X" draws a conclusion that is *supported* by her premises even if those premises are false or mistaken, consists in the way that the considerations she treats as premises give her action a purpose or *point*. These considerations thereby *show the goodness* that she sees in which she does—a sense of "goodness" which is, once again, not moral or ethical. It is rather the "goodness" of something that is *a good way* to get, do, or become something that one wants.

- And that the considerations that we list in representing an agent's practical reasoning are not considerations that *she* must represent "internally" either prior to action or as she carries it out. They are, however, considerations whose status as reasons for action the agent herself must understand—for they are just the considerations she would appeal to in answering Anscombe's question "Why?," and the means–end order displayed in a series of answers to such questions is the same as the order displayed in a syllogism that represents her practical reasoning.

This account raises many philosophical questions that are interesting in their own right, but remember that its immediate purpose is to position us to grasp "something that modern philosophy has blankly misunderstood: namely what ancient and medieval philosophers meant by *practical knowledge*" (§32, 57:3). Our next task is to see if we can close this gap, and then to see how it bears on the difficulties raised earlier concerning Anscombe's thesis that the knowledge of one's intentional actions is knowledge without observation.

Suggestions for further reading

- Anscombe discusses the validity of practical inference at greater length in her 1974 paper "Practical Inference."

- For interpretation and defense of the (ambitious) Aristotelian thesis that the conclusion of practical reasoning is an action, see Patricio A. Fernandez, "Reasoning and the Unity of Aristotle's Account of Animal Motion" and "Practical Reasoning: Where the Action Is."

- For a recent discussion of the "guise of the good" thesis, see Jessica Moss, "Aristotle's Non-Trivial, Non-Insane View That Everyone Always Desires Things under the Guise of the Good," and Sebastian Rödl, "The Form of the Will." For a dissenting view see Kieran Setiya, "Sympathy for the Devil."

- On the intrinsic teleology of practical reasoning, see Anselm Müller, "How Theoretical Is Practical Reason?"

- On the historical credentials of Anscombe's interpretation of the Aristotelian concept of practical reasoning, see A.W. Price, "Aristotle on Practical Reasoning."

- For an important discussion of the instrumentality of practical reasoning that draws heavily on Anscombe's interpretation of Aristotle and Aquinas, see Candace Vogler, *Reasonably Vicious*.

6

Practical Knowledge

The first thing we are to consider now is how Anscombe's account of practical reasoning relates to her claim that an agent has a distinctively practical form of *knowledge* of her intentional actions. Having done this, we can explore how this latter doctrine might illuminate "the utter darkness in which we found ourselves" (*I*, §32, 57:3) in considering whether it can be true, and if so how it is possible, that a person will necessarily know without observation what she intentionally does.[1]

Anscombe credits the concept of practical knowledge to Thomas Aquinas, who himself borrowed it from Aristotle, who writes in *De Anima* III.10 that *nous* can be among the sources of human movement: "thought, that is, which calculates means to an end, i.e. practical thought (it differs from speculative thought in the character of its end)" (433a14–15).[2] While this concept is clearly central to the argument of *Intention*, its significance has not been widely understood by Anscombe's interpreters[3]—a situation that she likely found quite unsurprising, given the "incorrigibly contemplative conception of knowledge" that she says is taken for granted in modern philosophical thought (§32, 57:3). But what is the alternative conception of knowledge that she wants us to adopt up instead?

As is usually the case with assumptions, the idea that knowledge is necessarily *contemplative* is put to work in philosophy much more often

---

[1] This chapter incorporates material drawn from my paper "Understanding 'Practical Knowledge,'" though I have changed my mind about a number of things since then—see section 6.5 for an especially significant retraction.

[2] Compare *NE* VI.2: "Intellect itself ... moves nothing, but only the intellect which aims at an end and is practical" (1139a35–b1).

[3] For example, at the end of a generally sympathetic discussion of Anscombe's critique of causal theories of action, Stewart Candlish and Nic Damnjanovic write that "Anscombe's account of 'practical knowledge' is hard to interpret ... and so it is difficult to see the alternative to either interior acts of intention or causalism that she has in mind" ("Reasons, Actions, and the Will," pp. 100–101). Less enthusiastically, David Velleman writes in *Practical Reflection* (p. 103) that Anscombe's conception of practical knowledge appears "not just causally perverse but epistemically mysterious." However, Velleman softens this assessment somewhat in pp. xxi–xxv of the preface to the 2007 reprinting of the book.

than it is explicitly stated. But the status of this assumption is revealed clearly enough in epistemologists' standard lists of sources of knowledge (perception, reason, introspection, testimony, etc.) and things we can thereby know (that this is a barn; that Jones owns a Ford; that $2 + 2 = 4$; and so on). Each of these examples is one in which, as Anscombe puts it, "[t]he facts, reality, are prior, and dictate what is to be said, if it is knowledge" (§32, 57:3)—for they are all cases where knowledge is of an *independent* reality that "sets the standard" for the correctness of one's judgment about it. And it seems clear enough that any knowledge a person can have of such a reality must be, as Thomas Aquinas puts it in a passage from the *Summa Theologiae* that Anscombe quotes in Section 48, somehow "derived from the objects known."[4] Thus it is generally assumed that in order to be knowledge, one's judgment of how things are must either be grounded in evidence or else be the result of some reliable process in which the knower's state of mind comes to reflect the state of the world.

However, especially in the medieval tradition where Christian, Jewish, and Islamic philosophers were concerned to understand how an impassible and unchanging God could possess all perfections, a range of thinkers appealed to concepts of practical or *productive* knowledge in trying to account for the distinctive character of God's knowledge of the created world. A central idea in all these accounts is that God's knowledge of creation is *prior in the order of being* to the existence of the things he knowingly creates. That is, the tradition that Anscombe refers us to holds that created things are as they are *because of how God knows them*, rather than that he knows them because of a suitable connection to how they anyway are. In this tradition, God's knowledge of created reality is taken to be of a fundamentally different character from the "contemplative," "speculative," or "theoretical" sort of knowledge that has been the focus of modern and contemporary philosophical theorizing.

Yet despite her recommendation that the concept of practical knowledge could be rediscovered through a return to these ancient and medieval sources, Anscombe does not do much to help the reader of *Intention* execute this *ressourcement*. Indeed, in the text itself her one direct reference to a medieval author points to a passage in Thomas Aquinas's *Summa Theologiae* in which the concept of knowledge that is *causa rerum intellectarum*, i.e., "the cause of what it understands" (§48, 87:4), appears in a brief argument offered

---

[4] Aquinas, *ST* I–II, q. 3, a. 5, obj. 1; quoted at *I*, §48, 87:4.

by an imagined objector in a discussion of the nature of human happiness.[5] But in fact, as I will argue in detail later, Anscombe's debt to Aquinas is far more extensive than this brief reference lets on, and the inspiration for her account of practical knowledge is not this cited passage but rather the much more thorough discussion of divine cognition in Part I, Question 14 of the *Summa Theologiae*—a discussion that contains a number of important concepts, distinctions, and examples that Anscombe echoes very deliberately. In order to support this interpretation and address the reader's likely unfamiliarity with this Thomistic framework, the first section of this chapter will turn away from the text of *Intention* to explore in some detail how, drawing on the Aristotelian concept of *nous praktikos*, Aquinas developed his own account of a form of knowledge that is *practical* or *productive* in character—a form of knowledge that is the *measure* of its object and "is 'cause of what it understands', unlike 'speculative' knowledge, which 'is derived from the objects known'" (*I*, §48, 87:4; quoting *ST* I–II, q. 3, a. 5, obj. 1).

6.1 The Thomistic background

I have noted that for Aquinas and other medieval thinkers, the concept of practical knowledge figures most prominently not in theories of human action, but in accounts of the distinctive nature of God's knowledge of the created world. In Part I, Question 14 of the *Summa Theologiae*, Aquinas frames his own discussion of these matters in terms of the idea that knowing is usually understood as a *receptive* act, where the form of the known object is apprehended by the mind of the knower. Aquinas insists, however, that such a thing cannot take place in God, whose acts are not dependent on anything outside himself.[6] And he goes on to address this seeming dilemma by arguing that knowledge may take different forms depending on the nature of the

---

[5] The argument is: "The ultimate end of any creature consists in becoming like God. But man is more like God with respect to his practical intellect, which is the cause of things thought of, than his speculative intellect, which derives knowledge from things. Therefore man's happiness consists in activity of his practical rather than his speculative intellect" (*ST* I–II, q. 3, a. 5, obj. 1). Aquinas denies the conclusion, arguing that human beings are more like God in our speculative capacity than our practical one, and moreover that "with respect to the principle thing known, which is his essence, God has only speculative knowledge, not practical" (ST I–II, q. 3, a. 5, obj. 1, ad. 1). He takes this to show that our *highest* intellectual good, i.e., the respect in which we are most like God in his intellectual perfection, is in speculative rather than practical intellectual activity.

[6] For an argument along these lines, see *ST* I, q. 14, a. 5, obj. 3.

knower,[7] and thus "since God's nature exists in a manner higher than that by which creatures exist, his knowledge does not exist in him in the manner of created knowledge" (*ST* I, q. 14, a. 1, ad. 3). In particular, Aquinas argues that since created things depend on God for their being, God can know his creation in virtue of knowing his own ideas of it, as they exist in his own mind: for God's own essence "contains a likeness" of the things that he has the power to make, and so his self-knowledge is sufficient for knowledge of everything that lies in his power (*ST* I, q. 14, a. 5c). This is why we need not suppose that God's knowledge of creation requires him to be *in reception* of anything, as in this knowledge "the principal object known … is nothing other than [God's] essence, which contains all the species of things" (*ST* I, q. 14, a. 5, ad. 1), much as fire contains the heat that it imparts to other objects.

This idea, that one may know an object not just by having one's mind reflect what is anyway there but also by being the one who through her knowledge brings that very object into existence, is at the center of Aquinas's account of practical cognition. He proposes in the *Summa* that knowledge may be either practical or speculative in any of several respects, mirroring in each case an element in Aristotle's treatment of practical thought in *De Anima* III.10:[8]

- First, as Aristotle claims that the object of appetite is always something attainable, or a "good that can be brought into being by action" (433a29–30[9]), so Aquinas writes that the *objects* of practical knowledge must be things "producible by the knower": thus, e.g., human knowledge of God or the natural world is necessarily speculative, whereas it is possible for us to have practical knowledge of human artifacts.

---

[7] The background to this distinction is the traditional principle *Omne quod est in aliquo est in eo per modum eius in quo est*: Whatever is in something, is in it according to the mode of that in which it is. For discussion of the legacy of this principle and its role in Aquinas's thought, see John F. Wippel, "Thomas Aquinas and the Axiom 'What Is Received Is Received According to the Mode of the Receiver.'"

[8] For the following distinctions, see *ST* I, q. 14, a. 16c. Though her reference there is to Aristotle, I suspect that this passage is in the background of Anscombe's threefold distinction in Section 33 of *Intention* between "the theoretical syllogism," the "idle practical syllogism which is just a classroom example," and "the practical syllogism proper," where in the last case "the conclusion is an action whose point is shewn by the premises, which are now, so to speak, on active duty" (*I*, §33, 60:1).

[9] In *Intention*, Anscombe quotes Aristotle as saying that practical reasoning must concern "what is capable of turning out variously" (*I*, §33, 60:1). She doesn't provide a reference, so I'm not sure if this is the same passage, but the underlying point seems to be the same. (As Nat Stein and Kim Frost have both pointed out to me, Aristotle says similar things at *NE* III.3 and VI.7.)

- Second, following Aristotle's claim that practical thought "calculates means to an end" (433a14), Aquinas identifies a practical *mode* of knowing, in which producible things are considered "as producible." By way of contrast he gives the example of an architect who "defines, analyses and examines the qualities proper to houses in general"—in this case the *object* of his knowledge is something that lies within his power, but the *mode* in which he knows it is speculative rather than practical, as it involves only ascertaining what a house is, independently of any concern with how to make one.

- Finally, following Aristotle's remark that practical thought "differs from speculative thought in the character of its end" (433a15–16), Aquinas says that knowledge can be either speculative or practical in terms of its *end or purpose*. According to Aquinas, knowledge is practical in respect of its end insofar as it aims at production or some other form of action, and speculative in this respect insofar as it aims just at "the consideration of truth." Thus, for example, the knowledge of builders who "consider how some house could be built, not with a view to building it but merely for the sake of knowing" will have a speculative end or purpose even though it is practical in its object and mode. Such knowledge is what we call "idle speculation" about how something *might* be done—but it is a way of considering means to an end that is not, as Anscombe puts it, "on active duty" (*I*, §33, 60:1). By contrast, for knowledge to be practical in respect of its *end* is for the knowledge to be directed toward the production or execution of the object or action that it represents.

For Aquinas, then, the distinction between practical and speculative knowledge is multifaceted. There are several respects in which knowledge might be called "speculative" rather than "practical" or vice versa, and two of these respects are independent of one another. Thus he offers the following division:

(1)   Knowledge is *purely speculative* whenever it is speculative with regard to its objects (the first sense in the previous list), as nothing that does not lie within the power of the agent can be the object of knowledge that is practical in either of the other two senses;

(2)   Knowledge is *purely practical* whenever it is practical with regard to both its mode and its end (the second and third senses in the

previous list), since in this case it must also be practical with regard to its objects; and

(3)   Knowledge is *partly speculative and partly practical* when it is practical with regard to its objects and either:

> (a) Practical in respect of its mode but not its end, as, e.g., when one considers what it *would take* to make something, though not in order actually to produce it; or
>
> (b) Practical in respect of its end but not its mode, as, e.g., when one defines *what it is* to be an artifact of a given kind in order later on to determine how best to make it.

Thus he concludes that God's knowledge is purely speculative where it concerns his own essence (for even God does not have the power to change this), and where created things are concerned it fits characterization (3(b)). These things lie within God's power, and his knowledge of them aims at bringing them about; but since we know created things speculatively, therefore God "knows (yet much more perfectly than we do) all that we speculatively know about things by defining and analysing," and therefore his knowledge of these things is speculative in respect of its mode (*ST* I, q. 14, a. 16c).[10]

The central idea, then, is that knowledge is practical to the extent that it is a *doer's* way of knowing. Practical knowledge always concerns something that one *is able* to bring about, and in knowing such a thing in a practical way one may either be thinking of *how* to bring it about, or be thinking of it *with the aim* of bringing it about, or both. As Aquinas writes in his commentary on *De Anima* III.15:

> the intellect that produces movement is the intellect that acts for the sake of something, not for the sake of reasoning alone. And this is practical intellect, which differs from theoretical intellect as regards its end. For theoretical intellect inquires into the truth not for the sake of something else, but for the sake of truth alone, whereas practical intellect's inquiry into truth is for action's sake. (Aquinas, *In De Anima* III.15, 43–49)

[10] This last point is somewhat obscure to a modern ear. Another way to draw this conclusion would be to say that given God's power he has no need to calculate means to his ends, and therefore his knowledge is never practical in its mode. I am not sure whether Aquinas would have endorsed this line of argument.

Elsewhere in the *Summa*, Aquinas emphasizes that this distinction between speculative and practical forms of intellectual activity does not require a distinction between two different intellects, or even two separate intellectual powers. Rather, his idea is that the very same cognitive faculty whose activity is sometimes speculative, because directed solely toward the apprehension of truth, can also be practical insofar as it not only knows, but also "relates the cognized truth to a task" (*ST* I, q. 79, a. 11, ad. 2[11])—i.e., takes action or production as its object and end. And it is in this way that the intellect of a human being can be "related to what it knows as God is to what He knows" (*ST* I–II, q. 3, a. 5, ad. 1): a person's knowledge of what she creates or otherwise brings about under the guidance of practical reason is similar to God's knowledge of the created world. This, as I will argue, is just what Anscombe has in mind when she says that the knowledge of intentional action is *practical knowledge*.

6.2 "A *form* of description of events" (§§46–48)

Here is the passage from Section 48 of *Intention* where the Thomistic conception of practical knowledge is referenced directly:

> where (*a*) the description of an event is of a type to be formally the description of an executed intention [and?] (*b*) the event is actually the execution of an intention (by our criteria) then the account given by Aquinas of the nature of practical knowledge holds: Practical knowledge is "the cause of what it understands," unlike "speculative" knowledge, which "is derived from the objects known." This means more than that practical knowledge is observed to be a necessary condition of the production of various results; or that an idea of doing such-and-such in such-and-such ways is such a condition. It means that without it what happens does not come under the description—execution of intentions—whose characteristics we have been investigating. (*I*, §48, 87:4–88:1)

In what follows I will attempt an exegesis of this difficult text, beginning with a discussion of what Anscombe means by saying that sometimes "the description of an event is of a type to be formally the description of an executed intention." With this in the background, in section 6.3 I will discuss

---

[11] Quoting from Pasnau's translation at https://spot.colorado.edu/~pasnau/westview/st1a78-7984-86.htm.

the *causal relation* that an agent's practical knowledge bears to its object. In sections 6.4 and 6.5 I will then relate this discussion to the question of how intentional action can be known without observation.

To begin, let us consider once more the case from Section 23 of the man who is operating a pump. A lot of things are happening here. Let us suppose that birds are chirping, the wind is blowing, the afternoon sun is beating down. Meanwhile blood is moving through the man's veins, sweat is dripping from his brow, neurotransmitters are being released in the contraction and relaxation of his muscles. Worms are tunneling through the earth. Water is flowing through the pipe. The piston of the pump is moving up and then down through its cylinder. And in the midst of all this there is *the action*: the man is *moving his arm* and so *operating the pump* as a way of *sending water to the cistern* and *filling it with poison,* in order thereby to *kill off the Nazi leaders* who live there and then *get some better men into power.* We saw previously that there is an *order* to this last set of descriptions: it comprises not just a *bunch* of descriptions but a *series* of them, in which "each description is introduced as dependent on the previous one, though independent of the following one" (§26, 45:6).[12] And we explored in chapter 5 how the Aristotelian concept of a practical syllogism, like Anscombe's imagined series of questions "Why?," gives us a way of making the order of this series explicit. For Anscombe, the concept of practical reasoning is the concept of a rational order inherent in intentional activity itself, an order that is there *in* the chaos of a person's movements and their effects. The content of the man's practical reasoning is given already in our description of what he is up to—in our description of his activity not just as a bunch of things that happen, but as that special variety of coherent and self-conscious movement in which means are ordered to the attainment of an end.

This way of conceiving her subject-matter sets Anscombe quite at odds with the dominant tradition in recent analytic philosophy, which usually assumes that the concept of intentional action picks out a distinctive *kind of event* whose distinguishing features the philosopher is supposed to discover. She criticized that assumption in Section 19, arguing that "an action is not called 'intentional' in virtue of any extra feature which exists when it is performed" (§19, 28:4), and that "in describing intentional actions as such, it will be a mistake to look for *the* fundamental description of what occurs—such as the movements of muscles or molecules—and then think of intention as something, perhaps very complicated, which qualifies this"

---

[12] These relations of dependency were analyzed in section 3.3.

(§19, 29:2). Instead, when we set out to describe what intentional actions are "[t]he only events to consider are intentional actions themselves, and to call an action intentional is to say it is intentional under some description that we give (or could give) of it" (§19, 29:2). In discussing that argument in section 3.1 I suggested that we should understand Anscombe's conclusion as a denial of the assumption that there is a *determinate kind* of physical event—such as a mere bodily movement—that occurs during intentional action but can also occur when a person does not act, so that to call some such event an intentional action is to postulate a further feature that accompanies it, or in virtue of which it is brought about.[13] As Anscombe puts the point now, when we are interested in understanding intentional action:

> It is not that we have a special interest in the movement of these molecules—namely, the ones in a human being; or even in the movement of certain bodies—namely human ones. *The description of what we are interested in is a type of description that would not exist if our question "Why?" did not.* It is not that certain things, namely the movements of humans, are for some undiscovered reason subject to the question "Why?" So too, it is not just that certain appearances of chalk on a blackboard are subject to the question "What does it say?" It is of a word or sentence that we ask "What does it say?"; and the description of something as a word or sentence at all could not occur prior to the fact that words or sentences have meaning. So the description of something as a human action could not occur prior to the existence of the question "Why?," simply as a kind of utterance by which we were *then* obscurely prompted to ask the question. (§46, 83:3; emphasis added)

The analogy with linguistic meaning is instructive. When we treat a group of sounds, marks, or movements as an "it" to which a question like "What does it say?" can be given application, we have *already* represented that group as a word or sentence, i.e., a unit of linguistic meaning. (This is not to say that each such unit must *be meaningful*—for there is plenty of nonsense that we can use our words to represent. The point is that words and sentences are the only things that are *candidates* for meaning—they are the only things to which a question like "What does it say?" can be given application.) And by the same token, this concept of linguistic meaning is not one that we can have independently of the idea that certain sounds, marks, or movements

---

[13] Remember: this is not the same as denying that many of the same physical processes involved in action also take place even when we do not act!

can say things, so that questions like "What does it say?" can be asked about them. This means that the question "What does it say?," asked of a group of sounds, marks, or movements, bears a very different relation to its object than does, e.g., a question like "What does it weigh?," asked of something like a bag of apples. In the latter case, the object of the inquiry has a unity independent of the form of description expressed in the question being asked about it, as there could have been bags of apples even if questions about weight had never occurred to anyone. But questions of meaning relate to words and sentences differently than this. The unity of a word or sentence is *semantic* or *propositional*, a unity not of matter but of meaning, and so the "it" whose significance we query when we ask "What does it say?" would not be anything unitary—would not be any *one* thing, as opposed to a mere aggregate—if the form of understanding embodied in this question did not exist. Because of this, to give such a question application by bringing some sounds, marks, or movements under a description of the form "It says ..." is *already* to characterize those things as constituting a word or sentence.

The same is true of the relation of Anscombe's question "Why?" to our concept of intentional action. As I will discuss in more detail in what follows, her position is that we give this question application simply by bringing what happens under descriptions involving words like *by, because,* and *in order to,* where these words are used in the sense that describes reasons for acting. To give a "Why?"-question application by bringing what happens under these concepts is *already* to characterize that happening as embodying the distinctive form of unity that is found in intentional action—a form of unity that is different from that of mere molecular or muscular movements. Our interest in human action does not start with a bunch of "movements of muscles or molecules" (§19, 29:2) which we identify as objects of interest and *then* find ourselves moved to pose "Why?"-questions about, any more than our interest in linguistic meaning begins by observing some sounds, marks, or movements whose peculiar character leads us *then* to consider whether there is anything that they say.[14] Instead, to describe someone's movements

---

[14] The point here is not that it cannot be an open question whether a given movement is an intentional action, or whether a given series of sounds, marks, or movements is linguistically meaningful. (On this point, see Anscombe's discussion of the biblical story of Belshazzar's feast in §46, 84:2.) But when we ask whether the sounds, marks, or movements made, e.g., by a non-human animal are a kind of speaking, writing, or signing, what we are asking is whether they are *suited* to the form of description that an account of meaning would provide—which is why the judgment "It's meaningless" has a different significance in reference to a nonsense poem than to the babble of a human infant. In the same way, to deny that an event was an action, or that it was something done intentionally, is to deny that it is so much as *suited* to the form of description

in a way that gives the "Why?"-question application to them is already to represent those movements as something more than a mere flurry of events, but rather as a coherent process that embodies the order of practical reason.

It is this last idea that Anscombe has in mind when she writes in Section 47 that that "the term 'intentional' has reference to a *form* of description of events," rather than representing "an extra property which a philosopher must try to describe" in explaining how certain events qualify as intentional actions (§47, 84:3–4). The alternative position that she develops in more detail now is that we characterize an event as an intentional action *simply* by subjecting it to the sort of teleological description explored in the preceding sections. That is, our concept of intentional action is brought to bear already in characterizing what happens as suited to reason-giving explanation, i.e., bringing it under the "*form* of description of events" whose essential characteristics are "displayed by the results of our enquiries into the question 'Why?'":

> Events are typically described in this form when "in order to" or "because" (in one sense) is attached to their descriptions: [e.g.] "I slid on the ice because I felt cheerful." (§47, 84:4–85:1)

The point here is that to say, e.g., "I slid on the ice because I felt cheerful" *is already* to characterize my sliding on the ice as an intentional action, since this use of "because" represents my cheerfulness as (in Anscombe's special sense) the *reason* why I slid.[15] In this way, descriptions of events that use words like "by," "because," or "in order to," meant in a way that would answer the questions "Why?" or "How?" whose sense we have discussed, are *in themselves*, or *as such*, descriptions of intentional actions. In addition, there are other cases where this form of description is *internal* to the sense of a single event-concept. Anscombe illustrates these possibilities with the two columns in her list on p. 85:

- First, a description may represent a kind of action which except in extraordinary circumstances (e.g., Anscombe mentions sleepwalking) "can only be voluntary or intentional" (§47, 85:2). These are

involved in reason-giving explanation—which is why "For no reason" means something different when we say it about an action rather than a cosmic event.

[15] Not that there isn't room for ambiguity here: perhaps my cheerfulness made me giddy and distracted, and so I lost my footing on the ice, etc. But that the statement is *ambiguous* between this (highly unlikely) reading and the reason-giving one is exactly the point—they postulate two quite different relations between how one feels and what one does.

the descriptions in Anscombe's right-hand column: they include *telephoning*,[16] *greeting, hiring, selling,* and *marrying,* which are all things that generally cannot be done involuntarily or by accident. Because of this, an unqualified description of someone as doing one of these things *is as such* a description of her as doing something intentionally, and so these are "*formally* descriptions of executed intentions" (§48, 87:2) in the same way that, e.g., "He said it was time to go" is *formally* a description of meaningful speech.

- Second, a description may represent a kind of action that can easily be performed unintentionally, but where our understanding of what it *is* to act in this way is dependent on the teleological or purposive form of description that we have been exploring. The left-hand column gives examples of this kind: we have *intruding, kicking, abandoning,* and *dropping,* each of which is such that the meaning of the description represents something as happening "immediately" *in order that* something further can be done or brought about. (To illustrate: "dropping" something means *letting* it go, *in order that* it falls (unless it is caught). The concept has application only where there is room to distinguish dropping a thing from throwing it, placing it down, and leaving it suspended in the air.) As such these concepts all "go beyond physics," and have a sense which is "basically at least animal" (§47, 86:1), for they "describe what *further* [an agent is] doing *in* doing something" (§47, 86:2). The outward- and forward-looking orientation characteristic of intentional action-explanation is internal to their sense.

If the significance of these categories is not clear, it may help to contrast them with a third column that Anscombe might have added, which would include descriptions like *lying* (e.g., across a path), *crushing, falling, rolling, breaking,* and *sliding.* All these describe things that can be done with a further purpose by human agents and others, but their meaning is not even implicitly teleological: they are all concepts we could apply, literally and without any anthropomorphism, to what happened in a world inhabited entirely by bricks, sticks, and stones. Unlike these, the descriptions in Anscombe's list

---

[16] Kim Frost reminds me that "telephoning" here must mean more than simply dialing someone's number on a phone—something easily done by accident, even in the days of rotary dials. The concept involves a communicative element too: to telephone someone is not just to dial their number into a phone, but to do this as way of *calling them up.*

are such that the teleological form of description embodied in purposive or reason-giving explanation is internal to their sense.

So the *"form* of description of intentional actions" (§47, 84:3) is a form of description that represents an event or series of events as embodying a means–end order. I argued in section 3.3 that since this order of means and ends is an explanatory order, it is in *some* incontrovertible sense an order of causes: thus, e.g., the man in Section 23 can be filling the cistern *by* operating the pump only if the rising level of water in the cistern *depends on* his pumping in some way. But there is something more to this dependence than is found in the causal relations between bricks, sticks, and stones, since even though facts about "what is the case, and what can happen ... if one does certain things" (§28, 50:3) are essential to everything we intentionally do, explanations involving words like "by," "because," or "in order to," used in the sense that interests us here, express a distinctive way of understanding what happens. The distinctiveness of this form of understanding came out in an important passage that we considered earlier on:

> Consider the question "Why are you going upstairs?" answered by "To get my camera." My going upstairs is not a cause from which anyone could deduce the effect that I get my camera. And yet isn't it a future state of affairs which *is going to be* brought about by my going upstairs? But who can say that it is going to be brought about? Only I myself, in this case. It is not that going upstairs usually produces the fetching of cameras, even if there is a camera upstairs—unless indeed the context includes an order given to me, "Fetch your camera," or my own statement "I am going to get my camera." (§22, 35:5–36:1)

The purpose of this example is to remind us that though statements like

(1)   I am getting my camera by going upstairs
(2)   I am going upstairs because I am getting my camera

and

(3)   When I go upstairs, I will get my camera

are similar in form to ones like

(4)   The flow of water (in the creek) is carrying that twig
(5)   That twig is moving because the water is carrying it

and

(6)   When the creek flows in that direction, the twig will go that way
            too,

in that each identifies two things (*getting my camera* and *going upstairs*;
the *motion of the twig* and the *flow of the water*) as standing in a relation
of explanatory dependence, the *sort* of dependence represented in the first
group of statements is different from the sort represented in the latter group.
While (4), (5), and (6) each represent one thing as *produced* or *brought about*
by another in virtue of some general connection that holds between events
of these kinds, statements like (1), (2), and (3) represent events as standing
in *teleological* relations in virtue of which the *point* or *purpose* of one event
is shown in relation to another. These teleological relations are, again, no
less causal or explanatory than those described in the second group: to say
that I am getting my camera *by* going upstairs, or going upstairs *because*
I am getting my camera, etc., is to say that one thing I do *depends on*, or
will be brought about by, my doing another. That is why "to say, in one form
or another: 'But Q won't happen, even if you do P,' or 'but it will happen
whether you do P or not' is, in some way, to contradict the intention" to do P
so that Q (§22, 36:3).[17] However, the intention is *not* similarly contradicted
just by saying that there's no general law to the effect that if P, then Q—a
statement that *would* be a way of contradicting the explanatory claims in (4),
(5), and (6). Statements like (1), (2), and (3) represent what happens within a
form of description that has application only in a world containing animate,
self-moving beings like ourselves.

6.3 The cause of what it understands (§§44–45, 48)

Let us turn again to the passage from Section 48. Here is part that we have
considered so far:

> where (*a*) the description of an event is of a type to be formally the
> description of an executed intention [and?] (*b*) the event is actually the
> execution of an intention (by our criteria) then the account given by
> Aquinas of the nature of practical knowledge holds: Practical knowledge is
> "the cause of what it understands," unlike "speculative" knowledge, which
> "is derived from the objects known." (*I*, §48, 87:4)

---

[17] Notice that this is the sort of contradiction that in section 4.3 I called practical *contrariety*.
It is not the direct or "head-on" (§52, 92:3) contradiction that would be found in the expression
of an opposing intention.

Anscombe's (*a*) refers to the concept that we just discussed. The description of an event is, or is of a type to be, *formally* the description of an executed intention if it is a description that represents the event as embodying a means–end order, such that Anscombe's question "Why?" is thereby given application to it. And her (*b*) requires that the event so described actually *be* an intentional action—that is, that it satisfy her conditions (C1) to (C5). It is, Anscombe says, when an event meets these criteria that the Thomistic account applies to it: the agent's knowledge of what she does, under the relevant descriptions, is the *cause* of that which it is knowledge of. She expands on this thesis in the next two sentences:

> This [*viz.*, that the Thomistic account holds] means more than that practical knowledge is observed to be a necessary condition of the production of various results; or that an idea of doing such-and-such in such-and-such ways is such a condition. It means that without it what happens does not come under the description—execution of intentions—whose characteristics we have been investigating. (§48, 87:4–88:1)

In order to understand what Anscombe says here, we need first to clarify these two characterizations of the possible causal roles of practical knowledge. What does it mean that practical knowledge[18] could be a *necessary condition of the production of various results,* and what does it mean that without practical knowledge *what happens does not come under the description whose characteristics we have been investigating*? Having clarified this, we can then consider how the two characterizations are supposed to relate to one another.

(1) What is the relation between these two things: an agent's own knowledge of what she intentionally does, and the nature of the action that she thereby knows? A paper that Anscombe published in 1963 considers a natural way of answering this question:

> What bearing can what [an] agent thinks have on the true description of what he does? Someone may want to say: if what he does is a happening, a physical event, something "in the external world," then that happening must be something that takes place, whatever the agent thinks. If you give a description of

---

[18] Or, perhaps, the mere idea of doing such-and-such a thing—a possibility that I will set aside until we consider it very closely in section 6.4.

it, for the truth of which it matters what the agent thinks, such as "He got married," "He swore an oath," "He murdered his father," then your description ought to be broken down into descriptions of thoughts and of purely physical happenings.

If we ask: Why? the answer is: because what an agent thinks simply cannot make any difference to the truth of a description of a physical fact or event.[19]

If the position expressed here were correct, then it would always be possible for the description of what happens when a person acts to be factored into two components: a "psychological" description of the content of the person's intention, and a "physical" description of what actually takes place when she acts—where the latter description characterizes something that could *also* have taken place "on its own," and not as the execution of an intention. As we have seen, however, this is just the position that Anscombe's account of intention stands opposed to. On her view, just as a person who expresses her intention for the future by saying what she'll do is speaking about *what will happen*, and not about her state of mind, so what we describe, when we describe what a person is doing, is an event in the world that *itself* embodies the means–end order that could be represented in a practical syllogism or the answers to a series of questions "Why?" or "How?" This came out already in an example from Section 4:

I am sitting in a chair writing, and anyone grown to the age of reason in the same world would know this as soon as he saw me, and in general it would be his first account of what I was doing. (*I*, §4, 8:2)

As Anscombe says there, *that she is writing* is an observable event that would be described "straight off" (§4, 8:2) in the characterization of her overt behavior—yet we should notice as well that it is *not* an event that could be taking place if she herself did not conceive of her action under this description. For if we "subtract" from this situation Anscombe's knowledge of what she is writing, and leave behind all the other true facts about her movements and their effects, then what remains will be only a bunch of bodily movements and marks of ink. Unlike the knowledge of an outside observer, Anscombe's own knowledge of what she herself is doing is not an *extra* feature of the case that is present *in addition* to the facts about what actually happens. It is rather something without which what actually happens

---

[19] G.E.M. Anscombe, "The Two Kinds of Error in Action," p. 4.

would not actually be happening at all. Her knowledge of her action is an integral element in the very process that it is knowledge of, and not "a mere *extra* feature of events whose description would otherwise be the same" (§48, 88:1; and cf. §19, 28:4).

Is this *constitution of action by thought*—that is, the dependence of the correct description of what happens when a person acts on the agent's own knowledge of what she does—a characteristic of intentional activity in general? The answer might appear to be "No," since many of the things that we sometimes do intentionally can also be done by accident. If *writing* is not like this, then maybe this is because "writing" is one of those special descriptions that belongs in the right-hand column of Anscombe's list on p. 85—it is the sort of action that can *only* be performed intentionally. So let us think instead of the man in Section 23 who is *poisoning the inhabitants of the house*. Clearly it is possible to pump a cistern full of poison without knowing that one does so, but does that show that the man's knowledge that he is poisoning the inhabitants is an "extra feature" of the case, existing "in addition" to the happenings in which his doing this consists? This will depend on how we are trying to understand *what happens* in the case at issue. As Anscombe writes:

> Why do we say that the movement of the pump handle up and down is part of a process whereby those people cease to move about? It is part of a causal chain which ends with that household's getting poisoned. But then so is some turn of a wheel of a train by which one of the inhabitants travelled to the house. Why has the movement of the pump handle a more important position than a turn of that wheel? It is because it plays a part in the way a certain poisonous substance gets into human organisms, and that a poisonous substance gets into human organisms is the form of description of what happens which here interests us; and only because *it* interests us would we even consider reflecting on the role of the wheel's turn in carrying the man to his fate. After all, there must be an infinity of other crossroads besides the death of these people. (§46, 83:4–84:1)

As I understand her, Anscombe's point here is that the question "How are the people getting poisoned?" expresses only one among many possible interests we could have in thinking about her case, and that it is only *because* this is our interest that the movement of the pump handle stands out as a salient feature of it. By the same token, it is only in the context set by a question like "*Who* (if anyone) is doing this to them?" that we are motivated to single out *the man* as a primary locus of activity, saying that *he is moving the handle* rather than that *it* is going up and then down. And finally, as I argued in section 5.5, the interest expressed in a question like "*Why* is the man doing this?," meant in Anscombe's special sense, provides the necessary context for thinking of the man as doing some *one* thing, and not merely a whole bunch of them, as he moves his arm up *and* down, up *and* down, resuming his task after stopping briefly to wipe his brow and then to break for lunch. It is true that even if the man does not have any idea that the water he is pumping is poisoned (or connected to the cistern of that house, etc.), nevertheless he may be *poisoning the inhabitants of the house*. But this description will be apt only if there are *some* things the man is doing in the self-knowing way that brings these events "under the description—execution of intentions—whose characteristics we have been investigating" (§48, 88:1). The concepts that constitute our interest in this situation, and which we use in the description of *what happens* in it, have application to those events only in virtue of the man's self-knowledge of his act.

Return now to the Thomistic formula we were considering: an agent's knowledge of her action is *practical* knowledge insofar as it is "cause of what it understands" (§48, 87:4). As several of her interpreters have noted, Anscombe's thesis that an agent's self-knowledge of her action is a *constituting principle* of action itself is likely meant to evoke the Aristotelian concept of formal causation. For Aristotle, a formal cause is the "form or achetype" accounting for the definition that a particular thing falls under.[20] In the case that interests us here, the relevant "definition" is the characterization of what happens as the execution of an intention—that is, the characterization bringing it under the "*form* of description of events" (§47, 84:3) wherein those events are characterized as an intentional action. Thus it is part of Anscombe's position that the knowledge of one's own intentional action counts as *practical* knowledge insofar as it is a *formal cause* of action itself:

(FC) It is in virtue of an agent's own knowledge of what she does that her action falls under the "form of description of events" that is the characterization of it as an intentional action.

(FC) is a plausible way to interpret Anscombe's second characterization of the causal role of practical knowledge, according to which this knowledge is something "without [which] what happens does not come under the

---

[20] Aristotle, *Physics* II.3, 194b27–30.

description—execution of intentions—whose characteristics we have been investigating" (§48, 88:1). But what about the other characterization that she offers? Anscombe says that the Thomistic formula "means more than that practical knowledge is observed to be a necessary condition of the production of various results" (§48, 87:4–88:1)—language that evokes the Aristotelian concept of an *efficient* cause, i.e., the "primary source of ... change or rest."[21] And while some of Anscombe's readers have claimed that in the lines just quoted she means to deny practical knowledge any efficient-causal role in action,[22] this reading receives only problematic support from that passage—for Anscombe's caution that her·thesis means *more* than that practical knowledge is "a necessary condition of the production of various results" is, at the very least, compatible with its *also* meaning that as well. Moreover, Aristotle himself treats an agent's craft or know-how as an efficient cause of the things that are produced by it,[23] and Aquinas says the same in characterizing the causal role of God's knowledge of creation:

> God's knowledge stands to all created things as the knowledge of artists stands to what they produce. But the knowledge of artists is the cause of their products because they work through their intellects. So, the form in their intellects much be the principle of their activity, as heat is the principle of heating. (*ST* I, q. 14, a. 8c)

Finally, both the formal and efficient varieties of causation seem to be at play in what Anscombe goes on to say next in Section 48:

> When we ordinarily speak of practical knowledge we have in mind a certain sort of general capacity in a particular field; but if we hear of a capacity, it is reasonable to ask what constitutes an exercise of it. E.g., if my knowledge of the alphabet by rote is a capacity, this capacity is exercised when I repeat these noises, starting at any letter. In the case of practical knowledge the exercise of the capacity is nothing but the doing

---

[21] Aristotle, *Physics* II.3, 194b32–33.

[22] For example, Kieran Setiya claims that "[w]hen Anscombe calls practical knowledge 'the cause of what it understands' she means formal not efficient cause" ("Knowing How," p. 151 n. 26), and Richard Moran writes that for Anscombe "the sense of the phrase from Aquinas is not about the efficient causal role of intention in producing movements, but rather concerns the formal or constitutive role of the description embedded in one's practical knowledge" ("Anscombe on Practical Knowledge," p. 228). (Setiya says the same thing in his entry on "Intention" in the *Stanford Encyclopedia of Philosophy*.)

[23] See *Physics* II.3, 195a6 and *Metaphysics*. V.2, 1013b12, where *andriantopoiêtikê*, i.e., the craft of sculpture, is identified as an efficient cause of a statue. (I think it was Kim Frost who first called this to my attention—and thanks to Nat Stein for helping me decipher the text.)

or supervising of the operations of which a man has practical knowledge; but this [is?] not *just* the coming about of certain effects, like my recitation of the alphabet or of bits of it, for what he effects is formally characterised as subject to our question "Why?" whose application displays the A–D order which we discovered. (*I*, §48, 88:2)

The first part of this passage may be a deliberate echo of Aristotle, who writes in *Physics* II.3 that causes

may be spoken of either as potential or as actual; e.g. the cause of a house being built is either a house-builder or a house-builder building. (195b5–7)

Aristotle's point, which Anscombe follows, is that the *general* capacity (or "potentiality") to do a certain thing, such as build a house or repeat the letters of the alphabet, is not on its own the efficient cause of an agent's doing such a thing on a given occasion—for the person will also possess this general capacity on occasions when she does something quite different. Rather, a given process of building, or recitation of the alphabet, is the actualization or *exercise*, on a particular occasion, of the agent's general capacity to do the thing in question. By the same token, the concept of practical knowledge that we are trying here to elucidate is not the concept of a general craft or "know-how," as the object of practical knowledge is something quite specific: it is knowledge, not merely of *how to do* such-and-such a thing, but of *what one is doing* as one does this, of *what is done* as one's intentions are carried out (for the latter formulation, see *I*, §45, 82:1–2).[24] And Anscombe goes on to remind us that in such a case the event that one has knowledge of is more than the mere "coming about of certain effects" (§48, 88:2), as it would be if in flailing about randomly one happened to bring some sticks together in a habitable form. For a person to *build* something, at least in the sense that interests us here, is for certain of her movements and their effects to be subject to our questions "How?" and "Why?": I am supporting a portion of the second story *by* erecting this load-bearing wall, the roof will be angled in this way *so that* water will run off effectively, and so on. When a person acts a way that falls under these forms of description, the means–end order of practical reasoning is embodied in her action itself.

[24] For further discussion of this point see Kim Frost, "A Metaphysics for Practical Knowledge."

I propose, then, to read Section 48 as characterizing an agent's practical knowledge of her action as both formal *and efficient* cause of its object.[25] So in addition to (FC) we have

(EC)   An agent's own knowledge of her action has a role in *producing* the movements by means of which she acts.

Attributing (EC) to Anscombe will seem untenable if we assume, as I have argued already that she herself did not, that the efficient-causal account of why an event takes place must always appeal to a separate event that stands to the *explanandum* as trigger to result. In *this* sense the knowledge of action is surely not an efficient cause of it: for the fact that a person knows she is doing something does not *cause* her bodily movements in the way that the impact of one object may causes movement in another. But this is not the only form that efficient causation can take. Rather, as Jennifer Hornsby writes, in explaining a person's action by reference to her own psychology we may only be appealing to "a network of intelligible dependencies between the facts about what an agent thinks, what she wants, and what she does":

> When we know why she did something, the fact that she did it may be seen as depending crucially on the fact that she wanted some particular thing and thought some particular thing. And the dependence is of a causal sort, of course.[26]

We find an example of Hornsby's "causal sort" of dependence in our now-familiar example of someone going upstairs to get her camera. While a statement like

(1)   I am going upstairs because I am getting my camera

---

[25] What about final and material causality? This is tricky. In most cases a person's knowledge of her action is not itself the end for the sake of which she acts (though cf. Velleman's *Practical Reflection* for an opposing position)—but as we have seen this knowledge does play a role in constituting her action as one that is ordered toward such-and-such an end. In an earlier version of this commentary I proposed that the material causes of human action were just the bodily states and processes studied by physiologists, but Will Small has suggested, plausibly, that the "matter" of action consists rather in the capacities for self-movement that are joined together in the exercise of skill. (Here it helps to bear in mind that for an Aristotelian the concept of materiality is relative: e.g., the body is the matter of a human being, organs the matter of the body, and tissue the matter of the organs. In each case the relevant material cause is determined relative to the set of capacities associated with the form in question. I thank Nat Stein for some helpful discussion of this.)

[26] Hornsby, "Agency and Causal Explanation," p. 289.

does not make any explicit reference to the speaker's thoughts or wants, nevertheless the truth of (1) *depends* on what the agent wants and thinks—for only if she *wants* to get her camera and *thinks* it is upstairs does it make sense for her to go upstairs to get it. This is why a response to (1) like

(2)   But your camera is in the cellar

functions to *contradict* the agent's statement of her intention:[27] if the challenge is effective,[28] it will undermine her confidence that the original statement (1) was really true, and *thereby* lead her to do something different. And so it is not as if "subtracting" from this case the agent's knowledge of her action will leave behind someone who is moving up the stairs but *not* as a way to get her camera—rather, without the knowledge she has of where her camera is and what she is doing to get it, the person would likely be moving around, or not, in an altogether different way.

The productive role of knowledge in action is also exhibited in the case of the man pumping poisoned water. As we saw, Anscombe says in Section 27 that if the man were to claim that he was not, after all, *intentionally* poisoning the inhabitants of the house, we might then test this claim by "eliciting some obviously genuine reaction by saying such things as ... 'Well, then you won't be much interested to hear that the poison is old and won't work'" (§27, 48:1). The way this test works is by undermining the man's claim to know that the inhabitants of the house are getting poisoned. If the man really is operating the pump only because it is his usual job, and not also in order to kill those people off, then lacking *this* knowledge should not make any difference to what he does. ("I am going upstairs to get my camera."—"But that's not what I asked you to go and get."—"So what? I did believe you had asked me for it, but was actually going to get it for myself.") As Anscombe admits (see §27, 48:1), such methods of determining a person's intentions are always imperfect, since the agent might either react in a way that disguises her true intentions or simply revise or abandon her intention upon learning that she is not succeeding in it. But the point that matters for now is that the logic of these tests is premised on the assumption that *intentional action is action that is responsive to the knowledge of what one is doing.*

---

[27] This is what Anscombe says at the end of Section 22: "to say, in one form or another: 'But Q won't happen, even if you do P,' or 'but it will happen whether you do P or not' is, in some way, to contradict the intention" (36:3). On the special variety of contradiction involved here, see my analysis in section 4.3.

[28] It might not be: for perhaps there is "a lift which [she] can work from the top of the house to bring the camera up from the bottom" (§22, 36:2).

(2) On the reading that I have offered of the passage from Section 48, a person's practical knowledge of her action is both formal and efficient cause of what she intentionally does. This mirrors the position of Aquinas, for whom God's knowledge is *productive* of the created things that are its objects, bringing them into being in accordance with their archetypal images in the divine mind. And it is just the image that Anscombe gives us at the start of Section 45, where her echo of Aristotle's and Aquinas's favorite example is surely no accident:

> Imagine someone directing a project, like the erection of a building which he cannot see and does not get reports on, purely by giving orders. His imagination (evidently a superhuman one) takes the place of the perception that would ordinarily be employed by the director of such a project. He is not like a man merely considering speculatively how a thing might be done; such a man can leave many points unsettled, but this man must settle everything in *a* right order. *His* knowledge of what is done is practical knowledge. (*I*, §45, 82:1)

Let us set aside for the moment whether this really is knowledge, and whether it can be knowledge if the man does not see what is going on—we will consider these questions in detail shortly. Putting things more neutrally, the thing to see is that the builder's *understanding* of what is done at the building site is a *maker's* way of understanding what goes on. He understands the process of construction, not just as something that happens, but as something that happens *under his control*; and he understands, not just *what* happens at the site, but *why* things happen as they do. Because of this, the builder's understanding of the process of construction embodies the calculative form that Anscombe discusses in Section 44. He understands, for example, that to finish the house it will have to have windows—and that these can be either sash or casement—and then in light of this he chooses "*an* alternative that fits, even though it is not the only one that would" (§44, 81:4). In giving the order to put in (say) casement windows the builder therefore understands that they are going in, and that this is taking place *because* the house is being completed. This is different from the knowledge that a passerby might have of the same thing: the passerby will have to observe or *figure out* what is going on and why, and if *she* is mistaken then the error is in her judgment. By contrast, the builder's directions, i.e., his *descriptions* of what is to be done, are what set the standard in relation to which the success of the project is evaluated—a point that Anscombe credits to Theophrastus (see §2, 5:1), but surely found in Aquinas as well:

> just as the knowable things of nature are prior to our knowledge, and are its measure, God's knowledge is prior to natural things, and is their measure. In the same way a house mediates between the knowledge of the architect who made it and that of those who get their knowledge of the house from the house itself once it is made. (*ST* I, q. 14, a. 8 ad. 3)

The concept of a "measure" here is evaluative: the measure of something is that in relation to which it counts as a success or a failure, an execution of an intention or a mistake. This is the same distinction we saw in the case of the shopper and the detective in Section 32, where the two lists were different in that the aim of the detective's list was just to *report* the man's purchases, whereas the shopper's list was meant instead to *direct* his activity. One aspect of this distinction is what Anscombe noted there (see *I*, §32, 56:1–2): if the detective writes down something that the man does not buy, then his *list* contains an error; but if the shopper fails to get something that is included on his list (and not because he couldn't find it, or didn't have the money, or decided it wasn't worth buying after all, etc.), this will constitute an error in *what he has done*, while his list may still be perfectly accurate. But now we can consider as well the distinctive *causal* role that the shopper's list plays in what he does. If, e.g., the shopper is picking up a stick of butter from a display case and intends to be buying butter and not margarine, then it seems that the following counterfactual must hold: all else being equal, if the shopper comes to believe that he is picking up margarine rather than butter, he will put the margarine down and look for some butter instead; whereas if he retains the belief that he is picking up a stick of butter, he will go ahead and put it in his basket.[29] In this respect, the shopper's knowledge that he is picking up butter rather than margarine is a causal constituent of the process whereby his activity unfolds: without this knowledge, he cannot manage to buy the things he means to—except in the unlikely event that he ends up with the right things just by accident (cf. §23, 39:1). And this situation contrasts with a different one, where the man selects something from the display case just in order to find out what it is: here, if the man believes at first that he is picking up a stick of butter and then realizes that it is margarine instead, this will be a reason to revise his belief, but not to put the margarine down and look for

---

[29] The point of the qualification "all else being equal" is to rule out a case where, e.g., the man's intentions also change, perhaps because he decides that he can just as well buy margarine.

something else. In this latter case the man's knowledge of what he is picking up will be speculative or *theoretical*: it is a case where "[t]he facts, reality, are prior, and dictate what is to be said, if it is knowledge" (§32, 57:3). By contrast, to have *practical* knowledge of a certain aspect of what one is doing is to know it in a way that plays a distinctive role in the execution of that very action, so described.

Return now to the Thomistic division that I outlined at the end of section 6.1. I propose that on Anscombe's view, the knowledge of what one is intentionally doing is *purely practical* in Aquinas's sense—that is, it is practical in respect of its *object*, *mode*, and *end*:

- The **object** of practical knowledge is something lying within one's power, namely *what one does* in acting in the manner in question.

- The **mode** of practical knowledge is the means–end order of practical reasoning. It is not an abstract knowledge only of *what* is happening or getting done, but of *how* and *why* those things are taking place.

- And the **end** of practical knowledge is achievement or production. It is knowledge that is on "active duty" (§33, 60:1) in guiding an action in pursuit of a goal (or, perhaps, something done "for no reason" or merely from a motive).

So now we can say: for Anscombe, the knowledge of one's intentional actions is a form of *practical* knowledge, different from knowledge of things whose being is independent of the knowledge of it, insofar as this knowledge does not idly accompany one's behavior as a mere representation of it, but is rather an integral component of its object, playing a distinctive causal role in the process by which a person tries to get what she wants. It is insofar as the knowledge of what one is doing plays such a role that it stands as "form" to the "matter" of a person's bodily movements and their effects, and is something without which she would not be acting intentionally as she is. Knowledge that lacks this characteristic cannot be practical knowledge, and what it is knowledge of cannot be one's own intentional action.

6.4 Doing without knowing?

It is time to consider the questions that have so far been kept to the side. The *argument from possible failure* that I presented in section 4.1 was as follows:

(P1) It is possible to do something intentionally and either (i) lack a confident and safe belief that one is doing this or (ii) believe confidently and safely that one is doing this only because this belief is based in observation.

(P2) Knowledge requires belief that is confident and safe from error.

(C) So it is possible to do something intentionally either (i) without knowing that one does this or (ii) without non-observational knowledge that one does this.

The conclusions (i) and (ii) in (C) are in conflict with Anscombe's conditions (C1) and (C2), respectively:

(C1) A person does something intentionally only if she *knows* that she is doing this.

(C2) A person does something intentionally only if she *knows without observation* that she is doing this.

Since the argument is deductively valid, in order to defend these conditions we must reject one or the other of its premises. How is the idea that the knowledge of intentional action is *practical* knowledge supposed to help us do this? The present section will explore this question in relation to condition (C1), and then I will take up condition (C2) in section 6.5.

(1) Concerning the practical knowledge that she says is possessed by the project supervisor described at the start of Section 44, Anscombe writes the following:

> what is this "knowledge of what is done"? First and foremost, he can say what the house is like. But it may be objected that he can only say "This is what the house is like, if my orders have been obeyed." [And] isn't he then like someone saying "This—namely, what my imagination suggests—is what is the case if what I have imagined is true"? (*I*, §45, 82:2)

This is followed by another example, in which Anscombe writes "I am a fool" on the blackboard while her eyes are shut:

> Now when I said what I wrote, ought I to have said: this is what I am writing, if my intention is getting executed; instead of simply: this is what I am writing? (§45, 82:3)

In each case the force of the question turns on the intuition that knowledge is the norm of outright assertion—that is, that a person who does not *know* that something is (or was or will be) the case cannot responsibly speak her mind simply by *saying* that it is. And the concern here is with the "mind" of a person who is doing something intentionally. Can such a person *always* say, simply and outright, that this is what she is doing, or should she sometimes say something less committal, thereby expressing a cognitive attitude that falls somewhere short of knowledge?

We can flesh out the concern by considering several forms of possible failure, corresponding to the distinctions that Anscombe drew in Sections 31–32:[30]

- First, in what I will call a *futile effort*, an agent acts in pursuit of an end which, though seemingly within her power, is actually impossible for her to attain, at least at present. As an example of this, suppose that there are not after all any people living in the house that a man is pumping poisoned water into, and so in poisoning the water-supply of that house he simply *is not poisoning* anyone who lives there. Anscombe says of such a case that the statement that one is doing the thing in question "falls to the ground," as, "unknown to the agent, something is not the case which would have to be the case in order for his statement to be true" (§32, 56:3–57:1). (It parallels the possibility of being sent into Oxford to buy tackle for catching sharks (§32, 56:2).)

- Second, in a case of *practical error* a person makes a mistake in practical reasoning, choosing as a means to her end a course of action that does not actually contribute to it, and because of this she fails to act as she intends to. As an example of this, suppose that the man pumping water has chosen the wrong pump from among several that were available, and so *is not filling* the cistern that is his target. This too will be a case where the man's statement that he is filling that cistern "falls to the ground": the case parallels one where someone constructing a shopping list includes on the list only things that are available for purchase at the place where the shopper is going, but mistakenly identifies *where* in this place a certain thing is. Thus we might speak in a case like this of "a mistake (an error of judgment) in constructing the list" (§32, 56:2).

[30] For my earlier discussion of these distinctions see section 4.3, especially Table 4.2 on p. 113. My paper "Understanding 'Practical Knowledge'" follows Sebastian Rödl ("Two Forms of Practical Knowledge and Their Unity") in distinguishing the second and third possibilities, but not the first and fourth.

- Third, in a case of *practical failure* an agent chooses a proper means to her end but simply fails to realize it in her bodily activity. This is harder to envision in the case of the man at the pump, but an example is "when I say to myself 'Now I press Button A'—pressing Button B—a thing which can certainly happen" (§32, 57:1). The source of one's mistake in a case like this is different than in the first two: it is not that one reasoned incorrectly, but rather that her action simply went off course. She chose the correct means to her end, but her action did not accord with that choice. This is what Anscombe calls "*direct* falsification" of the statement that one is doing something, i.e., "a case in which a man is *simply* not doing what he says" (§32, 57:1).

- Finally, let a *thwarted attempt* be a case where someone's intended activity is deliberately interfered with by another person—as if someone "sets out e.g. to make a hole in the pipe [through which one means to be pumping poisoned water] with a pick-axe" (§31, 55:2). Here again the statement that one is pumping will be false, but the source of the mistake is neither in one's practical reasoning nor a simple failure of action. Rather, in Anscombe's phrase, in a thwarted attempt a person's expression of what she takes herself to be doing is *directly* contradicted by the opposing statement of another person—i.e., someone else's statement that *she* is not going to do this, for *I* am going to stop her (see §31, 55:2).

It is important to emphasize that my description of these as possible cases of failed action doesn't rest on conflating *doing* something with *having done* it, or viewing actions as punctual events rather than temporally extended processes. That is, nothing in my description of these possibilities conflicts with Anscombe's observation that a person can "*be doing* something which he nevertheless does not *do*, if it is some process or enterprise which it takes time to complete and of which therefore, if it is cut short at any time, we may say that he *was doing* it, but *did not do* it" (§23, 39:2). (If the man at the pump is noticed by the police and arrested before the cistern is full, nevertheless he *was filling* the cistern up until then—and doing so intentionally and likely with an agent's self-knowledge of this.) It is also compatible with the way that progressive verb-forms can be used in what linguists call a "broad" sense, such that a person may count as doing something during breaks in action or stretches of time that contain what Anscombe calls "slips" (§48, 88:1), i.e., moments where things go off course and are no longer proceeding as the person intends. (If I make a wrong turn on the way to the store, I am still *driving to the store* even as I continue moving further away from it.) The crucial assumption I have made in laying out the previous cases, which Anscombe clearly shares, is only that there are *some* "material" limits on what a person can truly be said to be doing at a given moment, and that these in turn are also limits on what a person can *know* of what she does. According to this assumption a man cannot know that he is poisoning some party officials if in fact those officials no longer live in the house where the poison is going, since in such a case the thing that the man *takes* himself to know would not be something that is true. By the same token, someone pressing Button B cannot know that she is pressing Button A, someone pumping water into a broken pipe cannot know that he is replenishing a house's water-supply, and someone with a very obstinate uncle cannot know that he is making that uncle change his will.[31] If there weren't these limits on the self-knowledge of action, then knowing that one was doing one of these things wouldn't really be knowledge *of what happens* in the world.

As I've described them so far, however, the possibilities of practical error, practical failure, futile effort, and thwarted attempt are not incompatible with condition (C1). This is because (C1) requires only that a person who *is* doing something intentionally will know what she is doing, whereas in all these cases a person lacks self-knowledge of her action just because she *is not* doing what she intends to. But it is easy to modify these cases so that they challenge Anscombe's position directly. Let an *unfavorable situation* be one in which a person's power to act in a certain way is compromised, such that there is a significant likelihood of practical error or failure, or that her attempt will be thwarted or she'll unknowingly attempt something futile. Being in an unfavorable situation will not always leave a person *altogether* unable to act as she intends, nor need it be the case that a person in an unfavorable situation who manages to do what she intends to is not acting *intentionally* in that way, and instead can act in that way only by accident. This is because a person's doing X can be an intentional exercise of her power to do X, such that the question "Why are you doing X?" has application to it, even if she is in a circumstance where she cannot exercise this power infallibly. But the effect of being in an unfavorable situation on a person's *knowledge* of what she is doing seems to be different than this: for there appear to be circumstances in which a person's power to do X is reliable enough for her to do X intentionally, and where she is in fact exercising this

---

[31] For the last example, see *I*, §23, 40:1.

power in such a way that a "Why?"-question would be given application to her action, but still she is not reliable enough in this exercise for her belief that she is doing this to amount to *knowledge* of what she is doing. And by the same token, a person who reasonably *thinks* she is in an unfavorable situation may therefore lack the confidence in what she's doing for her belief in this to amount to knowledge. Either case will give us an instance of possibility (i) in the first premise of the argument from possible failure.

(2) Anscombe clearly wants us to resist the conclusion of this argument—but how? In a difficult paragraph in Section 45, she says the following in response to her example of writing on the blackboard (I have added the bracketed numbers and letters for ease of reference):

[A] Orders ... can be disobeyed, and intentions fail to get executed. That intention for example would not have been executed if something had gone wrong with the chalk or the surface, so that the words did not appear. [B] And my knowledge would have been the same even if this had happened. [i] If then my knowledge is independent of what actually happens, how can it be knowledge of what does happen? [ii] Someone might say that it was a funny sort of knowledge that was still knowledge even though what it was knowledge of was not the case! [C] On the other hand Theophrastus' remark holds good: "the mistake is in the performance, not in the judgment." (*I*, §45, 82:4)

This is an exceptionally challenging passage to unpack; so let us proceed a bit at a time:

(A)　　　The first two sentences remind us of possibilities like those I just discussed: they are cases in which a person's intention does not get executed, and so she *is not doing* what she intends to do.

(B)　　　Anscombe then says that in such a case the agent's "knowledge would have been the same"—but what does this mean? There are two possibilities:

　　　(i)　　　Perhaps the "knowledge" that is the same in such a case "is independent of what actually happens"—in which case *what happens* is not the object of this knowledge after all.

　　　(ii)　　　Perhaps instead this "knowledge" is "a funny sort of knowledge" that can *be* knowledge even when "what it [is] knowledge of [is] not the case."

(C)   And then we are reminded of the remark from the *Magna Moralia*, and the distinction between mistakes in judgment and ones in performance.

It seems clear that the position in (B(i)) would be in conflict with what earlier I called Anscombe's *factualist* account of the content of an agent's non-observational knowledge.[32] For Anscombe, a statement of the form

(1)   I am doing X

or

(2)   I am going to do X,

where this statement expresses the intention of acting in the way described, has the very descriptive content that it wears on its face: a statement like (1) or (2) *makes a claim about the world*. And the same thing is true of an agent's practical knowledge of her action: it is knowledge of the *same* object that can also be known through perception by an outside observer. That is emphasized in an important passage from Section 28 that sets the stage for the problem we are trying to resolve:

> Someone who hears me moving calls out: What are you doing making that noise? I reply "Opening the window." I have called such a statement knowledge all along; and precisely because in such a case what I say is true—I do open the window; and that means that the window is getting opened by the movements of the body out of whose mouth those words come. (§28, 51:2)

For Anscombe, *what I know* in knowing that I am opening a window is nothing short of the fact that *the window is getting opened by my movements*. That is, my knowledge of what I am doing is nothing short of knowledge of *what happens* when I act, insofar as what happens "is actually the execution of an intention" (§48, 87:4). But none of this would hold if practical knowledge were independent of what actually happens, as in that case it would not be knowledge *of* what happens after all.[33] So the position in (B(i)) cannot be hers.

---

[32] See the discussion in section 3.5, with reference to section 1.2.

[33] This is also the point of the paragraph that diagnoses "the temptation to make the real object of willing just an idea" (§45, 82:5–83:1)—this is a *temptation*, because what it tempts us to think is mistaken.

What about the position in (B(ii))? If Anscombe favored this position then perhaps she would have a reply to the argument from possible failure. She could reject premise (P2), since if it is possible to have practical knowledge of things that are not the case then this knowledge will not be governed by the usual safety condition, and a person who lacks confidence in what she is intentionally doing will only *think* that she lacks knowledge of her act. Anscombe might seem to endorse this response in some of what she says at the end of Section 32, namely that we need to get around the "incorrigibly contemplative" conception of knowledge as "something that is judged as such by being in accordance with the facts" (§32, 57:3)—for does this not suggest that we can know things even when our knowledge does not accord with them? But this is not a satisfying reading of Anscombe's position, and there are many passages in *Intention* that conflict with it. For example, when she introduces the concept of non-observational knowledge in Section 8 she says that there is a point of speaking of "knowledge" only where "there is a possibility of being right or wrong," i.e., only where "a contrast exists between 'he *knows*' and 'he (merely) *thinks* he knows' " (§8, 14:1)—and endorsing the position in (B(ii)) would conflict with this constraint. She echoes this point later on in the passage from Section 28 that we just considered: statements like (1) and (2), no less than corresponding "estimates" with the same descriptive content, stand the risk of being *falsified* if things in the world are not as they say them to be.[34] The idea that Anscombe would now turn this all on its head, holding that *practical* knowledge is not governed by this same constraint, is simply incredible. If practical knowledge is "funny" in this way, it does not live up to the name.

So we do not yet have a way around the argument from possible failure. The final sentence (C) in the paragraph from Section 45 reminds us of the special *sort* of falsity, or proneness to falsity, that we find in the cases at issue—it is a sort of falsity where "we do *not* say: What you *said* was a mistake, because it was supposed to describe what you did and did not describe it" (§32, 57:1). The reason for this is that the *aim* of practical knowledge is not to describe, but rather to *direct*, the action that is its object. And this accounts for why practical knowledge is not "judged as such by being in accordance with the facts" (§32, 57:3). For a person's intentional action is not an *independent* reality that her description of it aims to accord with, or "reflect," but rather a reality that is dependent on, and "measured" by, the

---

[34] For reference to other passages that challenge this interpretation of Anscombe's position, see my discussion of Sections 31–32 in section 4.3.

agent's own understanding of what she does. Nevertheless this understanding *is* a description of the agent's action—indeed, it is only because of this that an agent's self-knowledge can ever amount to knowledge of what happens.[35] So the reminder in (C) must not be a way of leading us down any of the false avenues that we just explored in connection with (B). But then it is hard to see what premise in the argument this passage invites us to reject.

(3) Let us consider a few other things that we might say on Anscombe's behalf in order to resist the argument from possible failure. A first thing to note is that the safety and confidence conditions appealed to in (P1) and (P2) are both anachronistic, and neither corresponds directly to anything in the text of *Intention*. One might argue further that these conditions are relevant only to *speculative* knowledge that is supposed to be "derived from the objects known" (*I*, §48, 87:4), and drop out of the picture when we are concerned with practical knowledge that is productive of its object. While the first point is correct as far as it goes, the use to which the concepts of confidence and safety are put in this argument does not carry a lot of philosophical baggage, and it is hard to find fault with the assumption that knowledge *in general* is governed by conditions like these. To the second point, it is hard to see why the fact that an agent's knowledge of her action aims at the production of its object, and that the reality of her action depends in turn on the way it is comprehended in her practical reasoning, means that this action can be *known* through her practical reasoning even when the agent is uncertain of what she is doing, or when her belief about what she is doing could easily have been wrong. If the thesis that intentional action is practically known means only that a person who is doing something intentionally must believe, with some degree of confidence, that she is doing this, then the thesis would be much less ambitious than we took it to be, and would not have required this extensive defense.

Another way to resist the argument is by questioning the assumption, implicit in premise (P2), that *belief* in what one does is a necessary component of practical knowledge.[36] Against this assumption, one might argue that belief is always a state of mind that is answerable to how things independently are—a state with respect to which "the facts, reality, are prior,

---

[35] Compare Aquinas, who writes that whereas "speculative reason only apprehends things, ... practical reason *not only apprehends but also causes them*" (*ST* II–II, q. 33, a. 1c; emphasis added).

[36] I'm grateful to Kim Frost for pointing out to me that the argument depends on this assumption, and for suggesting the response that I consider in what follows.

and determine what is to be [believed], if it is knowledge" (§32, 57:3). As we have seen, on Anscombe's view a person's knowledge of her own intentional actions does not have this *reflective, receptive* character—indeed, that is precisely the point of calling it *practical* knowledge. Can we, then, take her to reject the assumption that this knowledge always involves an appropriate sort of belief?

The initial difficulty with this response is simply that the practical intellect of a finite agent is necessarily fallible: we *can* be mistaken in what we take ourselves to be intentionally doing, and so it seems that there should be some concept to describe the cognitive state of a person who is in this position.[37] By the same token, it seems that we should be able to distinguish the cognitive state of someone who acts from *knowledge* that, e.g., the background conditions are in place that are necessary for her action to succeed, from the state of someone who acts from the mere *belief* that this is the case. (Remember that knowledge of these background conditions will be theoretical rather than practical, so there is no room for controversy in talking about belief in this context.[38]) In ordinary speech we would use the distinction between knowledge and mere belief to mark this contrast. For example, just as we might say of someone who is working furiously at a pump while, unbeknownst to him, the water flows out of a hole in the pipe, that

(3)   He *thinks* he is filling that cistern, but he is not

so it seems natural for a person who worries that he is in an unfavorable situation to describe what he is doing by saying, e.g., that

(4)   I *think* I am filling the cistern, but I am not really sure about that.

One does need to be careful in building a theory of knowledge from these claims about ordinary usage, but as long as talk of "belief" in the argument from possible failure is meant only to mark these pre-theoretical contrasts, it seems that the burden of proof will be on those who want to resist it.

A final reply says that just as a belief must be "safely" true in order to count as knowledge, so action must be executed "safely" in order to count as something intentionally done. So far this is surely right: if, e.g., I want to poison some Nazis and pick *at random* a pump that, as it happens,

---

[37] Another difficulty is that it is not at all clear that there cannot be such a thing as practical belief. For a detailed discussion of what practical belief could be, see my paper with Berislav Marušić, "Intending Is Believing."

[38] Thus Anscombe talks of "knowledge or opinion" pertaining to "the topic of an intention" (§28, 50:3).

supplies poisoned water to their house water-supply, then in operating the pump I am poisoning Nazis just as I intend, but not thereby poisoning them *intentionally*.[39] Could it be that all the cases of true but unsafe belief about what one is doing are also cases where the success of one's action is also too "lucky" or unsafe for it to count as intentional? In addition to the difficulty in stabilizing our intuitions about the ways that luck undermines knowledge and intentional agency, the problem with this response is that a statement like (4) seems *both* to deny knowledge of one's action under the description "filling the cistern" *and* to accept that the question "Why are you filling that cistern?" could be answered positively by giving a reason for acting, e.g., saying that

(5)   I am doing it in order to poison the inhabitants of that house.

This seems to show that knowledge that one is doing something is not, after all, necessary for a "Why?"-question to have application to this action, so described.

(4) I conclude, with some reluctance, that Anscombe's condition (C1) does not hold with perfect generality. In fact this conclusion could have been anticipated back when Anscombe first put forward her condition, supporting it by saying that her question "Why?"

> is refused application by the answer: "I was not aware I was doing that." Such an answer is, not indeed a proof (since it may be a lie), but a claim, that the question "Why did you do it (are you doing it)?," in the required sense, has no application. (*I*, §6, 11:4)

The problem with Anscombe's reasoning here is that in ordinary usage, the statement that

(6)   I did not know (/was not aware) that *p*

carries the implication that one had *no idea* that *p* was the case, and not just that one didn't have *knowledge* of this. For example, if I suspect that your spouse is being unfaithful and my suspicion turns out correct, it would be misleading for me to say that I didn't know she was being unfaithful, despite the fact that this is true—I *didn't* know, but only had a suspicion.[40] Or again,

---

[39] Cf. Anscombe's remark that "an intended effect just occasionally comes about by accident" (§23, 39:1).

[40] Of course I might say something like, "I didn't *know* that she was cheating—this is why I never shared the worry with you". But in this case the context, and the special emphasis on "know," cancel the usual implicature.

if I were being questioned about actions carried out under orders by my unreliable surrogates, whom I could not really trust to do what I said, it would be misleading for me to say that I didn't know that they were doing what I told them to. This shows that if we are using "know" in the sense that requires confidence and safety in one's grasp of a fact, the argument by which Anscombe introduces her condition (C1) fails to support that condition over a much weaker one like the following:

(C1*)   A person does something intentionally only if she *has some idea* that she is doing it.

It would, however, be a mistake simply to jettison Anscombe's (C1) for a weaker condition like (C1*). This is because the circumstances in which her condition (C1) is not satisfied are decidedly unusual: it takes some philosophical ingenuity to construct them, and we don't often encounter situations like these in ordinary life. Why is that? Likely it is not because we just *happen* usually to act in favorable circumstances rather than unfavorable ones. It seems instead as if self-knowing action is the *paradigmatic* form of intentional agency, so that when someone acts intentionally but without knowledge of her action there must be some special circumstance that accounts for why this is. This suggests a reading of (C1) as describing not a strictly necessary condition of intentional action, but rather a condition that holds, as Aristotle would have put it, "for the most part." It would thus have a force similar to many of our generalizations about things in the natural world, such as the scientifically supported statement that

(7)   The common fruit fly *D. melanogaster* has a lifespan of about twenty-one days.

The reason why (7) can be true even though the majority of fruit flies are killed before 21 days is that "killing" is an event that *interferes* with the usual or "normal" life of a fruit fly. The fact that a fruit fly was killed is a *special* explanation of why it lived, say, only a week, whereas no such explanation will be required for why a fruit fly lives longer than that. ("Why is that thing still around after two and a half weeks?"—"It's a fruit fly.") And a similar sort of explanation seems to be required for an agent's failure to know what she is doing in the cases that I have presented as counterexamples to (C1). It is *because* someone is in an unfavorable situation, such that he doesn't know (say) which pump is the right one, or can't operate the pump reliably, etc., and—this is something I will return to shortly—is barred from any evidence that would show that things are going just fine, that such a person may lack knowledge of what he is intentionally doing. Similarly for Davidson's carbon-copier, who is doing a difficult thing and can't see through to the bottom,[41] and also for one who writes on the board with her eyes closed or supervises a faraway project without any reports on how it is going. We can *understand why* these agents do not manage to know what they are doing, but this requires recognizing the features of the agents and their situation that *keep* them from knowing, such that there is something deviant or abnormal about these cases, in contrast to what happens usually and for the most part.[42] And no such explanation is required, concerning a person who does something intentionally and with knowledge of it, to explain why it is that she knows what she does. This suggests that even if there are exceptions to condition (C1), it can still succeed in characterizing the paradigmatic form of intentional activity that is the primary concern of the present inquiry.

6.5 Practical knowledge through perception?

The final thing to consider is how Anscombe's account of practical knowledge bears on her condition (C2):

(C2) A person does something intentionally only if she *knows without observation* that she is doing it.

The arguments of the preceding section explored whether acting intentionally requires having *knowledge* of what one is doing after all, so here we will focus our attention on the remainder:

(C2*) If a person does something intentionally, then if she knows she is doing this her knowledge is knowledge without observation, and if she merely believes she is doing this then her belief is not based in observation, etc.

---

[41] For this case, see section 4.1.

[42] Compare Anscombe's remark that it is "necessarily the rare exception ... for a man's performance in its more immediate descriptions not to be what he supposes" (§48, 87:2). But of course it is not just *these* descriptions that we are supposed to be concerned with—on this point see the discussion in section 4.2.

In order to give a counterexample to (C2*), we need to describe a case where (i) a person is doing something intentionally, (ii) the person knows or believes that she is doing this, and (iii) this knowledge or belief is reached *through observation*. This concept of what knowledge or belief is reached *through* is a justificatory concept: thus Anscombe writes that the knowledge of an intentional action is not "*based on* observation, inference, hearsay, [or] superstition" (*I*, §28, 50:3; emphasis mine), or not "*verified by* the senses" (§30, 54:1; emphasis mine). In what follows we will consider more closely why this restriction is so important.

Is it possible to act intentionally in a way that fails to satisfy condition (C2*)? In earlier work I presented what I took to be a counterexample to it.[43] Suppose that the man working at the pump has been informed that the pipe running from the pump to the cistern is frequently broken, but is given a device that can measure the quantity of poison in the party chiefs' water-supply. And suppose further that as he operates the pump, he sees on the device that the levels of poison are rising, and *thereby* knows that his pumping is replenishing the water-supply of the party chiefs' house. In this case, the man's knowledge that he is replenishing the water-supply seems like an instance of *practical* knowledge according to the account I gave in section 6.3: it is knowledge of what he does under the form of description given in the series A–D, and this knowledge plays an integral role in the man's execution of his intention. Nevertheless, it seems to be through *perception* that the man knows that he is doing this. That is, he relies on perception not just for background information "concerning what is the case, and what can happen ... if one does certain things" (§28, 50:3), but also in order to know *what he is doing*, i.e., that the event of his filling the poison with cistern "is actually taking place" (§28, 50:3). It seems, then, to be a case where the man's *practical* knowledge of what he intentionally does is nevertheless knowledge *through observation*.

This case *seems* to supply just what is needed for a counterexample to (C2*). When the man at the pump observes the device showing the rising levels of poison, he *thereby* knows that he is filling the water-supply with poisoned water. Absent this observation, the man would not have this knowledge. Moreover, if the man claims to be poisoning the water-supply and we ask him *how* he knows this, he may answer that he knows this because he can *see* that he is—that is, because he *observes* the rising levels of poison in the water-supply, as represented by the display of device. Doesn't this all

---

[43] For this case, see my paper "Understanding 'Practical Knowledge,'" p. 25.

go to show that the man's knowledge that he is filling the water-supply with poison, which is a description under which Anscombe's question "Why?" has application to his action, is based on what he observes?

To soften up this intuition, let's begin by reflecting on a somewhat different case, where the action that a person is considering is in the future rather than the present.[44] Suppose that I decide to meet you in New York on Tuesday, and I express this intention by saying that I'll be there. In order for me to *know* that this is what I am going to do, I will need to have a lot of background knowledge concerning such things as when the trains are running, how to buy a ticket, which train to take in order to get to my destination, and so on. All this background knowledge will be of "theoretical" matters that I ascertain through sources such as "observation, inference, [and] hearsay" (§28, 50:3)—and thus without those essential sources of information I cannot do more than make a lucky guess in saying where I will be. Does this show, however, that my knowledge (or belief) that I am going to meet you in New York is also based in observation? This would only be the case if the relevant background facts had the role of *evidence* in light of which I conclude that this is what I'll do. And that is not the relationship that is supposed to hold between premises and conclusion in an inference like the following:

(NY)   My friend X is in New York.
              There's a train to New York on Tuesday.
              So I'll go there then.

What makes (NY) a good inference is not that the premises *verify* the conclusion, or provide sufficient evidence for thinking that it is true. (They *could* provide such evidence, say if you know that I take the train to New York whenever I have a friend to see there. But that's not how it is *for me.*[45]) And the reason for that is that (NY) is a *practical* inference, not a theoretical one: in it, the conclusion is drawn because the premises show it to be good. Even in the case where this inference is such that its conclusion is *known* to be true, that will not be because this truth was *shown* by the considerations in light of which the conclusion was reached.

I want to suggest that the same point holds for present action, i.e., in the case of "an agent who says what he is at present doing" (§32, 56:3). In the alleged counterexample that I presented, the man's statement "I am filling the cistern with poison by pumping this water into it, etc." expresses his practical

---

[44] Thanks to Beri Marušić and Juan Piñeros for discussion of this parallel.
[45] Compare again what Anscombe says about getting one's camera: §22, 35:5–36:1; and cf. my discussion of these matters in section 3.3.

understanding of what he is doing, and it is in virtue of this understanding that his action is the execution of an intention of his, i.e., a movement in which he who moves is conscious of his own movement in relation to the end it is meant to serve. This action is grounded in, and made reasonable by, the considerations in light of which he acts, but *not* because those considerations provide evidence for the belief that he is doing this. For they are rather the considerations in light of which his action has a *point*: they show, or at least are supposed to show, that what he is doing is a way of getting something that he wants. This means that, insofar as these considerations include things that he knows only through observation, inference, etc., such as that this pipe runs to the house where the party leaders live, it may be only in light of what the man observes that he can act knowledgeably rather than as a shot in the dark. But again, this does *not* mean that it is in light of observation (or inference, hearsay, etc.) that the man's understanding of what he does is justified or "well-founded" (for this term see §2, 3:5). For this judgment is not a conclusion of theoretical inference that is meant to reflect an independent reality. It is not the *sort* of judgment that aims to be an appropriate response to evidence about some "prior" facts. All this is compatible with the fact that it may be only because of what the man observes, infers, etc., that he knows what he is intentionally doing. What accounts for this is the fact that bodily action takes place *within* a pre-existing situation, and knowledge of this situation is essential to the reasoning that grounds the understanding of what one does.

None of this should seem too mysterious. The fundamental point is simply that when we act, the reality that is our action is not independent of our own thinking about it. This does not mean that this thinking cannot be mistaken, nor that it can proceed without consideration of how things are in the mind-independent world. Anscombe makes this point clearly in a crucial paragraph of Section 28 whose phrasing I have echoed several times in the preceding pages, writing that

> the topic of an intention may be matter on which there is knowledge or opinion based on observation, inference, hearsay, superstition or anything that knowledge or opinion ever are based on; or again matter on which an opinion is held without any foundation at all. When knowledge or opinion are present concerning what is the case, and what can happen—say Z—if one does certain things, say ABC, then it is possible to have the intention of doing Z in doing ABC; and if the case is one of knowledge or if the opinion is correct, then doing or causing Z is an intentional action, and it

is not by observation that one knows one is doing Z; or in so far as one is observing, inferring etc. that Z is actually taking place, one's knowledge is not the knowledge a man has of his intentional actions. (§28, 50:3)

Anscombe is saying here that human agents are unlike God in that perception is often required for us to grasp various background facts—e.g., that this is a pump, that the water in the source is poisoned, that the pipe leads to the cistern of that house over there, that operating the pump will carry water from the source to the cistern, etc.—that are presupposed in the exercise of our agential powers.[46] This understanding of "what is the case, and what can happen ... if one does certain things" is an essential input into practical reasoning, as it is only through this grasp of our circumstances that we are able to calculate how to achieve our ends through action. And this understanding is speculative or *theoretical* in the sense discussed earlier: it is an understanding of how things are *independently* of our agency, such that in acting *on* these things we are able to adapt them to our ends. But the *reasoning* through which this theoretical understanding of how things are is put to work in action is not theoretical but *practical* reasoning: it is reasoning whose conclusion is an *action* that appears as a suitable means to our further ends. It is in virtue of this practical reasoning that "it is possible to have the intention of doing Z in doing ABC"—that is, the intention, e.g., to get some better leaders into power by operating this pump, thereby pumping poisoned water into that cistern, thereby poisoning the Nazi leaders who live there. And, by the same token, it is in virtue of this reasoning that it is possible to *act* with such an intention. When a person does this, her knowledge or belief concerning what she is doing—that is, the *understanding* of her action that is drawn on in the execution of it, and brings it under the form of description whose characteristics we have been investigating—is not based in "observing, inferring etc. that [her action] is actually taking place."

Let us now return to my alleged counterexample to (C2*). I imagined that the man at the pump is using a device that tracks the level of poison in the cistern. Thanks to its display the man knows that he is filling the cistern with poison, and thus that *by* moving his arm, and so operating the pump and sending water through the pipe, etc., he is doing this. So the man makes use of

---

[46] Aquinas makes this point as well: he says that practical reasoning "take[s] for granted" principles that are known in other ways, including "facts of sense observation, for example, that this is bread or this is iron," as well as "general principles" that may be known speculatively, e.g., "that adultery is prohibited by God or that man cannot live without sufficient nourishment" (*ST* I–II, q. 14, a. 6, c). I thank Fr. Stephen Brock for pointing me to this passage.

his senses to inform him of whether poison is getting into the cistern—that is, to inform him not only of "background" facts about the circumstances of his action but also of what is actually happening as he acts.[47] It is also true that *without* making use of his senses in this way, the man would not know that he is poisoning the water-supply—even if, perhaps, he would still be doing this intentionally. This shows that the man's knowledge that he is poisoning the water-supply *depends* on what he learns through the senses. But does this entail that it is *based in observation?* It does not—no more than the dependence of the reasoning in my inference (NY) on observational knowledge of its premises shows that the conclusion of that inference is observationally known. For the man's knowledge that he is poisoning the water supply by filling the cistern, . . ., etc., is knowledge that is *grounded in his practical reasoning.* And the role of observation in practical reasoning is not to provide evidence in support of its conclusion. The man's understanding of what-he-is-doing-and-why is something that he possesses *in light of* what he observes, but this does not show that it is an observational understanding.

This distinction, between observational knowledge of the premises of a practical inference and practical knowledge of its conclusion, is central to what Anscombe says in Section 48 about her case of the project supervisor:

> Naturally my imaginary case, in which a man directs operations which he does not see and of which he gets no information, is a very improbable one. Normally someone doing or directing anything makes use of his senses, or of reports given him, the whole time: he will not go on to the next order, for example, until he knows that the preceding one has been executed, or, if he is the operator, his senses inform him of what is going on. This knowledge is of course always "speculative" as opposed to "practical." Thus in any operation we really can speak of two knowledges—the account that one could give of what one was doing, without adverting to observation; and the account of exactly what is happening at a given moment (say) to the material one is working on. The one is practical, the other speculative. (§48, 88:3–89:1)

The talk of "two knowledges" in this passage echoes Anscombe's discussion of the "difficulty" with her account in Sections 29 and 32. The difficulty had

---

[47] That is, his senses help to verify or ground his "account of exactly what is happening at a given moment . . . to the material [he] is working on" (§48, 89:1). The use of "exactly" here makes it seem as if the account that is verified by the senses might be at a finer level of detail than the descriptions under which it is intentional, but I don't believe this is what Anscombe has in mind.

been to understand how, if, e.g., *opening a window* is "making such-and-such movements with such-and-such a result," and therefore *knowing* that one is opening the window is "knowing that that is taking place," this knowledge of one's action could be knowledge without observation (§29, 51:3). This is difficult because such a thing very often *is* known by observing it, as she reminded us in Section 4: e.g., "I am sitting in a chair writing, and anyone grown to the age of reason in the same world would know this as soon as he saw me" (§4, 8:2). She went on there to contrast this ordinary observational knowledge with recondite knowledge of, e.g., "precisely how I was affecting the acoustic properties of the room" (§4, 8:2)—the point being that our usual knowledge of what a person is doing is not of the "chaos" of her movements and their effects, but rather of the practically rational order that is there *in* it.[48] Still, the *object* of this knowledge is not "just" the order itself, but also *what is going on*, insofar as "what is going on is the execution of an intention" (§48, 87:3). And the challenge was to understand how the *same* thing that can be known in this way can also be known or understood "from the inside," i.e., practically and without observation, by the one who acts.

We explored earlier how the paradoxical-sounding slogan that in acting "I *do* what *happens*" (§29, 52:6) is meant to guard against what Anscombe sees as tempting but mistaken ways of responding to this difficulty.[49] I do what happens, and I know what I do: so what I know *is* what happens, insofar as what happens is the execution of my intention. Thus there are not two objects of knowledge, but only one. The *object* of an observer's knowledge is the same as the object of an agent's: the former knowledge is speculative and the latter practical, but in each case the object known is nothing other than *what is happening* when a person acts as she intends. The passage that I just quoted clarifies this point without qualifying it: Anscombe says now that while of course a person usually "makes use of his senses" in acting, the object known or understood in this speculative or theoretical way is not *what she does*, but only "what is happening ... to the material [she] is working on." By contrast, the object of practical knowledge is nothing other than "what one [is] doing."

Notice how the conclusion that Anscombe reaches here is not the same as the conclusion of the problematic argument from the end of Section 29, which I argued earlier is an argument against her considered position in the

---

[48] Thus she writes: "Of course we have a special interest in human actions: but *what* is it that we have a special interest in here? It is not that we have a special interest in the movement of these molecules—namely, the ones in a human being; or even in the movements of certain bodies—namely human ones" (§46, 83:3). For discussion of this passage, see section 6.2.

[49] I identified these mistakes, and argued against them, in section 4.2.

voice of an imagined interlocutor, rather than Anscombe's articulation of the view she favors.[50] The argument in Section 29 says that in intentional action "the essential thing [a person] does, namely [e.g.] to write such-and-such, is done without the eyes," and that in *this* sense "without the eyes he knows what he writes" (§29, 53:1)—but that led to the verdict that knowledge of action is *not* knowledge of what actually happens, but only of this "essential" bit for which perceptual input is not needed. By contrast, in Section 48 Anscombe says just the opposite. Of course a person's action usually depends on what is known by observation, inference, hearsay, etc., insofar as these are often indispensable sources of input to practical reasoning. Her conclusion is that what a person *knows* "without the eyes" is the very same thing that is *done with them*: it is nothing but her action, informed by a practical understanding that "makes use of the senses" in calculating what to do. While one who acts intelligently and with a purpose will indeed *draw* on considerations made manifest by observation, inference, etc., in calculating how to act, this calculation is not a form of reasoning whose conclusion supposed to be *supported* by the considerations in light of which it is drawn. Instead it is reasoning through which an action is identified as a suitable means to an end, and the object that is apprehended as the conclusion of this reasoning is not a mere representation of what to do, but rather her action itself.

6.6 Summary discussion

Let us return to the paragraph that concluded Section 32:

> Can it be that there is something that modern philosophy has blankly misunderstood: namely what ancient and medieval philosophers meant by *practical knowledge*? Certainly in modern philosophy we have an incorrigibly contemplative conception of knowledge. Knowledge must be something that is judged as such by being in accordance with the facts. The facts, reality, are prior, and dictate what is to be said, if it is knowledge. And this is the explanation of the utter darkness in which we found ourselves. For if there are two knowledges—one by observation and the other in intention—then it looks as if there must be two objects of knowledge; but if one says the objects are the same, one looks hopelessly for the different

---

[50] See fn. 6 on page 106.

mode of contemplative knowledge in acting, as if there were a very queer and special sort of seeing eye in the middle of acting. (*I*, §32, 57:3)

At the end of section 4.3 (see p. 114) I distinguished four important ideas here:

- First, that the knowledge of one's intentional actions is knowledge *without observation.*

- Second, that the *normative relation* of this knowledge to what it is knowledge of is different from that of knowledge that is supposed to be an accurate record or representation of its object.

- Third, that a person's knowledge of her actions has a kind of *priority* with respect to the reality that it is knowledge of.

- Fourth, that this knowledge is *practical* rather than "contemplative."

We are now in a position to put these pieces together, and also to see why this could not be done until we understood the nature of practical reasoning. The claim in Section 31 that when a person fails to act in accord with her judgment "the mistake is not one of judgment but of performance" (§31, 55:1) does not mean that in such a case the person's judgment is knowledgeable nevertheless. Nor does Anscombe's denial that in the case of intentional action the reality known is "prior" to the knowledge of it mean that this knowledge can be properly "judged as such" even when it is *not* "in accordance with the facts" that it describes. Rather, her claim is that a person's understanding of what she is doing is the standard or—this was Aquinas's term—*measure* of its object, since it is in relation to this understanding that the failure or success of her action is determined. And it is likewise the *cause* of its object, since she who acts intentionally does so *from* her understanding of what she is doing and why, and her exercise of the capacity to act is "nothing but the doing ... of the operations of which [she] has practical knowledge" (§48, 88:2). As such, the *ground* of this knowledge is not reasoning in which a conclusion is "derived from the objects known" (§48, 87:4) in a way that aims to reflect what is anyway the case, but reasoning that concludes in an action that is performed for the sake of an end, in light of what an agent knows about herself and her circumstances. The "seeing eye" in acting is the eye of the agent herself, who discerns her material situation and reasons to action in light of what she knows. When all goes well she acts as she intends, and does so in a self-knowing manner. The object of this knowledge *is* her action—a single reality that is known practically, without observation, "in intention" by the agent and, perhaps, also through observation by others.

Suggestions for further reading

- On the contrasting roles of belief and intention in theoretical and practical knowledge, respectively, see Lucy Campbell, "An Epistemology for Practical Knowledge."

- For argument that Anscombe's requirement of non-observational knowledge can accommodate the possibilities of "slips" and failures in action, see Kevin Falvey, "Knowledge in Intention," Adrian Haddock, "The Knowledge That a Man Has of His Intentional Actions," and Michael Thompson, "Anscombe's *Intention* and Practical Knowledge."

- On the role of perception in practical reasoning and the execution of action, see Anton Ford, "Praktische Wahrnemung" and "On What Is in Front of Your Nose."

- On whether practical knowledge of action involves any *judgment* that one is doing such-and-such, see Kim Frost, "A Metaphysics for Practical Knowledge."

- For careful exegesis of Sections 44–48 that reaches interpretive conclusions different in some ways from my own, see Eylem Özaltun, "Practical Knowledge of What Happens" and Kieran Setiya, "Anscombe on Practical Knowledge."

- For an important account of how practical reasoning can be the ground of the knowledge of one's act, see Sebastian Rödl, *Self-Consciousness*, chapter 2.

- For discussion of conditions like (C1*) as possible necessary conditions on intentional action, see Kieran Setiya, "Practical Knowledge," Sarah K. Paul, "Intention, Belief, and Wishful Thinking," and Setiya, "Practical Knowledge Revisited."

- On the implicitly normative character of generalizations about living beings, see Part I of Michael Thompson's *Life and Action*. For a dissenting view of this matter, see Sarah Jane Leslie, "The Original Sin of Cognition."

7

Concluding Discussion

Intention ends in a flurry. Section 49 discusses the difference between voluntary and intentional action, and Sections 50–52 return to the topic of expression of intention for the future. The final sections especially are important in the way they reinforce the *factualist* elements of Anscombe's position that I introduced in discussing Section 2 and have revisited many times since then.

7.1 Intentional and voluntary (§49)

Anscombe said in Section 5 that her question "Why?," asked in a sense "in which the answer, if positive, gives a reason for acting" (*I*, §5, 9:3), *has application* only to what a person intentionally does. She might seem to take this back in the first thing she says in Section 49 about the difference between the voluntary and the intentional:

> (1) Mere physical movements, to whose description our question "Why?" is applicable, are called voluntary rather than intentional when (*a*) the answer is e.g. "I was fiddling," "it was a casual movement," or even "I don't know why" [or?] (*b*) the movements are not considered by the agent, though he can say what they are if he does consider them. (§49, 89:3)

Is Anscombe saying here that in conditions (*a*) or (*b*) her "Why?"-question has application to an action even though this action is not intentional? In fact she does not: her claim is rather that in these conditions we *call* movements voluntary rather than intentional even though they satisfy her condition. That is compatible with holding that they *are* in fact intentional—the point is only that it would be somehow misleading to say this about them, given the relatively low stakes.

The next two distinctions that Anscombe draws in the remainder of this paragraph are more philosophically significant, however:

(2) Something is voluntary though not intentional if it is the antecedently known concomitant result of one's intentional action, so that one could have prevented it if one would have given up the action; but it is not intentional: one rejects the question "Why?" in its connexion ...

(3) Things may be voluntary which are not one's own doing at all, but which happen to one's delight, so that one consents and does not protest against them. (§49, 89:3)

The point in both (2) and (3) is that though these actions (or happenings) are known, they are not *practically* known: that is, they are not known in a way that fits them into the order of means and ends. With (2) Anscombe reiterates the distinction between intention and foresight that she explored in Sections 25 and 27; and with (3) she makes room for the possibility of voluntary passivity.[1]

Another thing that Anscombe says in connection with the distinction in (2) permits talk of intentional but *in*voluntary actions. We may, she says, call intentional actions involuntary "if one regrets them very much, but feels 'compelled' to persist in the intentional actions in spite of that" (§49, 89:3). I take her to have in mind the sort of case that Aristotle discusses in Book III, Chapter 1 of the *Nicomachean Ethics*:

with regard to the things that are done from fear of greater evils or for some noble object (e.g. if a tyrant were to order one to do something base, having one's parents and children in his power, and if one did the action they were to be saved, but otherwise would be put to death), it may be debated whether such actions are involuntary or voluntary. Something of the sort happens also with regard to the throwing of goods overboard in a storm; for in the abstract no one throws goods away voluntarily, but on condition of its securing the safety of himself and his crew any sensible man does so. (1110a4–11)

As John Hyman has argued convincingly, the concept of voluntariness according to which an action performed under duress is classified as involuntary is essentially an *ethical* concept—that is, a concept whose function "is to inform the appraisal of individual conduct and in particular the assessment of innocence and guilt."[2] Anscombe emphasized earlier,

---

[1] For a valuable discussion of this last concept, see chapter 4 of John Hyman's *Action, Knowledge, and Will*.

[2] Hyman, *Action, Knowledge, and Will*, p. 76.

however, that the concept of intention that concerns her in *Intention* is one whose scope is *not* primarily "ethical or legal" (*I*, §25, 45:3). This is why she says that even though the man she imagined will not be poisoning the inhabitants *intentionally* by her criteria if he doesn't care about the poison and is only doing his usual job, nevertheless this difference "will not absolve him from guilt of murder" (§25, 45:3). And by the same token, if instead the man were doing this with a gun to his head, the fact that, by her criteria, he would still be poisoning the water-supply intentionally would not suffice to show that he was a murderer—for "murder" is an ethical and legal concept that usually we do not apply to actions that are carried out under duress. *Intention* is a work of philosophical psychology rather than philosophical ethics. As such, concepts like this one fall outside its scope.

7.2 Intention for the future (§§50–52)

Section 50 begins by reiterating what was argued earlier: that the expression of intention for the future is a kind of *prediction*, i.e., a statement whose descriptive *content* is the same as that of a mere "estimate" of what is going to happen (for this position, see *I*, §50, 90:2). But then in Section 52 Anscombe considers the possibility of conjoining an expression of intention together with an estimate that says the opposite, as, e.g., in

(1)   I am going for a walk—but shall not go for a walk.[3]

It is helpful to read this passage in light of Wittgenstein's discussion in Part II, Section x of the *Philosophical Investigations* of statements that have the "Moore-paradoxical" form "*P*, but I believe that not-*p*." For Wittgenstein, part of what gives Moore's paradox its bite is that in its ordinary use a statement of the form

(2)   I believe that *p*

is not *merely* a description of the speaker's state of mind. Thus he writes that

> the expression "I believe that this is the case" is used like the assertion "This is the case"; and yet the *hypothesis* that I believe that this is the case is not used like the hypothesis that this is the case. (*PI*, II.x, p. 190)

[3] See §52, 92:2.

It seems appropriate to gloss the difference that Wittgenstein points to in the second part of this quotation by recalling Anscombe's distinction in Section 2 between "the types of ground on which we call an order, and an estimate of the future, sound":

> The reasons justifying an order are not ones suggesting what is probable, or likely to happen, but e.g. ones suggesting what it would be good to make happen with a view to an objective, or with a view to a sound objective. In this regard, commands and expressions of intention are similar. (*I*, §2, 3:5–4:1)

Wittgenstein's corresponding point in the passage just quoted is that whereas the reasons in virtue of which one forms or expresses what he calls the *hypothesis* that one believes something are considerations relevant to the interpretation of one's present state of mind, the reasons in virtue of which one expresses a *belief* through a hesitant assertion with the form of (2) are considerations relevant to the truth of what is believed. And so while Wittgenstein allows that sometimes "it *looks* as if the assertion 'I believe' were not the assertion of what is supposed in the hypothesis" (*PI*, II.x, pp. 190, 191), he ultimately rejects this in favor of the view that "the statement 'I believe it is going to rain' has a meaning like, that is to say a use like, 'It's going to rain' " (p. 190): it is "a hesitant assertion" about the weather rather than "an assertion of hesitancy" about one's mind (p. 192). Therefore, while "'I believe it is so' throws light on my state, [...] so does the assertion 'It is so'" (p. 191). *Both* statements have the dual roles of expressing one's state of mind and describing how things are (believed to be). And Anscombe says something similar about the case that interests her:

> If I say I am going for a walk, someone else may know that this is not going to happen. It would be absurd to say that what he knew was not going to happen was not the very same thing that I was saying was going to happen.
>
> Nor can we say: But in an expression of intention one isn't saying anything is going to happen! Otherwise, when I had said "I'm just going to get up," it would be unreasonable later to ask "Why didn't you get up?" I could reply: "I wasn't talking about a future happening, so why do you mention such irrelevancies?" (*I*, §52, 92:4–5)

As I argued in section 1.2, the idea here is that just as one *expresses belief by talking about what is believed*, so one *expresses an intention by talking about what is going to happen*—that is, by saying what one is going to do. This is why there is a "contradiction of a sort" in a statement of the sort she considers, even in those circumstances where the statement is intelligible:

> "I am going for a walk—but shall not go for a walk" is a contradiction of a sort, even though the first part of the sentence is an expression of intention, and the second an estimate of what is going to happen. ...
>
> The contradiction consists in the fact that if the man does go for a walk, the first prediction is verified and the second falsified, and vice versa if he does not go. And yet we feel that this is not, so to speak, a head-on contradiction, like that of pairs of contradictory orders, contradictory hypotheses, or opposed intentions. (§52, 92:2–3)

The right analysis to give here is along the lines of my reading of Section 31: that the "kind of contradiction" present in this case is just that the second part of the assertion must be false if the first part is true, and vice versa. So the two parts are related as "contraries" in the Aristotelian sense: they cannot both be true at once. It is, however, because of the difference in what *grounds* the two parts of the statement that this is not a "head-on contradiction" in the way that the expression of two opposing orders, hypotheses, or intentions would be.

While much of this discussion is a reiteration of the position that Anscombe staked out in Section 2, the subsequent inquiries into the sense of "Why?" allow her to address a difficulty she left unresolved there, namely that of explaining what is the "different sort of reason" (§3, 7:2) that justifies a statement when it is an expression of intention rather than an estimate. In light of these inquiries, she can say now that this sort of reason is a *reason for acting*, i.e., a consideration in relation to which an action is shown to be good or worthwhile.[4] Thus it is that "quite generally, the applicability of the question 'Why?' to a prediction is what marks it out as an expression of intention rather than an estimate of the future" (§50, 90:2).

Yet this resolution of the earlier difficulty raises important questions of its own. On Anscombe's view, to express an intention is to say that something

---

[4] Recall, however, that on Anscombe's view what makes a consideration a "reason for acting" does not concern the content of the reason itself, but rather the *form of reasoning* in which it plays a role. Depending on whether one engages in practical or theoretical reasoning, the very same consideration, e.g., that I am a man of such-and-such an age, can figure equally as a reason for action or a reason for belief.

is going to happen—but the *grounds* on which one says this (and so thinks it, presumably) do not provide any *evidence* that things will happen as one says (or thinks). They are rather, as she put it earlier, grounds "suggesting what it would be *good to make* happen with a view to an objective" (§2, 4:1; emphasis added). One thing we therefore need to ask is how such grounds can be grounds for thinking or saying that the thing in question *will happen*, and not just that it would be good if it did. And another is why, given that we sometimes *fail* to do what we intend to, we shouldn't express our intentions only by saying, e.g., that we will do such-and-such "unless I am prevented, or I change my mind" (§52, 92:6).

While Anscombe does not address the first question directly, the place to begin answering it is by recalling that on the Aristotelian–Thomistic view of practical reasoning that she has drawn on and developed, the *object* of such reasoning must be something that lies within the agent's power.[5] Put another way, the *question* that a person uses practical reasoning to answer—that is, the question "What will I do?"—is one whose answer is *up to that person* to determine. Because of this, the reasoning by which a person arrives at her answer to this question cannot regard that answer as a matter of settled fact. For this is a case where *what the agent will do depends on her reasoning about it*, and thus she is in such a position such that, by evaluating an action as good or worthwhile, she can make it the case that she will perform it.[6]

In answer to the second question Anscombe grants that practical reasoning is of course fallible in these respects—that is, it is possible to reason practically to a *mistaken* belief about what one will do. However, she adds, the possibility of being wrong will be present in just about any case where a person makes a claim about how things are, or were, or are going to be (for this argument see §52, 92:7–93:1). Yet it would be absurd to add a clause like "unless I am wrong" (or "unless my memory deceives me," etc.) after *everything* we say, and impossible to add such a thing in all and only the *right* cases—since there are bound to be times when we think we couldn't be wrong but, as it turns out, we are. This shows that while *sometimes* it will

[5] For discussion of this concept, see section 6.3. Another way to get at this idea is to say that the truth in a statement of one's action is *practical* truth, i.e., "truth which you make true by acting. For some reason, people find this idea very difficult. In lecturing I have sometimes tried to get it across by saying: 'I am about to make it true that I am on this table.' I then climb on the table. Whether I have made it true that my hearers understand, I do not know" (Anscombe, "Practical Inference," p. 145 n. 14). Anscombe has more to say about this concept, which she borrows once again from Aristotle and Aquinas, in her essay "Practical Truth."

[6] This paragraph condenses a line of reasoning that Berislav Marušić and I develop at much greater length in our paper "Intending Is Believing."

be appropriate to say something like "I am going to do this ... unless I do not do it," this will only be when "the fact that one may not do what one is determined to do" is something that one considers (§52, 93:3)—that is, when the possibility of failure is *salient* or *relevant* in a way that warrants explicit mention.

Following this discussion, in her final paragraph Anscombe recalls a series of divisions that we encountered before,[7] in identifying three ways a person may fail to execute her intention. These are:

- Cases in which the intended action fails or is prevented;
- Cases in which the agent changes her mind about what to do; and
- Cases like that "of St. Peter, who did not change his mind about denying Christ, and was not prevented from carrying out his resolution not to, and yet did deny him" (§52, 93:3; and cf. §2, 5:1)—but not because of any *mistake* in what he did.

The first and second possibilities here are those that we discussed earlier in connection with Sections 31 and 32. But the third is so far unfamiliar, and Anscombe's diagnosis of it is difficult to follow:

St. Peter might perhaps have calculated "Since he says it, it is true"; and yet said "I will not do it." The possibility in this case arises from ignorance as to the way in which the prophecy would be fulfilled; thus St. Peter could do what he intended not to, without changing his mind, and yet do it intentionally. (§52, 94:1)

The thing that makes Peter's *ignorance* an essential element in his case is that when a person intends to do something but anticipates that in such-and-such circumstances there is a good chance that she will change her mind or fail to what she intends, she is then in a position to address this possibility through practical reasoning. For example, if I plan to pick you up at the airport and see that there is not enough gas in the tank for me to drive there, then I can fuel up first; if I recognize that I am liable to start drinking if I go out to a bar with my colleagues, then I can choose to spend my evening watching a movie instead; and so on. And it is because Peter does not have this sort of knowledge of *how* he is liable to violate his intention that he is not able to determine what he should do in order to avoid this. Indeed, even as Peter thrice does the

---

[7] For these divisions, see Table 4.2 on page 113.

very thing he intends not to do, he fails in each case to recognize that this is happening:

> Then they seized [Christ] and led him away, bringing him into the high priest's house, and Peter was following at a distance. And when they had kindled a fire in the middle of the courtyard and sat down together, Peter sat down among them.
>
> Then a servant girl, seeing him as he sat in the light and looking closely at him, said, "This man also was with him." But he denied it, saying, "Woman, I do not know him."
>
> And a little later someone else saw him and said, "You also are one of them." But Peter said, "Man, I am not."
>
> And after an interval of about an hour still another insisted, saying, "Certainly this man also was with him, for he too is a Galilean." But Peter said, "Man, I do not know what you are talking about."
>
> And immediately, while he was still speaking, the rooster crowed. And the Lord turned and looked at Peter. And Peter remembered the saying of the Lord, how he had said to him, "Before the rooster crows today, you will deny me three times." And he went out and wept bitterly. (*Lk* 22, 54–62 RSV)

Does the fact that Peter realizes only afterward that he has denied Christ show that at each moment of denial he was ignorant of what he was doing—and thus that in each case he did this unintentionally? This would be an implausible verdict, and if it followed from condition (C1) we would have reason to reject the requirement that intentional action be self-known. But this is emphatically *not* how Anscombe meant for that requirement to be understood. This point is unfortunately left implicit in *Intention*, but it comes out clearly in an unpublished manuscript that Anscombe was writing around the same time, where she discusses the possibility of "knowledge without realisation":

> "I did not think of that" or "I did not think of it like that" do not disprove knowledge. At least the condition "knowledge and consent," if it is really requisite [for the voluntariness of an act], does not mean that the matter must present itself to the [agent] as such-and-such—the condition must hold in the narrower sense,

> in which e.g. a man cannot be accused of deliberate murder
> unless he conceived himself to be engaged in killing someone.[8]

While Anscombe's concern in that paper is with the Catholic doctrine that mortal sin requires knowledge of one's wrongdoing, she clearly means to draw the same distinction in *Intention* in relation to the case of St. Peter. While Peter does not bring his actions explicitly under the concept "denial," at the time he speaks he has practical knowledge of what he is doing under a description that he understands to be equivalent to it: for he knows that he is *telling someone that he is not a follower of Jesus.* (Notice that the concept "telling" belongs in the right-hand column of Anscombe's two lists in Section 47 (see 85:3): it is something that *cannot* be done except intentionally or voluntarily. The concept "denying" surely belongs here as well.) To tell someone such a thing *is* to deny Christ, and not because of some contingent aspect of Peter's circumstances that he happens to be unaware of. Because of this, the crow of the rooster is not a means by which Peter *discovers* that he has denied his teacher, but rather a sign through he becomes *mindful* of what he has done. In saying what he did to the people in the courtyard Peter knew what his words meant, and knew whom he spoke them in reference to. Knowing this, he knew what he was doing, and did it intentionally despite not having abandoned the intention not to do it.

Anscombe's account of Peter's conflicted calculation is a bit harder to accept. One thing that is strange in Peter's case is that he takes the "estimate" in the words of Jesus to be infallible: it is not just a warning, but a guarantee, that things will be the way he says. As long as Peter understands the prophecy in this way, it is hard to see how he can reason practically to the conclusion that he will do anything other than what Christ says; and as long as he reasons *sub specie boni* it is hard to see how he can take Christ at his word—at least not without an incoherence in his view of the future. But perhaps this incoherence is exactly what we are supposed to take away. Peter is in conflict with himself. His view of the future is unstable in a similar way to the experience of an ambiguous percept, as neither appearance is unequivocal and he cannot see things *at once* in both of the ways he judges them to be. In this respect his conflict is even more direct than that of the person who makes the Moore-paradoxical judgment "*P*, but I believe that not-*p*", since there it is possible to interpret the second half of the thought as the mere attribution to oneself of a certain state of mind. But then it is also a sign of his seriousness that Peter does not rest content with the judgment that he has a

---

[8] Anscombe, "On Being in Good Faith," p. 105.

good intention.[9] As Peter looks forward to his own future, the only question he has to answer is that of what he will actually *do*.

Suggestions for further reading

- On the relation between intention and belief, and the limits of the knowledge of one's future actions, see Berislav Marušić, *Evidence and Agency*.

- For accounts of practical reasoning and intention for the future that take their bearing from Anscombe's argument in *Intention*, see Berislav Marušić and John Schwenkler, "Intending Is Believing: A Defense of Strong Cognitivism."

- On the possibility that a person's knowledge of her action may be "masked" due to the painfulness or discomfort of thinking about what she is doing, see Eric Marcus, "Reconciling Practical Knowledge with Self-Deception."

- For illuminating discussion of the parallels between self-knowledge of belief and self-knowledge of one's future actions, see Richard Moran, *Authority and Estrangement*, chapters 3 and 4 especially.

---

[9] The comedian Louis CK has a routine in which he describes sitting in the first-class cabin on an airplane and watching other passengers shuffle past him to their seats in coach. (To watch it, visit https://youtu.be/grjMbV64q60.) One of these passengers is a soldier in uniform, and as the soldier is walking past Louis considers offering him his seat—at which point he credits himself for his kindness, and decides that he deserves to stay where he is. The point would not be different if Louis had gone so far as to form an *intention* to get up. On the pathology of this sort of self-regard, see Richard Moran, *Authority and Estrangement*, chapter 5.

Glossary of Terms

A–D order The order in a series of descriptions under which an action is intentional. At one end of the series are descriptions of the agent's bodily movements, and at the other are descriptions of these movements' further effects, insofar as these effects fall within the scope of the agent's intention. The order of the series represents the means–end relations among these descriptions: e.g., if a person colors a wall (call this action "C") *by* painting it with a roller ("B") that she moves with her arm ("A"), and *because* she is redecorating ("D"), then the series "A–B–C–D" represents A and B as means of doing C and D, C and D as further intentions with which the person does A and B, and so on.

"break" The division between what a person *is doing* and what she *is going to do*. The location of this break is flexible and dependent on context: e.g., someone putting a pot of water on to boil can equally well be described as "making tea" or "boiling the water because she is going to make tea." There are limits to this, however: e.g., someone presently filling out a law school application cannot be described as *going* to law school except in a very loose sense.

calculation The form of reasoning that identifies a suitable means toward a given end. The contrast here is with reasoning whose premises are supposed to provide a *proof* of the conclusion that is drawn from them.

"cause of what it understands" A phrase from St. Thomas Aquinas that characterizes the relation of an agent's self-knowledge to the action that it is knowledge of. In doing something intentionally, a person acts as she does *because of her knowledge* of her action, and the reality of her action depends on her own knowledge of it.

desire The first principle or *arché* of practical reasoning must be something that the agent desires. For example, a person who reasons "Jersey cows give excellent milk, and they have some good ones for sale at Hereford market" will conclude by *going* to Hereford only if she wants to buy a milking cow. Anscombe argues further that in order for desire to rationalize action it must be a way of seeing the desired object "under the aspect of some good."

estimate   A description of the world that is justified, if at all, by considerations showing that what it describes is likely to be true. For example, the statement "I am going to be awake all night" will be an *estimate* of what one will do if it would be supported by saying that one feels restless and has had a lot of coffee to drink, etc.

expression of intention   A description of one's present or future action that is justified, if at all, by considerations showing that it would be good to act in the manner described. For example, the statement "I am going to be awake all night" will *express the intention* to do this if it would be supported by saying that one needs to be up studying for a test.

"for no reason"   The statement that one is doing something "for no reason" (or "just because I thought I would," etc.) is not a way of refusing application of the question "Why?"—and so things can be done intentionally even if one has no reason for doing them. But it would be impossible to have a robust concept of intentional action unless this question "Why?" could *sometimes* be answered positively by giving reasons for acting.

form of description   An event is characterized as an intentional action whenever it is brought under the form of description that gives application to the question "Why?" Sometimes this is done through the use of words like "by," "because," and "in order to": e.g., if I say that someone jumped in order to get over an obstacle, I have thereby characterized her jumping as an intentional action. Many other action concepts have this teleological structure internal to their sense: e.g., to describe someone as *paying* for something is already to say that she is giving a person money *in order to* compensate them for a purchase, etc.

further intention   A thing that one is doing, or is going to do, that can be described in answer to the question "Why are you doing such-and-such?" We describe the further intention with which a person does A whenever we say that she is doing A *because* she is doing B (e.g., signing her name because she is filling out a contract), or that she is doing A *in order* to do C (e.g., going to the store in order to buy some milk).

intentional action   Intentional actions are defined preliminarily as those actions to which a question like "Why are you doing that?," asked in a sense that would be answered positively by giving one's reasons for acting, has application. This question is given application by describing one's motives or further intentions, or by saying that one is doing the thing "for no reason." Its application is refused by saying that one did not know that she was acting in the way in question, or knew this only by observation, or that the action was the result of a mere cause or a side-effect of something else that was intentionally done. This culminates in an account of intentional action as that which is *practically known* in the execution of an intention.

mental cause If I say, e.g., that I knocked over a glass because I was startled by a loud noise, I have described the noise as a *mental cause* of what I did. Mental causes differ from reasons for acting in being necessarily conscious and episodic, and action due to merely mental causes is not subject to the same kind of *normative* appraisal as action for a reason: thus "It isn't good to be so easily startled—maybe you should do some calming exercises" expresses a different sort of criticism than "Don't get your vitamins by eating that awful food—you can have some of this better tasting dish instead."

mistake in performance A person's description of her own intentional action will be inaccurate if she fails to act in the manner that she describes, as when, e.g., I say that I'll be in class but then sleep through my alarm clock, or say that I'm putting a call on hold when in fact I press the button to hang up. In such a case we do not necessarily impugn the person for having *said* something mistaken—for the mistake may lie rather in what she *did*.

motive Anscombe distinguishes four ways that a "Why?"-question may be answered by giving a motive for action. A motive explanation is *backward-looking* if it describes a past circumstance that the action is a response to (e.g., "I killed him because he killed my father"), *forward-looking* if it describes a future objective of the action (e.g., "I did it from the motive of gain"), *interpretative* if it aims to put the action in a certain light (e.g., "I did it out of admiration"), and *mixed* if it involves a combination of the above. Motives are distinguished from dispositions and mental causes, and treated as a species of reason for acting—though it is argued that the concepts of backward-looking and interpretative motive are not enough on their own to ground a robust concept of intentional action.

observation Observation, inference, and hearsay are all ways we have of knowing what happens in the world. They are not, however, possible routes to *self*-knowledge—so they cannot be ways that a person knows what she herself does intentionally, and nor can they be ways that she knows her own reasons for acting.

practical knowledge Not just a general capacity or knowledge of how to do such-and-such a thing, but a special manner of knowing *what one does* on a particular occasion. This knowledge is practical, rather than contemplative, due to its role in producing the action that it is knowledge of. And its basis in the agent's practical reasoning means that it is knowledge without observation.

practical reasoning The reasoning through which a person decides what to do. The *form* of this reasoning is different from that of reasoning whose premises are supposed to prove the truth of the conclusion that is drawn from them, as, e.g., in "This man is a beggar, and all beggars need money, so this man here must need some money." This is not how we reason to action: e.g., one who reasons "People like me need Vitamin X, and there is a lot of Vitamin X in this food, so I'll have some" has not even attempted to give a proof of what she will (or should) do. Rather, the conclusion "So I'll have some" is drawn insofar as this is *calculated* as a way of getting some Vitamin X.

prediction A description of what is going to happen—specifically, in the present case, of what one is going to do. Anscombe argues that both estimates *and* expressions of intention are kinds of prediction. In expressing the intention to do something, a person describes her present or future action, and not the state of mind from which she speaks.

reason for acting A consideration is treated as a reason for acting when it is used to explain why a person did (or is doing, is going to do) a certain thing intentionally—or, equivalently, when someone does (or decides to do) something intentionally because of it. For example, in "She is turning right onto Main Street because she is driving to the store" and "I am driving to the store, so I will turn right here," the fact that the person is *driving to the store* is treated as her reason for turning right.

refusing application A question like "Why did you do that?" is refused application by a statement indicating that the action in question was not intentional. For example, in answer to "Why did you wake up the baby?," the statements "I didn't know she was sleeping!" and "I was trying not to—but needed to get something out of her bedroom" both admit doing the thing in question, but deny that this was part of one's intention.

under a description A person may be doing X intentionally and not doing Y intentionally even though "doing X" and "doing Y" describe one and the same action. For example, if A drinks from B's cup because she thinks that it is her own, then her action is intentional under the description "drinking from the cup" but not under the description "drinking from B's cup."

"Why?" There is a sense of "Why?" in which a question like "Why did you do X?" can be given a positive answer only if X was done intentionally. This is different from the sense of "Why?" that can be answered positively by giving a mere cause or describing the action in question as a side-effect. To answer a "Why?"-question by giving a reason for acting is already to characterize the action as intentional: thus, e.g., in the exchange "Why did you look that way?"—"To see if the parade was coming," the answer represents *looking that way* as something one intentionally did.

Bibliography

Alvarez, Maria and John Hyman. 1998. "Agents and Their Actions." *Philosophy* 73: 219–245.

Annas, Julia. 1976. "Davidson and Anscombe on 'the Same Action.'" *Mind* 85: 251–257.

Anscombe, G.E.M. 1963. *Intention.* 2nd edn. Harvard University Press.

Anscombe, G.E.M. 1981a. "Causality and Determination." In *Metaphysics and the Philosophy of Mind: Collected Philosophical Papers, Volume II,* 133–147. Basil Blackwell.

Anscombe, G.E.M. 1981b. "The First Person." In *Metaphysics and the Philosophy of Mind: Collected Philosophical Papers, Volume II,* 21–36. Basil Blackwell.

Anscombe, G.E.M. 1981c. "The Intentionality of Sensation: A Grammatical Feature." In *Metaphysics and the Philosophy of Mind: Collected Philosophical Papers, Volume II,* 3–20. Basil Blackwell.

Anscombe, G.E.M. 1981d. "Modern Moral Philosophy." In *Ethics, Religion and Politics: Collected Philosophical Papers, Volume III,* 26–42. Basil Blackwell.

Anscombe, G.E.M. 1981e. "Mr Truman's Degree." In *Ethics, Religion and Politics: Collected Philosophical Papers, Volume III,* 62–71. Basil Blackwell.

Anscombe, G.E.M. 1981f. "On Promising and Its Justice, and Whether It Need Be Respected *in Foro Interno.*" In *Ethics, Religion and Politics: Collected Philosophical Papers, Volume III,* 10–21. Basil Blackwell.

Anscombe, G.E.M. 1981g. "The Two Kinds of Error in Action." In *Ethics, Religion and Politics: Collected Philosophical Papers, Volume III,* 3–9. Basil Blackwell.

Anscombe, G.E.M. 1981h. "Under a Description." In *Metaphysics and the Philosophy of Mind: Collected Philosophical Papers, Volume II,* 208–219. Basil Blackwell.

Anscombe, G.E.M. 1981i. "War and Murder." In *Ethics, Religion and Politics: Collected Philosophical Papers, Volume III,* 51–61. Basil Blackwell.

Anscombe, G.E.M. 2005a. "Practical Inference." In *Human Life, Action and Ethics: Essays by G.E.M. Anscombe,* edited by Mary Geach and Luke Gormally, 149–158. Imprint Academic.

Anscombe, G.E.M. 2005b. "Action, Intention and 'Double Effect.'" In *Human Life, Action and Ethics: Essays by G.E.M. Anscombe,* edited by Mary Geach and Luke Gormally, 207–226. Imprint Academic.

Anscombe, G.E.M. 2005c. "Does Oxford Moral Philosophy Corrupt Youth?" In *Human Life, Action and Ethics: Essays by G.E.M. Anscombe,* edited by Mary Geach and Luke Gormally, 161–167. Imprint Academic.

Anscombe, G.E.M. 2005d. "Glanville Williams' *The Sanctity of Life and the Criminal Law*: A Review." In *Human Life, Action and Ethics: Essays by G.E.M. Anscombe*, edited by Mary Geach and Luke Gormally, 243–248. Imprint Academic.

Anscombe, G.E.M. 2005e. "Practical Truth." In *Human Life, Action and Ethics: Essays by G.E.M. Anscombe*, edited by Mary Geach and Luke Gormally, 149–158. Imprint Academic.

Anscombe, G.E.M. 2008. "On Being in Good Faith." In *Faith in a Hard Ground: Essays on Religion, Philosophy and Ethics by G.E.M. Anscombe*, edited by Mary Geach and Luke Gormally, 101–112. Imprint Academic.

Aquinas, T. 1999. *Commentary on Aristotle's De Anima*. Yale University Press.

Aquinas, Thomas. 1983. *Treatise on Happiness*. University of Notre Dame Press.

Aquinas, Thomas. 2006. *Summa Theologiae: Questions on God*. Cambridge University Press.

Aristotle. 1984. *Complete Works*. Princeton University Press.

Armstrong, D.M. 1981. "The Nature of Mind." In *The Nature of Mind and Other Essays*, 1–15. Cornell University Press.

Austin, J.L. 1956–1957. "A Plea for Excuses." *Proceedings of the Aristotelian Society* 57: 1–30.

Boyle, Matthew and Douglas Lavin. 2010. "Goodness and Desire." In *Desire, Practical Reason, and the Good*, edited by Sergio Tenenbaum, 161–201. Oxford University Press.

Bratman, Michael E. 1999a. "Davidson's Theory of Intention." In *Faces of Intention: Selected Essays on Intention and Agency*, 209–224. Cambridge University Press.

Bratman, Michael E. 1999b. *Intention, Plans, and Practical Reason*. CSLI Publications.

Campbell, Lucy. 2018a. "An Epistemology for Practical Knowledge." *Canadian Journal of Philosophy* 48: 159–177.

Campbell, Lucy. 2018b. "Two Notions of Intentional Action? Solving a Puzzle in Anscombe's *Intention*." *British Journal for the History of Philosophy* 26: 578–602.

Candlish, S. and N. Damnjanovic. 2013. "Reasons, Actions, and the Will: The Fall and Rise of Causalism." In *The Oxford Handbook of the History of Analytic Philosophy*, edited by Michael Beaney, 689–708. Oxford University Press.

Cavanaugh, T.A. 2016. "Anscombe, Thomson, and Double Effect." *American Catholic Philosophical Quarterly* 90: 263–280.

Coope, Ursula. 2007. "Aristotle on Action." *Aristotelian Society Supplementary Volume* 81: 109–138.

Dancy, Jonathan. 2000. *Practical Reality*. Oxford University Press.

Dancy, Jonathan. 2018. *Practical Shape: A Theory of Practical Reasoning*. Oxford University Press.

Davidson, Donald. 1980a. "Agency." In *Essays on Actions and Events*, 43–62. Oxford University Press.

Davidson, Donald. 1980b. "Freedom to Act." In *Essays on Actions and Events*, 63–82. Oxford University Press.

Davidson, Donald. 1981. "Actions, Reasons, and Causes." In *Essays on Actions and Events*, 3–19. Oxford University Press.

Davidson, Donald. 1982. "Intending." In *Essays on Actions and Events*, 83–102. Oxford University Press.

Donnellan, Keith S. 1963. "Knowing What I Am Doing." *Journal of Philosophy* 60: 401–409.

Doyle, James. 2018. *No Morality, No Self: Anscombe's Radical Skepticism*. Harvard University Press.

Falvey, Kevin. 2000. "Knowledge in Intention." *Philosophical Studies* 99: 21–44.

Fernandez, Patricio A. 2014. "Reasoning and the Unity of Aristotle's Account of Animal Motion." *Oxford Studies in Ancient Philosophy* 47: 151–205.

Fernandez, Patricio A. 2016. "Practical Reasoning: Where the Action Is." *Ethics* 126: 869–900.

Ford, Anton. 2011. "Action and Generality." In *Essays on Anscombe's* Intention, edited by Anton Ford, Jennifer Hornsby, and Frederick Stoutland, 76–104. Harvard University Press.

Ford, Anton. 2013. "Praktische Wahrnehmung." *Deutsche Zeitschrift für Philosophie* 3: 403–418.

Ford, Anton. 2015. "The Arithmetic of Intention." *American Philosophical Quarterly* 52: 129–143.

Ford, Anton. 2016. "On What Is in Front of Your Nose." *Philosophical Topics* 44: 141–161.

Ford, Anton. 2017. "The Representation of Action." *Royal Institute of Philosophy Supplement* 80: 217–233.

Ford, Anton. 2018. "The Province of Human Agency." *Noûs* 52: 697–720.

Frey, Christopher and Jennifer A. Frey. 2017. "G.E.M. Anscombe on the Analogical Unity of Intention in Perception and Action." *Analytic Philosophy* 58: 202–247.

Frey, Jennifer. Forthcoming. "Practical Knowledge and Double Effect." In *Intention and Double-Effect: Theoretical and Practical Challenges*, edited by John O'Callaghan and Craig Iffland. University of Notre Dame Press.

Frost, Kim. 2014. "On the Very Idea of Direction of Fit." *Philosophical Review* 123: 429–484.

Frost, Kim. 2019. "A Metaphysics for Practical Knowledge." *Canadian Journal of Philosophy* 49: 314–340.

Geach, Mary. 2011. "Introduction." In *From Plato to Wittgenstein: Essays by G.E.M. Anscombe*, edited by Mary Geach and Luke Gormally, xiii–xx. Imprint Academic.

Haddock, Adrian. 2005. "At One with Our Actions, but at Two with Our Bodies." *Philosophical Explorations* 8: 157–172.

Haddock, Adrian. 2011. "The Knowledge That a Man Has of His Intentional Actions." In *Essays on Anscombe's* Intention, edited by Anton Ford, Jennifer Hornsby, and Frederick Stoutland, 147–169. Harvard University Press.

Hanser, Matthew. 2005. "Permissibility and Practical Inference." *Ethics* 115: 443–470.

Hare, R.M. 1952. *The Language of Morals*. Clarendon Press.

Hornsby, Jennifer. 1997. "Agency and Causal Explanation." In *The Philosophy of Action*, edited by Alfred R. Mele, 283–307. Oxford University Press.

Hornsby, Jennifer. 1998. "Dualism in Action." *Royal Institute of Philosophy Supplement* 43: 377–401.

Hornsby, Jennifer. 2011. "Actions in Their Circumstances." In *Essays on Anscombe's Intention*, edited by Anton Ford, Jennifer Hornsby, and Frederick Stoutland, 105–127. Harvard University Press.

Hornsby, Jennifer. 2013. "Basic Activity." *Aristotelian Society Supplementary Volume* 87: 1–18.

Hubbs, Graham. 2016. "Anscombe on Intentions and Commands." *Klesis* 35: 90–107.

Hursthouse, Rosalind. 2000. "Intention." *Royal Institute of Philosophy Supplement* 46: 83–105.

Hyman, John. 2015. *Action, Knowledge, and Will*. Oxford University Press.

Kaveny, M. Cathleen. 2004. "Inferring Intention from Foresight." *Law Quarterly Review* 120: 81–107.

Kenny, Anthony. 2016. "Elizabeth Anscombe at Oxford." *American Catholic Philosophical Quarterly* 90: 181–189.

Lavin, Douglas. 2013. "Must There Be Basic Action?" *Noûs* 47: 273–301.

Lavin, Douglas. 2015. "Action as a Form of Temporal Unity: On Anscombe's *Intention*." *Canadian Journal of Philosophy* 45: 609–629.

Leslie, Sarah Jane. 2017. "The Original Sin of Cognition: Fear, Prejudice, and Generalization." *Journal of Philosophy* 114: 393–421.

Malle, Bertram F. 2006. "Intentionality, Morality, and Their Relationship in Human Judgment." *Journal of Cognition and Culture* 6: 87–112.

Marcus, Eric. 2012. *Rational Causation*. Harvard University Press.

Marcus, Eric. Forthcoming. "Reconciling Practical Knowledge with Self-Deception." *Mind*.

Marcus, Eric and John Schwenkler. Forthcoming. "Assertion and Transparent Self-Knowledge." *Canadian Journal of Philosophy*.

Marušić, Berislav. 2015. *Evidence and Agency: Norms of Belief for Promising and Resolving*. Oxford University Press.

Marušić, Berislav and John Schwenkler. 2018. "Intending Is Believing: A Defense of Strong Cognitivism." *Analytic Philosophy* 59: 309–340.

Moran, Richard. 2001. *Authority and Estrangement*. Princeton University Press.

Moran, Richard. 2017. "Anscombe on Practical Knowledge." In *The Philosophical Imagination: Selected Essays*, 219–240. Oxford University Press.

Moran, Richard and Martin Stone. 2011. "Anscombe on Expression of Intention: An Exegesis." In *Essays on Anscombe's Intention*, edited by Anton Ford, Jennifer Hornsby, and Frederick Stoutland, 33–75. Harvard University Press.

Moss, Jessica. 2010. "Aristotle's Non-Trivial, Non-Insane View That Everyone Always Desires Things under the Guise of the Good." In *Desire, Practical Reason, and the Good*, edited by Sergio Tenenbaum, 65–81. Oxford University Press.

Müller, Anselm W. 1979. "How Theoretical Is Practical Reason?" In *Intention and Intentionality*, edited by Cora Diamond and Jenny Teichman, 91–107. Cornell University Press.

Özaltun, Eylem. 2016. "Practical Knowledge of What Happens: A Reading of §45." *Klesis* 35: 52–73.

Paul, Sarah K. 2009a. "How We Know What We're Doing." *Philosophers' Imprint* 9: 1–24.

Paul, Sarah K. 2009b. "Intention, Belief, and Wishful Thinking: Setiya on 'Practical Knowledge.'" *Ethics* 119: 546–557.

Price, A.W. 2011. "Aristotle on Practical Reasoning." In *Virtue and Reason in Plato and Aristotle*, 189–250. Oxford University Press.

Prichard, H.A. 2002. "Acting, Willing, Desiring." In *Moral Writings*, edited by Jim MacAdam, 272–281. Oxford University Press.

Quinn, Warren. 1989. "Actions, Intentions, and Consequences." *Philosophy and Public Affairs* 334–351.

Rödl, Sebastian. 2007. *Self-Consciousness*. Harvard University Press.

Rödl, Sebastian. 2010. "The Form of the Will." In *Desire, Practical Reason, and the Good*, edited by Sergio Tenenbaum, 138–161. Oxford University Press.

Rödl, Sebastian. 2011. "Two Forms of Practical Knowledge and Their Unity." In *Essays on Anscombe's* Intention, edited by Anton Ford, Jennifer Hornsby, and Frederick Stoutland, 211–241. Harvard University Press.

Ross, W.D. 2002. "What Makes Right Acts Right?" In *The Right and the Good*, edited by Philip Stratton-Lake, 16–64. Oxford University Press.

Ryle, Gilbert. 2009. *The Concept of Mind*. 3rd edn. Routledge.

Schwenkler, John. 2015. "Understanding 'Practical Knowledge.'" *Philosophers' Imprint* 15.

Setiya, Kieran. 2008. "Practical Knowledge." *Ethics* 118: 388–409.

Setiya, Kieran. 2009. "Practical Knowledge Revisited." *Ethics* 120: 128–137.

Setiya, Kieran. 2010. "Sympathy for the Devil." In *Desire, Practical Reason, and the Good*, edited by Sergio Tenenbaum, 82–110. Oxford University Press.

Setiya, Kieran. 2016a. "Anscombe on Practical Knowledge." In *Practical Knowledge: Selected Essays*, 156–167. Oxford University Press.

Setiya, Kieran. 2016b. "Knowing How." In *Practical Knowledge: Selected Essays*, 135–155. Oxford University Press.

Setiya, Kieran. 2018. "Intention." In *The Stanford Encyclopedia of Philosophy*, Fall 2018 edn., edited by Edward N. Zalta. https://plato.stanford.edu/archives/fall2018/entries/intention/.

Sidgwick, Henry. 1907. *The Methods of Ethics*. 7th edn. Macmillan and Co.

Stout, Rowland. 2010. "What Are You Causing in Acting?" In *Causing Human Action*, edited by Jesús H. Aguilar and Andrei A. Buckareff, 101–113. The MIT Press.

Teichmann, Roger. 2008. *The Philosophy of Elizabeth Anscombe*. Oxford University Press.

Thompson, Michael. 2008. *Life and Action: Elementary Structures of Practice and Practical Thought*. Harvard University Press.

Thompson, Michael. 2011. "Anscombe's *Intention* and Practical Knowledge." In *Essays on Anscombe's* Intention, edited by Anton Ford, Jennifer Hornsby, and Frederick Stoutland, 198–210. Harvard University Press.

Thomson, Judith Jarvis. 1991. "Self-Defense." *Philosophy and Public Affairs* 20: 283–310.

Ullmann-Margalit, Edna and Sidney Morgenbesser. 1977. "Picking and Choosing." *Social Research* 44: 757–785.

Velleman, David. 2007. *Practical Reflection*. 2nd edn. Princeton University Press.

Vogler, Candace. 2002. *Reasonably Vicious*. Harvard University Press.

Vogler, Candace. 2016. "Nothing Added." *American Catholic Philosophical Quarterly* 90: 229–247.

White, Roger. 2005. "Epistemic Permissiveness." *Philosophical Perspectives* 19: 445–459.

Wippel, J.F. 2011. "Thomas Aquinas and the Axiom 'What Is Received Is Received According to the Mode of the Receiver.'" In *Metaphysical Themes in Thomas Aquinas II*, 113–122. Catholic University of America Press.

Wiseman, Rachael. 2016a. *Guidebook to Anscombe's Intention*. Routledge.

Wiseman, Rachael. 2016b. "The Intended and Unintended Consequences of Intention." *American Catholic Philosophical Quarterly* 90: 207–227.

Wiseman, Rachael. 2017. "Who Am I and What Am I Doing?" *Journal of Philosophy* 114: 536–550.

Wittgenstein, Ludwig. 1958. *The Blue and Brown Books*. Basil Blackwell.

Wittgenstein, Ludwig. 2001. *Philosophical Investigations*, trans. G.E.M. Anscombe. 3rd edn. Blackwell.

Concordance

§1	1:1	"Very often, when"	3, 4
§2	1:3/2:1	"The distinction between"	4, 5, 107n7
	2:2	"If, however, we"	6, 12
	2:4/3:1	"Now by this"	6n3, 107n7
	3:5/4:1	"Orders are usually"	10, 133n22, 194, 204
	4:2	"It is natural"	7
	4:3	"If I do not do"	7, 12
	4:4	"A lie, however"	7
	4:5/5:1	"One might not"	7, 10, 11–12, 96, 111, 178, 207
	5:3	"Intention appears to"	8n4
§3	5:4/6:1	"We need a better"	3, 8, 14
	6:2	"Looking at the verbal"	3, 8, 15
	6:3	"We might attempt"	10, 11
	7:2	"Now our account"	11, 205
§4	7:3/8:1	"I therefore turn"	13, 151
	8:2	"I am referring"	14, 29, 94, 151, 170, 197
	8:3/9:1	"In this way"	151
	9:2	"Now it can easily"	3, 13, 89, 101
§5	9:3	"What distinguishes actions"	17, 18, 19, 32, 201
	9:4/10:1	"To see the difficulties"	17, 19, 24, 31, 62
	10:2	"It will hardly"	17, 39, 42
	10:3/11:1	"Nor can we say"	17
	11:2	"It is very usual"	17
§6	11:4	"This question is"	20, 22, 23, 189
	11:5/12:1	"Since a single action"	21n4, 22

§7	12:2	"It is also clear"	24
	12:3	"Here, digressing for"	24n7

§8	13:4/14:1	"What is required"	104, 109n10, 186
	14:2	"Now the class"	29
	14:3/15:1	"But the class"	30

§9	15:4/16:1	"I first, in considering"	31
	16:2	"Now we can see"	33n13, 33n15

§10	16:3	"I will call"	33

§11	17:1	"Now one might"	34–35
	17:2/18:1	"A 'mental cause'"	33

§12	18:3	"Popularly motive and"	37
	18:4/19:1	"Nevertheless there is"	37
	19:2	"When a man"	37n19

§13	20:2	"Revenge and gratitude"	37, 134
	20:3	"Motive-in-general"	37
	20:4/21:1	"The account of motive"	36–37
	21:2	"To give a motive"	37–38, 134
	21:3	"The motives admiration"	38, 47

§14	21:5/22:1	"Now the most"	39–40
	22:2	"These facts are"	40
	22:4/23:1	"We have now"	41, 62

§15	23:4/24:1	"Is this a cause"	41, 75n22, 82
	24:2	"This, however, does not"	41, 42, 59

§16	24:3/25:1	"It will be useful"	47

§17	25:2	"I can now"	30, 34n16, 44
	25:3	"Now of course"	21n5, 43
	25:4/26:1	"An answer of"	43, 44, 45
	26:2	"'I don't know why'"	44–45
	26:3	"I myself have"	44n28, 46

§18	28:2	"The answers to"	47

§19	28:3	"We do not add"	56
	28:4/29:1	"That an action"	50–51, 162, 171
	29:2	"And in describing"	50, 52–53, 55, 90, 162–163, 164
	29:3/30:1	"The question does not"	18, 82n29

§34	62:2/63:1	"But, we may ask"	132, 135
	63:2	"This is so, of course"	135

§35	64:1	"(a) Dry food suits"	135, 142
	64:2/65:1	"The first three"	136n24, 143, 147–148
	65:2	"Thus, there is nothing"	135
	65:3	"But it is misleading"	134
	65:4/66:1	"It may be said"	134–135
	66:2	"Then 'I want this'"	135, 136, 136n25, 150

§36	67:2	"It is a familiar doctrine"	139
	67:3	"'Wanting' may of course"	139
	67:4/68:1	"The wanting that interests"	135, 139
	68:2	"The primitive sign"	135, 139
	68:3/69:1	"The primitive sign"	135, 139
	70:1	"Thus the special"	139, 146

§37	70:3	"Are there any further"	136, 138–139, 145
	70:4/71:1	"But is not anything"	140–141
	71:2	"But cannot a man"	141
	71:3	"It is not a mere matter"	141
	71:4/72:1	"Then Aristotle's terms"	143

§38	72:3	"Let us now consider"	146
	72:4/73:1	"Aristotle would seem"	131–133
	74:2	"But in saying this"	146–147

§39	74:3/75:1	"A (formal) ethical"	147
	75:2/76:1	"'Evil be thou my good'"	140, 141n30, 142, 143, 145, 153

§40	76:2/77:1	"The conceptual connexion"	144
	77:4/78:1	"In this enquiry"	143

§41	78:2	"It will have become clear"	136, 146
	79:1	"Of course"	95, 131, 134, 147

§42	79:3/80:1	"It has an absurd appearance"	148–149

§43	80:2	"Consider a question"	151

§44	80:4/81:1	"(a) The man has no end"	147
	81:3	"(c) The same man has"	147
	81:4	"This trivial case (c) is"	130, 146, 177

§45	82:1	"We can now consider"	174, 177
	82:2	"But what is this"	174, 180
	82:3	"I wrote 'I am a fool'"	180
	82:4	"Orders, however, can be"	184–185
	82:5/83:1	"Hence we can understand"	185n33

§46	83:3	"Of course we have"	163, 197n48
	83:4/84:1	"Why do we say that"	171
	84:2	"So the description"	164n14

§47	84:3	"Thus there are many"	165, 167, 172
	84:4/85:1	"In fact the term"	165
	85:2	"The class of such"	165
	85:3	"Intruding; Offending; . . . "	165–166, 171, 209
	86:1	"With what right do I"	166
	86:2/87:1	"Since I have defined"	8n4, 66

§48	87:2	"We can now see"	166
	87:3	"Surprising as it may seem"	67, 191n42, 197
	87:4/88:1	"If we put these"	156, 156n4, 161, 168–169, 171, 172, 182, 185, 187, 199
	88:2	"'Practical knowledge' is"	173–174, 199
	88:3/89:1	"Naturally my imaginary"	195n47, 196–198

| §49 | 89:3/90:1 | "The distinction between" | 201–202 |

| §50 | 90:2 | "I have completed" | 203, 205 |

§52	91:7/92:1	"Let us consider"	110
	92:2	"'I am going for a walk—'"	110, 203n3, 205
	92:3	"The contradiction consists"	109, 110, 168n17, 205
	92:4	"If I say I am going"	110, 204
	92:5	"Nor can we say"	110, 204
	92:6	"Ought one really always"	206
	92:7/93:1	"In the small activities"	206
	93:3	"But if one is considering"	206, 207
	94:1	"It is for this reason"	207–210

Index